# INSTRUCTOR'S MANUAL AND TEST BANK TO ACCOMPANY KAMIEN

# MUSIC
## AN APPRECIATION

## SECOND BRIEF EDITION

**RAOUL F. CAMUS**
*Queensborough Community College*
*of the City University of New York*

**McGraw-Hill, Inc.**
New York   St. Louis   San Francisco   Auckland   Bogotá   Caracas
Colorado Springs   Hamburg   Lisbon   London   Madrid   Mexico City
Milan   Montreal   New Delhi   Oklahoma City   Panama
San Juan   São Paulo   Singapore   Sydney   Tokyo   Toronto
Sydney   Tokyo   Toronto

Instructor's Manual & Test Bank to Accompany Kamien
**MUSIC**
AN APPRECIATION
Second Brief Edition
Raoul F. Camus

ISBN 0-07-034822-7

1 2 3 4 5 6 7 8 9 0 BKM BKM 9 0 9 8 7 6 5 4 3 2

# CONTENTS

## Part 1
## INSTRUCTOR'S MANUAL

## Part 2
## TEST BANK

# ABBREVIATIONS

EAV      Clearvue/eav, 6465 N. Avondale, Chicago, IL 60631-1909.

HAM      *Historical Anthology of Music*. Edited by Archibald T. Davison and Willi Apel. Cambridge: Harvard University Press, 1950.

HAMW      *Historical Anthology of Music by Women*. Edited by James R. Briscoe. Bloomington: Indiana University Press, 1987.

MOG      Metropolitan Opera Guild, 1865 Broadway, New York, New York 10023. (Opera study guides, silent and sound filmstrips, and opera boxes available for many standard operas, including those so indicated)

MHS      Musical Heritage Society, Tinton Falls, New Jersey 07724.

MM      *Masterpieces of Music Before 1750*. Edited and compiled by Carl Parrish and John F. Ohl. New York: W. W. Norton, 1951.

MWW      *Music in the Western World: A History in Documents*. Selected and annotated by Piero Weiss and Richard Taruskin. New York: Schirmer Books, 1984.

NS      *The Norton Scores*. Edited by Roger Kamien. 4th ed. New York: W. W. Norton, 1984.

SSR      *Source Readings in Music History from Classical Antiquity through the Romantic Era*. Edited by Oliver Strunk.. New York: W. W. Norton, 1950.

WMM      *Women Making Music: The Western Art Tradition, 1150-1950*. Edited by Jane Bowers and Judith Tick. Urbana: University of Illinois Press, 1986.

# INTRODUCTION

The publication of an instructor's manual may seem presumptuous and unnecessary, for frequently it is merely relegated to the bookshelf or "circular file" with only a cursory glance by the receiver. Perhaps that will happen to this pamphlet as well, but we hope you will give it a chance to help in planning for the course, and in preparing each day's class.

If asked what I teach, I try to remember that the answer should be students, not music. Sometimes we get so involved in our subject, or so bogged down by the many administrative chores demanded of us, that we loose sight of our primary responsibility to our students. They are the audiences of the present, and the future. What sense is there in training performers and composers if there will be no listeners? It is up to us, in these "introduction" courses, to provide experiences for our students that will encourage and excite them to love music, and realize that it is a vital and integral part of our whole culture and civilization. In short, we must prove to them that *Music makes the Difference!* The text, and all the supporting materials, are designed to help in that attempt.

## THE MATERIALS

### THE INSTRUCTOR'S MANUAL AND TEST BANK

This manual is intended to accompany the second brief edition of Roger Kamien's *MUSIC: An Appreciation*. It is divided into two basic parts, the *Instructor's Manual* and the *Test Bank*.

#### PART 1. THE INSTRUCTOR'S MANUAL

This Introduction deals with the course as a whole, discussing course outlines, special features of the text, examinations, the accompanying record set, the test bank, and the *Study Guide and Student Workbook*.

Paralleling the organization of the text, the *Instructor's Manual* begins with a summary of the OBJECTIVES of each section, including a brief summary of the major points covered. There then follow SUGGESTIONS for classroom activities and listening experiences, topics for discussion, supplementary information, timings of the selections included in the accompanying record sets, projects for classroom participation, and additional or alternate musical examples and record information. Each section concludes with QUESTIONS AND TOPICS that may be used to encourage classroom discussions, as topics for student papers, or as essay questions for written examinations.

#### PART 2. TEST BANK

The *Test Bank* is available in two forms: the printed hard copy (part 2 of this manual), and computer software. Each of the 1093 multiple-choice questions in the Test Bank, all directly related to the text, is accompanied by the following information:

Ans. a    The correct answer for the question
p. 376    Page of the text where the correct answer may be found
SG        Question taken from the *Study Guide and Student Workbook*

There is considerable variation in the length of each section, and the number of sections in each of the seven parts of the text. The number of questions will therefore depend on the length of the section and the relative importance of the materials covered.

The *Computerized Testmaker* provides an easy means for instructors to use a computer in preparing exams based on items from this test bank. No specialized computer background is necessary for this system, and the instructions are so clear and user-friendly that exams can be developed and printed in a matter of minutes. The program provides unique flexibility by including both a "quick test" mode, which allows the instructor to create a test and answer key quickly and easily, and a "full features" mode that allows the instructor to use more advanced features such as editing, adding, and deleting questions, scrambling and randomly selecting questions when creating tests, and more. The Testmaker is available for IBM, Mac, and Apple computers. For information about the Computerized Testmaker, please contact your local McGraw-Hill representative.

The great debt to Dr. Arthur M. Daniels, who prepared the first edition of this Manual, is sincerely acknowledged. Special thanks are also due to Roger Kamien and Amy Camus for patiently reading the drafts of both the Manual and the Study Guide, and providing encouragement and many valuable suggestions. Readers are encouraged to send comments and suggestions to the author (Music Department, Queensborough Community College, Bayside, NY 11364).

## THE TEXT

*MUSIC: An Appreciation* was designed to offer the instructor great flexibility in developing the course outline. Consequently, it contains more material than would normally be used in a semester or quarter course.

Part I, *Elements*, introduces basic musical concepts and exposes the student to five short and attractive compositions from a variety of style periods. As in later parts of the book, the sections of part I are relatively self-contained and may be studied in an order different from that of the text. The consideration of certain topics may be postponed to later points in the course.

Parts II to VI survey the style periods of western music and discuss specific composers and representative pieces. Part VII is an introduction to nonwestern music. Here too, the text is designed for maximum flexibility, and the sections are relatively self-contained. The instructor is free to rearrange or omit topics as desired.

The text also includes some special teaching aids that should be mentioned:

*Listening Outlines.* These are not technical analyses, but guides designed to be read while listening to the music. They are tools that help the listener concentrate more easily on the main musical events. These outlines may be used in the classroom, as well as outside class. In class, outline numbers can be called out or written on the chalkboard from time to time to ensure that the students' attention is accurately focused. Difficult passages in an outline should be discussed in advance by the teacher. Students may be asked to raise hands when a particular number in the outline has been reached, and the instructor is encouraged to make frequent spot-checks during a piece. Take care not to break moods by too frequent or indiscreet interruptions. It is recommended that the outlines be introduced on the first day of class. It must be emphasized, however, that while the Listening Outlines are valuable teaching aids, the text can be profitably used without them.

*Annotated Vocal Texts.* These teaching aids are designed to help students follow the music and understand the relationship between words and music by providing song texts, choral texts, and segments of opera libretti with English translations and brief comments about the musical content. As with the Listening Outlines, the annotated vocal texts may be used in class or for outside listening.

*Glossary and Musical Example Locator.* A new glossary allows readers to combine a review of musical terms with easy reference to clear musical examples of the terms.

THE STUDY GUIDE AND STUDENT WORKBOOK

A *Study Guide and Student Workbook* has been prepared to accompany the basic text. As the title indicates, the work has a twofold purpose:

The *Study Guide* is intended to help the student prepare for class by reviewing the materials in the text through multiple-choice, matching, or fill-in questions. Students are urged to read the assignment, answer the questions in the Study Guide, check the answers with the answer key printed in the rear of the Workbook, and then reread the text for any passages or concepts they did not fully understand.

The *Student Workbook* contains pages for use in classroom discussions, for listening or written assignments, for surveys or reports, for broadening the scope of understanding music in relationship to the cultural period and the other art forms, or for reviewing biographical details of some of the major composers. There are also questions posed for review of concepts and topics covered, some of which may be exploratory, others argumentative, but all designed to encourage thought and interaction in and out of class. Some pages are also devoted to materials designed to supplement topics discussed in the text. Finally, there is a quiz on each of the seven major units of the text. The answers to these questions are not contained in the Workbook, but are included in this Instructor's Manual at the end of each unit. The answers are also included at the end of this manual, so that you may duplicate the page for the students if you decide not to use the quizzes as true examinations. The pages of the Workbook are perforated so that they may be collected in class, and the students may then reassemble them after grading. Other pages of the Workbook intended for your convenience in collecting from the students include a pre-course questionnaire and a listening exercise to be done in the first class session, with the same exercise at the end of the Workbook to be done the last class session for comparison (see Section I-1 below). There are also three concert report forms, and a final course evaluation sheet for those who wish to avail themselves. Also for your convenience, please note that the "Contents" in the Study Guide has been provided with sufficient space to enter class sessions or calendar dates for those sections you wish to assign. According to the recent copyright law, you may duplicate the Contents in the Workbook, provided they are used in connection with the basic text.

RECORDINGS

The Second Brief Edition is accompanied by a Brief Set of three CD and cassette recordings that include many of the works discussed in the text. The Basic Set that accompanies *MUSIC: An Appreciation*, Fifth Edition, consists of eight CDs, cassettes, or Lps and is also available for use with the second brief edition, for those who want their students to study a larger body of works. An expanded Supplementary Set of four CDs, cassettes, or Lps is available to faculty members adopting the text and is available for student purchase. References to record sides and bands are included in the margins of the text, next to the works discussed, and the timings of the selections are included in this manual.

# THE COURSE

COURSE OUTLINES

Traditionally, introductory music courses emphasize the repertoire heard most frequently in our concert halls—music from the baroque period to the present. Consequently, the parts of the book devoted to the Middle Ages and the Renaissance are quite condensed. Even so, instructors with limited time at their disposal may choose to begin with the baroque period or even with the music of Bach and Handel. For the same considerations of time, the last four sections of the book—jazz, the American musical, rock, and nonwestern music—may also have to be condensed.

While it is difficult to imagine a unit on classical music without Haydn, Mozart, and Beethoven, Part IV, *The Classical Period*, may be abbreviated by omitting certain works from the course coverage. The parts of the text devoted to romantic and twentieth-century music offer greater possibilities for abridgment, and the choice of what to eliminate is best left to the instructor.

The sections dealing with jazz, rock, and nonwestern music allow for greater flexibility of presentation. They may be studied at the end of the course, as suggested by the text, integrated into other topics, or at the beginning of the course with or immediately after the elements.

It is suggested that class time be devoted as much as possible to specific compositions rather than to material—such as biography—best left for outside reading. For example, when beginning a new historical period, play a representative composition and ask the students to describe it in terms of the elements of music already studied. In later stages of the course, students can be asked to compare the new work with one from the preceding historical period. Students can then be assigned readings from the text in which characteristics of the new historical style are surveyed.

As in any well-organized course, the instructor should determine his or her own goals and make them clear to the students. A successful introductory music course is one that promotes a positive attitude toward music. Students should come away with a basic knowledge of the evolution of music, and with the ability to recognize aurally specific forms, musical techniques, and historical styles. This text provides material for various approaches, and for different levels of rigor. The degree of musical sophistication required of the student is a matter for the individual instructor to decide.

The time devoted to each topic will depend on the goals set by the instructor. The following three options are some possibilities for planning a one-semester course meeting three hours per week for fifteen weeks. All three plans budget the first two weeks for the elements of music. Two weeks may seem hopelessly inadequate, but remember that basic musical concepts are reviewed throughout the text.

| One-semester, Fifteen-week Course | Options | | |
| Three hours per week (45 hours) | A | B | C |
| --- | --- | --- | --- |
| Introduction/administration/motivation | 1 | 1 | 1 |
| Elements of Music | 6 | 6 | 6 |
| Medieval and Renaissance Music | 4 | 2 | 2 |
| Baroque Music | 6 | 6 | 5 |
| Classical Music | 8 | 9 | 8 |
| Romantic Music | 9 | 9 | 9 |
| Music of the Twentieth Century | 8 | 8 | 8 |
| Jazz and Rock | 1 | 2 | 3 |
| Nonwestern Music | 1 | 1 | 2 |
| Examination (midterm or final) | 1 | 1 | 1 |
| | 45 | 45 | 45 |

A quarter-long course meeting three hours per week for ten weeks and a one-semester course meeting twice a week for fifteen weeks share the same total numbers of class hours (thirty). They also pose the same difficult problems of scheduling. Assuming that the basic content of the course reflects the repertoire most frequently encountered in the concert hall, the following plan seems feasible:

One-semester, fifteen-week course, two hours per week (30 hrs)
*or* one-quarter, ten-week course, three hours per week (30 hrs)

| | |
|---|---|
| Elements of Music | 6 |
| Medieval and Renaissance Music | 1 |
| Baroque Music | 4 |
| Classical Music | 5 |
| Romantic Music | 6 |
| Music of the Twentieth Century | 6 |
| Nonwestern Music | 1 |
| Examination (midterm or final) | 1 |
| | 30 |

If one is fortunate enough to have an entire year for the introductory music course, one of the semester-long options can be used for the first half-year. The second semester will then be available for a more in-depth study of the historical periods, for work in particular genres, or for the pursuit of any other combination of specific interests of faculty or students. It is also possible to devote the first semester to parts I through IV, and the second semester to parts V through VII.

## EXAMINATIONS

The text is designed to develop the listening abilities of students and to heighten their interest in music. It seeks to establish music as a lifelong source of pleasure, inspiration, and cultural enrichment. It seems unfair then to assign a grade to changes in listening habits, or to how successfully we have overcome student ignorance and prejudice, yet in most academic situations a grade is a necessary finale to the course. Some suggestions for student evaluation are therefore in order.

In examinations, it is advisable to restrict the number of questions concerning minute details of composers' lives, personal (as opposed to period) styles, and specific compositions. An examination should contain a good number of listening questions, either essay or short answer or both. The text has many Listening Outlines aimed at helping the students to concentrate more easily on the fruits of this aural art form. While they are valuable teaching tools, the text can profitably be used without them, but some form of listening evaluation should be included in the overall scope of the course. This may take the form of specialized listening exams on assigned works, or general questions added to traditional exams. It is recommended that listening questions deal with musical techniques, forms, and style periods as well as with the identification of works previously studied. The first twenty questions in the Test Bank are sample multiple-choice questions that can be used for musical excerpts played in class.

Note that the *Study Guide and Student Workbook*, discussed above, has self-help questions for each section of the text, and a larger cumulative quiz at the end of each major unit. These quizzes can be used to prepare for major examinations, or, since they are perforated, can be handed in for grading. The answers to these unit quizzes are contained in this Instructor's Manual, and not in the Student Workbook. In each case some listening questions should be added. The Workbook also contains other pages, such as concert reports, biographical sketches, listening assignments, and research projects that can be used for grading purposes.

# Part 1

# Instructor's Manual

# I. ELEMENTS

## I-1. SOUND: PITCH, DYNAMICS, AND TONE COLOR

OBJECTIVES

The elements of music are approached through a general discussion of sound; its antithesis, silence; its subdivision into those sounds that are pleasant or interesting and those that are not; and its production by the vibration of an object through a medium. Using the student's ability to sing our national anthem and the familiar "do-re-mi" scale, the concepts of pitch, interval, and octave are introduced. The use of dynamics in music is explained, as are the standard dynamic indications from *pp* to *ff* and the signs for crescendo and diminuendo. Timbre is defined, and the function of tone color in composition is discussed. The section ends with two Listening Outlines, each designed to illustrate concepts introduced in the text: Wagner's Prelude to Act III of *Lohengrin*, and *Hotter Than That* by Louis Armstrong and his Hot Five.

SUGGESTIONS

1. Assuming this to be the first class session, it is an opportunity to become familiar with the students and have them talk about music. If you have decided to use the accompanying *Study Guide and Student Workbook*, there are several pages in the front intended for the opening session:

a. The *Table of Contents* can be used as a course outline by filling in the class sessions and/or dates in the space provided next to each section, and then either giving the assignments class by class, or duplicating the complete table for distribution (see above, p. ix).

b. The *Pre-Course Questionnaire* can be used to gain insight into the student's musical knowledge at the beginning of the semester. It is suggested that the questionnaire be completed, and then collected and held until the end of the course, when it can be discussed to see differences in responses.

c. In addition to the self-test multiple choice questions based on the first section, the Workbook contains three exercises for classroom use. *Pitch discrimination* asks the student to determine if the second of two pitches played on the piano is higher, lower, or the same as the first. *Tone colors and combinations* asks them to recognize individual voice ranges or instruments, while *Performing Media* gives the students an exercise in differentiating between groupings of sounds as exemplified by the orchestra, band, chorus, and other standard combinations. These exercises can be used to encourage the students with regard to their abilities, or show areas that need further development. It is suggested that the exercises be put on cassette, if possible, so that they can be administered quickly and not cause an unnecessarily disorganized first session.

d. Finally, in the first section of the Workbook, there is a page for student responses to hearing Wagner's Prelude to Act III of *Lohengrin* and comparing it to Louis Armstrong's *Hotter Than That*. It is suggested that this page also be collected and retained until the last session, as there is a similar page in the rear of the Workbook (Post-Course Listening Analysis). It is to be hoped that the students, on hearing the same compositions, will be able to express themselves with much greater understanding and musical terminology. Saving these two pages (the Questionnaire and the Listening Analysis) and then returning them to the students at the end of the course after they have completed the post-course version should prove to them the higher level of achievement reached as a result of the course. (The works were chosen because they are the first works discussed in Section 1, and are included in the basic and brief sets)

2. In discussing pitch, consider bringing in a siren whistle (readily available as a percussion sound effect) to demonstrate the full pitch range, and a tuning fork to show organization and scientific standardization.

3. The text refers to "the familiar scale" and then gives the solfege syllables. This would be an opportune time to have the class sing Richard Rodgers's "Do-Re-Mi" from *The Sound of Music*. A nice icebreaker, it will also show the students that the syllables are familiar, and that music classes are not necessarily spectator sports.

4. To illustrate timbre, one might ask two or more students (female if you are a woman, male if you are a man) to come to the front of the room. Have each student sing or say the same short phrase, trying to match the approximate pitch of your voice. Then have the students close their eyes, change the order of where each person stood (so voices will be recognized by timbre, not by location), and have each person, including yourself, sing or say the same phrase again. The class should be able to identify the order of statements by the timbre of each voice. (It also helps to break the ice, and encourages students to participate, rather than merely sit back and listen/vegetate/daydream.)

5. Some explanation of the Listening Outlines should be given, with the intent of making the students self-sufficient in their listening assignments outside as well as in class. Two examples are provided in this first section, and the sets include both. As they are quite short, you probably can fit them both in for variety, especially stressing the terms introduced in this first section: pitch, dynamics, and timbre.

QUESTIONS AND TOPICS

1. Compare and contrast the use of dynamics in the two works discussed in this  section.

2. Discuss the use of solo instruments in Wagner's Prelude, and compare with the use of solo instruments in Armstrong's *Hotter Than That*.

3. Musical terminology and the science of acoustics.

4. The use of electronic amplification at rock concerts.

5. Pitch ranges of musical instruments and voices compared.

6. Timbre and the harmonic series.

7. Compare and contrast the use of dynamics in any two compositions, especially between different musical styles.

# I-2. PERFORMING MEDIA: VOICES AND INSTRUMENTS

OBJECTIVES

The principal goal of this section is to familiarize the student with the SATB classification of human voices and the classification of the various families of instruments. The mechanisms of the various instruments are described, their ranges noted, and their functions in solo or ensemble capacities discussed.

SUGGESTIONS

1. The Student Workbook has several pages to help in covering the materials in this section:

a. four charts designed for review or use in class, on which the various families and their members are to be arranged according to vocal ranges. The amount of material to be included depends on how deeply you wish to delve into the subject of instrumental classification;

b. blank seating plans for orchestra, symphonic band, and chorus adaptable to local circumstances to help prepare the students for live performances.

2. If possible, demonstrate the various major instruments. If this is not possible, introduce some minor accessories, such as an old mouthpiece or single and double reeds that could be passed around for all to see and feel. There are also many videos and filmstrips available (some by EAV, for example) that would help with the unfamiliar instruments.

3. Zubin Mehta's film demonstration and performance of Ravel's *Bolero* (Pyramid Films) has proven to be quite successful in illustrating some of the elements of the previous lesson (timbre, dynamics, pitch), as well as demonstrating the instruments of the orchestra in actual rehearsal and performance.

4. In discussing the groupings of instruments, you may wish to include the nonwestern instruments found in section VII of the text. The Student Workbook has a page devoted to nonwestern instruments that could be used at this time (see VII-1 below).

5. In discussing vocal ranges and performance styles, you may wish to include nonwestern models. Compare, for example, the voices in the Puccini excerpt with Bessie Smith's blues and the African examples, all included in the basic set.

6. If time permits, test the students on instrument and voice classification recognition. Urge them (if you allow the use of the Workbook during the exercise) to think first of the vibrating element, locate the correct family in the chart, then think of the pitch range, and by simply going down the chart to the proper category, they will most likely hit the proper instrument. It is assumed that this exercise would be for those who need help; students who have a good musical background should be able to do the exercise without assistance.

7. Time should be left for a major work in the orchestral repertoire, Britten's *Young Person's Guide to the Orchestra* (included in the supplementary set, 17:12). You might also mention the great popularity of this work as the ballet *Fanfare*.

8. If older students complain about learning to recognize the sounds of the instruments, urge them to provide their own children with such standard compositions designed to aid children in instrument recognition as *Peter and the Wolf, Tubby the Tuba, Peewee the Piccolo*, and others. While these are charming works, they would be somewhat out of place in a college class, but if the complaining students had learned the instruments when they were four, they wouldn't be struggling now . . . (a commercial to build our future audiences).

9. The best plan for illustrating this section would be to arrange a visit by your class to an actual rehearsal, either on campus with one of the college or college-community groups, or at an open rehearsal of the local professional orchestra (these latter are usually open performance-- rehearsals, however, so they would not be as valuable as an actual working rehearsal).

10. It is to be hoped that some exposure to live music will be required as a part of the course. For that purpose, the Appendix of the Student Workbook includes some practical considerations on "Going to a Concert," "Some Pre-Concert Suggestions" to help in writing concert reports, and three "Concert Report" forms. The "Suggestions" are intended for those wishing to require fully written concert reports, and should be adapted to suit your personal preference. The form is quite simple by intent, and you may wish to elaborate, but since the pages are perforated, you might find it easier simply to use the printed forms. Some discussion of the format should be made, as there may be some question as to the meaning of medium or historical style this early in the semester.

11. Some discussion should be devoted to the question of live versus recorded performances. You might, for example, ask the students to remember when they saw a live performance of their favorite group. Was it as technically perfect as the recorded versions they were used to? If not, why not? Was there a compensating factor, such as presence? (Note the illustration "Concert by the Grateful Dead" in the color section) Compare, for example, a popular musician with a popular ball player: while we think the ball player is outstanding if he has a 300 batting average,

imagine what we would think if the musician hit only one out of every three notes! We expect an average of 1,000, despite the physical or emotional conditions of the player before and during the concert (i. e., a plane ride, perhaps jet-lag, a quick taxi to the local fast-food place, then on to the bandstand, play the show, some quick sleep probably caught on the next plane or bus ride instead of a comfortable hotel or motel, then the local fast-food place, then . . .). We could also suggest that recordings are like the *Playboy* centerfolds: perfected as much as can be by modern techniques. Unfortunately life is seldom perfect, but would we want to live just looking at the pictures without some opportunity for the real thing? (This analogy may be too strong, but it usually makes for a lively discussion.)

12. In discussing the relative merits of live versus recorded performance, do not overlook the photo of the audience at a concert of the United States Marine Band included in the color plates. Why do so many people turn up at an outdoor concert, uncomfortable and musically unrewarding as they frequently are, when they could easily listen to the same music on recordings in the comfort of their own homes?

QUESTIONS AND TOPICS
1. Compare the mechanisms of the piano, organ, and harpsichord.
2. Discuss the various techniques employed in playing string instruments.
3. Describe briefly the physiology of singing.
4. Describe the components of a string instrument.
5. Discuss the resources and manipulative techniques of the electronic composer.
6. The present revival of "obsolete" instruments.
7. Musical instruments before 1600.
8. Discuss the advantages and disadvantages of live and recorded performances.
9. Discuss the functions of the orchestral conductor.
10. Discuss the pros and cons of the career of the professional musical performer.
11. The evolution of electronic instruments.
11. The modern recording studio: synthesizers, samplers, computers, and MIDI.

# I-3. RHYTHM

OBJECTIVES
This section introduces the student to the various topics subsumed under the general heading of rhythm. By using such familiar tunes as *America* and *Mary Had a Little Lamb* such terms as beat and the various meters (duple, triple, quadruple, and sextuple) are defined, as are measure, accent, and syncopation. The concept of tempo is explained, and a list of the principal tempo indications is provided. The section ends with a description of a metronome.

SUGGESTIONS
1. Ask the students to find their own heart beat, the pulse. (As a practical matter, correct any students who do so with their thumbs instead of their first three fingers; nursing students in the class are a great help, if there are problems.) Quoting from the text, "the beat is a regular recurrent pulsation . . .," and certainly they should all be aware of their own heartbeat. This can be used later in the discussion of tempo in providing a built-in metronome. Organize the pulsations into groupings by adding accents, and discuss duple, triple, and quadruple meters. Apply these simple steps to the familiar songs suggested in the text, and then illustrate with musical examples taken from the selections already played in class, or new works. (The brief and

basic sets have a great variety, including Varèse's electronic composition, that can illustrate a barely noticeable beat)

2. It is often helpful to demonstrate the various basic conducting patterns for the meters discussed in the text. After showing the patterns, encourage the class to conduct along with you. Choose a variety of tempi as well as meters, and perhaps even some romantic works with obvious rubati. Some simple examples: the minuet from Mozart's *Eine Kleine Nachtmusik* (3/4), Bach's *Brandenburg* Concerto No. 5 (4/4), and Bizet's *Farandole* from *L'Arlesiénne* (C, then 2/4), all contained in the brief and basic sets.

3. In discussing syncopation, you might return to Armstrong's *Hotter Than That* discussed previously, or introduce Joplin's *Maple Leaf Rag*, on the basic set.

QUESTIONS AND TOPICS
    1. Discuss manifestations of rhythm in life and nature.
    2. Discuss the characteristics of duple, triple, quadruple, and sextuple meter, showing the location of secondary accents where appropriate.
    3. Outline the tempo changes from "very slow, broad" to "as fast as possible," using the appropriate Italian terms.
    4. Syncopation as a characteristic feature of jazz.
    5. Three different conductors' approaches to the tempo of the slow movement of Brahms's First Symphony (or any other favorite symphonic movement).
    6. The invention of the metronome.

# I-4. MUSIC NOTATION

OBJECTIVES
    Using the familiar tune *Farmer in the Dell*, the various aspects of pitch notation (notes, staves, clefs, ledger lines, etc.) and rhythmic notation (stems, flags, beams, etc.) are defined and illustrated. The section ends with a page of the orchestral score of Tchaikovsky's *Romeo and Juliet* Overture.

SUGGESTIONS
    1. The Student Workbook contains a page of exercises for drawing notes, rests, accidentals, and clefs, and some simple pitch recognition word games. A page of blank staves is included for your convenience in developing other exercises.
    2. The text contains other simple musical examples, especially on pages 36, 37 and 42 that can be used as further examples of printed notation.
    3. A vast body of well-known tunes provides an excellent source of drill material in notation. Supplement the tunes in the book with those of your own choice to provide additional practice material.

QUESTIONS AND TOPICS
    1. Discuss the elements of pitch notation.
    2. Discuss the elements of rhythmic notation.
    3. Illustrate the time signatures for various duple, triple, and compound meters.
    4. Early stages in the development of musical notation.
    5. The notation of popular sheet music.
    6. The notation of avant-garde concert music.

## I-5. MELODY

### OBJECTIVES

Using such familiar tunes as *Row, Row, Row your Boat, Mary Had a Little Lamb,* and *America,* such aspects of melody as phrase structure, complete and incomplete cadences, and sequence are defined and illustrated. The student is introduced to the practice of indicating the larger and smaller formal units of a work by means of capital and lowercase letters.

### SUGGESTIONS

1. Between this section and the last, several familiar old songs have been introduced, and all can be discussed with regard to phrases, cadences, and form. The text defines melody as "a series of single notes which add up to a recognizable whole." If we consider the "recognizable whole" as a thought or idea, we can build on the students' knowledge of grammar. A complete thought would be a sentence; melody can then be considered a *musical* sentence, the composer's thought or idea. A part of a sentence/melody is a phrase, and cadences are punctuation marks. Consider especially incomplete and complete cadences, drawing an analogy with interruptive and terminal punctuation marks. Discuss also conjunct and disjunct melodies, and illustrate with the simple folksongs.

2. For more complex examples, consider Tchaikovsky's *Dance of the Reed Pipes* (see Listening Outline, p. 50; recording in basic and brief sets, 2:34), which contrasts a melody with wide range, many leaps, and a variety of rhythmic patterns (1b) with a stepwise melody with narrow range and one basic rhythmic pattern (2a). Both melodies are primarily staccato. Other examples from the basic set suitable for use include Bach's Air (legato), Beethoven's Fifth Symphony, first movement (sequence and repeated notes), and Chopin's Prelude in C Minor (melody unified by a single rhythmic pattern - - - . - ).

### QUESTIONS AND TOPICS

1. Describe the manner in which musical phrases may be unified.
2. Discuss the symbols used in analyzing musical phrases and sections.
3. Contrast the effect of stepwise melodies with those that move mostly by leaps.
4. Phraseology in music and language.
5. The prevalence of aa'ba' form in familiar tunes.
6. Repeated rhythmic patterns in familiar tunes.

## I-6. HARMONY

### OBJECTIVES

This section considers harmony and the various topics traditionally subsumed under this heading. The concept of harmony is explained, as are harmonic progression, consonance and dissonance, and the resolution of dissonances. The functions of the tonic and dominant triads are explained, as is the use of broken chords (arpeggios).

### SUGGESTIONS

1. Since the text includes an illustration of Tracy Chapman accompanying herself on the guitar, perhaps one of her recordings might prove of interest to the students in discussing harmony. Illustrate the various concepts introduced in the section, such as consonance, dissonance, and triads. There was a time when half the class would have been interested in the

guitar, but those times seem to have faded into the past. There may still be a few students, however, who could discuss the chords they have been learning to play. Ask them which chord they learned first, and then which second. Chances are they were tonic-dominant, with the third chord a sub-dominant, allowing many opportunities for classroom discussion and demonstration of what you can do with just three chords.

2. You might play one of the *Music Minus One* or sing-a-long recordings of accompaniments to popular vocals. In this way they can understand the concept of accompaniment to a melody, and at the same time those in the class who like to sing or play might be thankful for your having introduced them to a new teaching/performing possibility.

QUESTIONS AND TOPICS
1. Describe the functions of the tonic and dominant triads.
2. Discuss the effects of consonances and dissonances.
3. The acoustical basis for consonance and dissonance.
4. The concept of dissonance in music history.
5. Harmonization traditions of folksongs.

## I-7. KEY

OBJECTIVES
This section defines and illustrates various terms having to do with key. The topics covered include the tonic and tonality, the structure of the major, minor, and chromatic scales, whole and half steps, key signatures, and modulation.

SUGGESTIONS
1. Using *America*, presented in section 5 above as an example of a melody in major, ask the class, or individual students, to sing the first phrase to give them a feeling of tonality and the tonic. After introducing the concept of major tonality, play or sing the same song in minor. If you have the time, encourage them to sing along a second time, thereby reinforcing the differences. Intervals can then be introduced, with a reference to the piano octave illustrated previously in the text.

2. *Joshua Fought the Battle of Jericho* is presented as an example of a song in minor, and the same technique as above could be used: first have them sing it in minor, and then again in major. Introduce the concepts of minor tonality and key signatures. By comparing C major with A minor, for example, you can also introduce the concept of relative keys. The Student Workbook has some blank staves to practice writing scales.

3. Chromaticism and modulation can be demonstrated simply on the piano, or by referring back to the examples played in previous classes.

4. Some examples of compositions that contrast major and minor that can be discussed  are Tchaikovsky's *Dance of the Reed Pipes*, Haydn's *Surprise* Symphony, second movement,  and Bizet's *Farandole* (minor to major; Listening Outlines for all three selections in text). It might be helpful to have the class hum the tonic until after the modulation to help them identify the change of key or mode.

5. If you wish to add a humorous note to this discussion, and at the same time impress upon the students how strongly the ear expects (even demands) proper pitch relationships in certain styles of music, play a selection from Florence Foster Jenkins's recording *The Glory (????) of the Human Voice* (Victor LM-2597). Her interpretations of the "Queen of the Night" aria from

Mozart's *Magic Flute* or the "Bell Song" from Delibes's *Lakme*, for example, are simply indescribable!

QUESTIONS AND TOPICS
1. Compare the interval patterns of the major and minor scales.
2. Discuss the factors that contribute to a sense of tonality.
3. Discuss the structure and expressive effect of the chromatic scale.
4. The historical evolution of the major scale as the basis of western music.
5. Scale patterns other than major, minor, or chromatic.
6. Tonality in nonwestern music.

# I-8. MUSICAL TEXTURE

OBJECTIVES
This section defines and illustrates the three basic types of musical texture: monophonic, polyphonic, and homophonic. Imitation is defined and illustrated by the familiar round *Row, Row, Row your Boat*, and then the song is presented with chordal accompaniment. The *Farandole* from Bizet's *L'Arlesienne* Suite no. 2, with a Listening Outline, is presented as an example of changing textures.

SUGGESTIONS
1. The most common, and the original meaning of the word texture deals with the weaving of fibers. Using the analogy then of weaving strands of melody in the cloth of sound, we can develop the three possibilities of musical texture. The text uses *Row, Row, Row your Boat* as an example, and the class could sing the song in unison to demonstrate monophonic texture (the acceptance of octaves must be explained in this regard, assuming there are men and women singing). The song can then be done as a round, demonstrating polyphonic texture. Finally, to illustrate homophonic texture, the simple chords in the book could be used, or if you wish to keep the singing a cappella, ask a few of the basses to sing "Row, Row, Row" on tonic, dominant, and tonic, while the rest of the class sings the complete melody in unison.
2. Some additional examples of musical texture from the record sets:
 monophonic: Gregorian chant *Alleluia: Vidimus stellam*, Bach, *Little* Fugue (opening)
 polyphonic, with imitation: Josquin, *Ave Maria*, Bach, *Little* Organ Fugue
 polyphonic, with different melodies: Bach, *Wachet Auf*, fourth movement
 homophonic, rhythmic accompaniment different from melody: Chopin, Prelude in e
 homophonic, rhythmic accompaniment same as melody: Tchaikovsky, *Romeo and Juliet*
3. A Listening Outline is provided for Bizet's *Farandole*, and the work is included in the brief and basic sets (3:01). Not only will it illustrate texture, it will reinforce the discussion of minor/major tonalities from the previous class.

QUESTIONS AND TOPICS
1. Explain the difference between contrapuntal texture and imitation.
2. Discuss the varying functions of the accompaniment in homophony.
3. Polyphony in jazz.
4. Texture as an element of variety in _____ (supply one of the works previously discussed in class).
5. The difficulty of ascribing the terms "homophonic" or "polyphonic" to certain selected musical excerpts.

# I-9. MUSICAL FORM

OBJECTIVES

The functions of repetition, contrast, and variation in the delineation of musical form are discussed. Two of the most common formal types are explained and illustrated by means of Listening Outlines: ternary, or ABA, by the *Dance of the Reed Pipes* from Tchaikovsky's *Nutcracker* Suite, and binary, or AB, by the *Badinerie* from Bach's Suite No. 2 for Flute and Strings.

SUGGESTIONS

1. The text refers back to some of the simple melodies that introduced the concepts of form, repetition, and contrast. At this time you can discuss one of the basic problems inherent in all creative endeavors: how to provide variety, and yet maintain unity in a work, whether it be musical, architectural, sculptural, literary, or any other phase of human creativity. Using the simple ABA form, one can show variety through the contrasting section, and unity by the return. Note the simple ABA form of the Palace of Versailles illustrated in the text (p. 79). One can deal similarly with other forms, such as theme and variations, rondo, or the minuet and trio.

2. In introducing ABA form, you might return to Wagner's Act III Prelude to *Lohengrin*, discussed in the first class. You might also ask the students individually or as a class to sing a simple song such as *Twinkle, Twinkle, Little Star*, and identify the form. From a practical point of view, especially if the students are more mature, ask them to sing the *Alphabet Song* as heard in school or on *Sesame Street*. Chances are most of them will get through the alphabet and then break down on the return section, having run out of letters. Helping them to learn the song will encourage them to help their own children to learn the alphabet in a pleasant and musical way.

3. Tchaikovsky's *Dance of the Reed Pipes* from *The Nutcracker* is presented as an example of ABA' form, and is included in the brief and basic sets (2:34). If not confusing to the students this early, there are several video cassettes available of *The Nutcracker* that can be used to reinforce form, and also introduce ballet. As a variation of ABA, the basic set also has the Benny Goodman Band's version of Irving Berlin's *Blue Skies*, which illustrates AABA form.

4. Regarding binary form, *America* has already been discussed in the section on key (I-7). The text provides a Listening Outline for the *Badinerie* from Bach's Suite No. 2 for Flute and Strings (in brief set, 1:23). Other examples include the themes of Haydn's *Surprise* Symphony and Schubert's *Trout* Quintet. Both the Air and the Gigue in Bach's Suite no. 3 are in AABB form, and the Student Workbook asks the student to find familiar melodies in binary and ternary form.

QUESTIONS AND TOPICS

1. Discuss the functions of repetition, contrast, and variation in musical form.
2. Compare and contrast binary and ternary form.
3. Discuss the difference between literal and developmental repetition.
4. Problems in perceiving form.
5. Solutions to the creative problem of variety versus unity.
6. An analysis of contemporary rock forms.

# I-10. MUSICAL STYLE

OBJECTIVES

Style is defined as a characteristic way of using melody, rhythm, tone color, dynamics, harmony, texture, and form; *i.e.*, all the elements treated in this opening part of the text.

Approximate dates are given for the major style periods of western music, and the role of music in society is briefly touched upon.

SUGGESTIONS

    1. This section is intended as an introduction and overview of the remainder of the course. The Student Workbook has two pages devoted to making connections with historical or cultural events and famous personalities in the various periods in the hope of helping the student memorize as painlessly as possible the various approximate dates. (It was once said about Americans that they knew only two dates in history, 1066 and 1492, but lately even the latter date seems to be universally unknown by the students!) By associating with events and personalities, especially in relating them to other subjects such as their history and language classes, the burden may be lightened somewhat.

    2. Style is quite difficult to put into words, and you might consider approaching style visually before aurally. Choose two works of art with a similar theme, such as Michelangelo's *David* (p. 65) and Gianlorenzo Bernini's *David Slaying Goliath* (p. 79). The timelessness, balance, symmetry, order, logic, and restraint of the one is clearly contrasted with the emotional violence and "moment-in-time" viewpoint of the other. Whether you use the terms classical-romantic, Apollonian-Dionysian, or ethos-pathos, the contrast is the same, and many examples can be found without too much difficulty. In music, for example, contrast the *Dies Irae* and *Tuba Mirum* sections of the Mozart Requiem with the same sections in the Verdi or Berlioz Requiems. The text is the same, but the style of composition is obviously quite different.

    3. In discussing the worksheet in the Workbook, or just in mentioning the various periods, you might play a brief portion of a musical work representative of that period, thereby illustrating differences in style.

    4. Another approach to style would be to compare the treatments given the same song by two different artists. The very pleasant-sounding treatment given *Where Have all the Flowers Gone* by Peter, Paul, and Mary, for example, is in marked contrast to the stark monophonic treatment given by Pete Seeger. You might ask the students which they prefer, musically speaking, and then discuss the message each is trying to convey. Considering that the song is an antiwar protest, does not the one lull us into a state of complacency, while the other forces us to concentrate on the message?

QUESTIONS AND TOPICS
    1. What are the elements whose sum forms a musical style?
    2. Describe some of the social uses of music.
    3. The social uses of music in contemporary American society.
    4. Style periods in the visual arts compared to those in music.
    5. The role of pictorial evidence in the history of music.

# II.
# THE MIDDLE AGES AND RENAISSANCE

## II-1. MUSIC IN THE MIDDLE AGES (450-1450)

OBJECTIVES

The section provides a brief overview of the medieval period (dark ages, romanesque, and gothic periods) and defines the roles of the three principal social classes of the time: nobility, peasantry, and clergy. The uses of instruments in the predominantly vocal music of the period are discussed, as is the ambivalent attitude of the church authorities toward musical instruments. The church modes are defined, and the role of Pope Gregory in chant organization is explained. One chant, the *Alleluia: Vidimus stellam*, is singled out for study and presentation in both modern and medieval chant notation. The secular music of the period is then briefly introduced. The life of the jongleur is described, as is that of the musical poet of this age of chivalry, the knight. An estampie is discussed as an example of instrumental music. The evolution of polyphony is traced from its beginnings in simple parallel organum, through the addition of contrary motion and rhythmical independence, to the complex creations of the members of the Notre Dame school, Leonin and Perotin. The *ars nova* in France and Italy during the fourteenth century is then briefly discussed, the mass ordinary defined, and the Agnus Dei from Machaut's *Notre Dame* Mass given as an example.

SUGGESTIONS

1. Discuss the prejudice inherent in the term "Middle" Ages. Can we conceive of 1,000 years of western history (thirty generations!) in which virtually nothing of significance occurred? Using the chart in the Student Workbook, try to develop a picture of medieval life. Personalities should also include legendary ones, for often the students can associate more quickly and closely (assuming the associations are correct). Robin Hood, Richard, John, and the Magna Carta can be discussed briefly (and humorously too if you ask the students to tell the story, for frequently bits of Errol Flynn, Douglas Fairbanks and Kevin Costner from TV showings get mixed in), for they bring the time alive, and anchor the people and events to a specific date (1215). The heroes of the medieval romances (a genre that will serve as the impetus for romanticism) such as Roland, Siegfried, Ilya Mourometz, el Cid, Leminkeinen, *et. al.*, could also be mentioned.

2. Discuss the social groupings of the Middle Ages, and then compare to present day America. Do we have a nobility and a peasantry? How does the power of the church today compare with then? (Note, for example, the many prominent clergymen in the present African American movement.) If there are classes today, are there musical associations? (Lawrence Welk vs. the BeeGees?)

3. The mention of Hildegard of Bingen should whet one's appetite for more information on the status of women in music. There is no question that women have been ignored in standard writings on the subject, and it is time that their role be recognized by examples of women composers and performers. A highly recommended resource for further information is *Women Making Music*, edited by Jane Bowers and Judith Tick (Urbana: University of Illinois Press, 1986, hereafter referred to as WMM). One learns, for example, that not only did Hildegard compose a significant number of antiphons, responsories, and sequences, but also the earliest extant liturgical morality play, *Ordo virtutum*, which "predates by about two centuries any other works

in this genre" (p. 28). Three of her compositions are included in *Historical Anthology of Music by Women* edited by James R. Briscoe (Bloomington: Indiana University Press, 1987, hereafter referred to as HAMW). All three have been recorded, and Hildegard would certainly be worth including in any discussion of medieval music.

4. In discussing the restrictions, formulas, and sacred emphasis of the Middle Ages, consider that the pictorial arts were under similar restraints. The Byzantine icon *Madonna and Child Enthroned*, included in the color plates, is a perfect example of how an anonymous painter transcended the strict formal rules. As described by H. W. Janson (*History of Art*, Prentice Hall, 1966, p. 178), the work, although painted in the thirteenth century, "reflects a type several hundred years earlier. Echoes of the Classicism of the Second Golden Age abound: the graceful pose, the rich play of drapery folds, the tender melancholy of the Virgin's face, the elaborate, architectural perspective of the throne (which looks rather like a miniature replica of the Colosseum). But all these elements have become oddly abstract. The throne, despite its foreshortening, no longer functions as a three-dimensional object, and the highlights on the drapery resemble ornamental sunbursts, in strange contrast to the soft shading of hands and faces. The total effect is neither flat nor spatial but transparent, somewhat like that of a stained-glass window." The text compares this icon to a Gregorian chant's "otherworldly feeling." Can even further analogies be fruitfully discussed?

5. Discuss the church modes and their use. As a basis for comparison, play the major and minor scales first, and then help the students to sing several of the modes. Explain that the modes can be defined by means of the white notes on the piano, and help them write the scales in their Workbooks (p. 29).

6. Compare the medieval chant notation of the *Alleluia: Vidimus stellam*, its modern transcription, and standard notation. Since there are no bar lines, how can there be rhythm? Quickly review the basic rules for pronouncing church Latin, and then ask a student to read the text. (Since many college students today have difficulty reading English, we should be patient when confronting them with another language.) After following the transcribed notation, encourage the students to follow the chant notation (recording in brief and basic sets, 2:09).

7. Discuss the importance of dancing to the nobility, and the use of music for accompaniment. Possibly some of the students have had experiences with country or square dancing that they can share. Have the students ever seen, heard, or danced to music provided by only one or two musicians? Play the estampie and review the above comments (recording in basic set, 1:15). Is it danceable? What element of music is most important for dancing? Must there be harmony?

8. Discuss the concept of the nobility as composer-poets. How does this compare with the standard conception of the Age of Chivalry? As examples, see the trouvère virelai *Or la truix* and the minnelied *Willekommen Mayenschein* by Neidhart von Reuenthal, both included in Parrish and Ohl's *Masterpieces of Music Before 1750* (music and recording; hereafter referred to as MM). Both pieces are quite short.

9. Recorded examples and illustrations of medieval instruments can be found in David Munrow's *Instruments of the Middle Ages and Renaissance* (Angel SBZ-3810) with the Early Music Consort of London. The book contained in the record set has many illustrations, which should be used while the recording is played. See also *Instruments of the Middle Ages and Renaissance* (Vanguard 71219/20) by the Musica Reservata of London. Comparisons can be made, both favorable and unfavorable, with modern instruments.

10. The brief passing mention of Beatriz de Dia is another opportunity for bringing in the role of women in music. Information is scant, but her portrait and her song *A chanter m'er de so*, the only surviving example of a troubadour song composed by a woman, are included in WMM,

pp. 48-49 (see also HAMW, pp. 11-13). Considering that half your class is probably female, the poem, contrasted with the typical male themes, should make for a lively discussion.

11. Review texture by asking the class to sing a familiar song (*America, Mary Had a Little Lamb,* etc.) in unison. Discuss the natural division of voices, and the perfect intervals (octaves between sexes, fourths and fifths between registers S, A, T, B). Introduce parallel organum, and ask them to sing the song again, this time concentrating on the organum, or use the examples of parallel organum found in HAM (I, 25; recording MHS OR-350).

12. Discuss Machaut's career as priest, secretary, courtier, and church official, as described in the text. If you wish to relate this to modern times, how does his career compare with that of today's "serious" composer? In what sense has the university replaced the court and cathedral as a patron of music? How does a priest come to write a love song?

13. Discuss the importance of the mass in the Roman Catholic church, and its various sections (see the Student Workbook, p. 30). Point out the sections of the mass ordinary, and the importance of Machaut's setting as the first polyphonic treatment by a known composer. Draw attention to the Agnus Dei, as discussed in the text, then play the work (recording in brief and basic sets, 3:18).

QUESTIONS AND TOPICS
1. What was the attitude of the church toward the use of musical instruments?
2. Describe the musical life of a major cathedral.
3. What are the characteristics of Gregorian chant?
4. How are the church modes different from the major and minor scales?
5. What is the general structure and character of the chant *Alleluia: Vidimus stellam*?
6. The liturgy of the Roman Catholic church.
7. Music in the Roman Catholic church today.
8. How authentic is the portrayal of the song contest in Wagner's *Tannhäuser*?
9. Compare the rhythm of the Gregorian chant with that of the trouvère songs.
10. Instrumental accompaniment in the troubadour-trouvère repertory.
11. Trace the evolution of organum from its simplest to its most complex style.
12. Describe the rhythmic innovations of the Notre Dame composers.
13. Describe the career of Guillaume de Machaut.
14. Discuss the rhythmic innovations of the "New Art."
15. Describe the form and stylistic characteristics of Machaut's *Notre Dame* Mass.
16. Musicians at court in the fourteenth century.

## II-2. MUSIC IN THE RENAISSANCE (1450-1600)

OBJECTIVES

This section describes the European Renaissance as a period of exploration and humanism and as a time when the Protestant Reformation greatly weakened the dominance of the Catholic church. It was a period that saw the invention of printing and the idealization of the "universal man," among whose attributes was proficiency in music. The music of the period, predominantly a cappella vocal music, is characterized by word-painting, polyphonic texture, and gently-flowing rhythm. The two important forms of Renaissance sacred vocal music, the motet and the mass, are described and illustrated, respectively, by Josquin's *Ave Maria . . . Virgo serena* and the Kyrie of Palestrina's *Pope Marcellus* Mass. The madrigal is then discussed, with Thomas Weelkes's *As Vesta Was Descending* as an example. The development of instrumental music as a genre independent of vocal music is outlined, and Andrea Gabrieli's Ricercar in the Twelfth Mode is discussed as an example of instrumental polyphony.

SUGGESTIONS

1. Gunpowder, the compass, and the invention of moveable type have been credited as some of the major factors in bringing about the Renaissance. Through student responses, discuss life before and after each, and their effectiveness for change. The end of feudalism through gunpowder (as demonstrated by the battles of Agincourt and Crecy), the ability to navigate more securely when out of sight of land, and the possibility of mass production of books are only a few of the many points to consider. (Imagine the effect on education if each student had to copy the text by hand before commencing the course?) The Student Workbook has a chart that can be filled in before class and then discussed, or used in class concurrent with discussion. See also the video cassette *The Flowering of Harmony,* program 2 in *The Music of Man* series (Home Vision MUS09).

2. Using Shakespeare as an example of a major personality of the Renaissance, discuss the use of music as an integral part of his plays. To what extent does he assume an audience knowledgeable in music in order for his words to be understood and appreciated? The New York Consort of Viols' recording *The Sweet Power of Musick* (MHS 4123) has a delightful selection of quotations and musical examples.

3. The Student Workbook contains a worksheet for comparing medieval and Renaissance styles. Choose any three compositions, and see if the students can correctly identify the styles of each after hearing. Be sure to give them the titles and record information when completed, in the hope they may wish to hear other examples.

4. The text stresses the importance of the "pagan cultures of ancient Greece and Rome" in the emergence of Renaissance humanism. Just how were the literary masterpieces transmitted from the ancient world to Renaissance Europe? Since only the clergy were literate during the Middle Ages, were these pagan manuscripts preserved, copied, and translated by monks, or is there another explanation (old manuscripts still preserved, translations from Arabic copies, etc.)? What do we mean by the Greek and Latin classics? Is a classic really "a book everyone talks about but nobody reads"?

5. Play as much of Josquin's *Ave Maria* as you have score on page 69 of the text. Can the students identify the imitation, and separate the octaves from the unison? (Reactions will vary, depending on the amount of polyphonic music covered previously.) Quickly review the basic rules for pronouncing church Latin, and then ask a student to read part of the text. Play the selection again, this time continuing (recording in brief and basic sets, 4:43). Can the words be understood, and is the pronunciation correct? To what extent does stepwise motion predominate

over the use of skips? Are there any instances of word painting? (Note the annotated vocal text reference to "increased rhythmic animation" to reflect "new joy.")

6. Discuss the statement that "every educated person was expected to play an instrument and read musical notation" made on page 66. Can the students name other personalities of the past and present who were also competent musicians, proving that this attitude toward music did not hold for the Renaissance alone? (Jefferson, Franklin, Hopkinson, Truman, and Clinton, are some examples just from American history.) How many students sing or play instruments regularly? Has the stereo or TV replaced live music in the American home? How many students feel that an educated person today should be able to perform musically? (You might wish to give a commercial at this point for any opportunities for instrumental instruction available at your school, such as group classes, ensembles for beginning and intermediate instrumentalists, community orchestras, bands, or choruses, Suzuki programs in which the parent learns along with the child, etc.)

7. Relating to the above discussion, present Weelkes's madrigal as if one were finishing supper and the part books were brought out. A first playing of the madrigal would give the students a general familiarity with a cappella singing in English, the plot of the text, the polyphonic texture, and an appreciation of the skill demanded from the educated person of the time. The various word-paintings could then be discussed and illustrated, followed by a second playing for full comprehension (recording in brief and basic sets, 2:53; music in NS, and in E. H. Fellowes, *English Madrigal School*, vol. 22)

8. Instrumental music and the church may be discussed using Gabrieli's Ricercar as an example (recording in basic set, 2:02). If using a stereophonic recording, does separating the speakers help achieve an antiphonal effect? Compare this version with a recording made using recorders (see record set, second edition), brass (see record set, third and fourth editions), or other combinations.

9. The Student Workbook has a research project devoted to some of the more important Renaissance instruments. It would be most helpful if you could provide illustrations of some of the instruments listed, along with recordings to illustrate the timbres. The recordings mentioned in section II-1.9 above can serve here as well.

10. The text states "a wealth of [Renaissance] dance music has come down to us," but gives no examples. The record set contains Praetorius's *La Bourrée* from *Terpsichore* (basic set, 1:54). While a delightful work to listen to, as the text suggests, it would be more interesting and relevant to see some Renaissance dances performed. An excellent video cassette, *Le Gratie d'Amore: European Court Dance of the Late Renaissance*, contains performances of dances from Thoinot Arbeau's *Orchesography*, Fabritio Caroso's *Il Ballarino* and *Nobiltà di Dame*, and Cesare Negri's *Le Gratie d'Amore* (available from the Historical Dance Foundation, 31 Union Square West, New York, NY 10003). It would be even more fun, and unquestionably more effective in bringing the topic to life, if some Renaissance dances could be *danced*. A classroom with movable chairs could easily provide sufficient space for one or more couples, perhaps even the whole class. The Student Workbook has a research project devoted to some of the more important dances of the Renaissance. While time will probably not permit illustrating all of them in class, there may be some dance majors who would be interested in explaining this fascinating subject further, and helping in the demonstration. Even without such help, some simple dances could be attempted in class. The recording *May I have the Pleasure?* (TWR-771-2, Towne Waytes Society, Vancouver, Canada) not only has the music, but has a small booklet with instructions for each dance. Other records you might explore are *Dance Music of the Renaissance* (Archive 2533111), *Gothic and Renaissance Dances* (MHS 761), and *Dance Music Through the Ages* (Archiv 2723051). Some popular basse danses, bransles, pavanes, allemandes, and tourdions may be found on the recording *French Dances of the*

*Renaissance* (Nonesuch H-71036). The Broadside Band's CD *Danses populaires françaises* contains a number of Arbeau's dances (Harmonia Mundi 901152). Historical background, music, and full descriptions (including Labanotation) may be found in the excellent little publication by the Dance Notation Bureau of Ingrid Brainard's *Three Court Dances of the Early Renaissance*.

QUESTIONS AND TOPICS

1. What was the movement called humanism? How did it originate, and what were its main characteristics? (Are the major personalities included in the chart in the student's workbook?)
2. Was life for professional musicians in the Renaissance different from the Middle Ages?
3. Shakespeare and music.
4. Flemish composers in Renaissance Europe.
5. Word-painting in Renaissance vocal music.
6. What are the basic elements of Josquin's technique?
7. How does the career of Josquin Desprez reflect the life of a musician in the Renaissance?
8. The secular vocal music of Josquin Desprez.
9. What are the characteristics of the Renaissance madrigal?
10. Similarities and differences in the madrigal and the motet.
11. Compare the number and variety of Renaissance instruments to those in use today.
12. Humor and earthiness in the English madrigal.
13. The dances of the Renaissance and their music.

# III. THE BAROQUE PERIOD

## III-1 BAROQUE MUSIC (1600-1750)

### OBJECTIVES

This section opens with a general characterization of baroque style as one that "fills space—canvas, stone, or sound—with action and movement." Baroque style is set against a backdrop of seventeenth-century scientific discovery. The baroque in music is divided into three periods—early, middle and late—and the general style characteristics of each are briefly defined. The main body of the section treats in turn each of the following elements of late baroque style: unity of mood, rhythm, melody, terraced dynamics, texture, the basso continuo, text setting, the baroque orchestra, and baroque forms.

### SUGGESTIONS

1. Discuss the general characteristics of the baroque, and how the "age of grandeur" differed from the Renaissance. You might wish to use the color illustrations in the text: compare the calm, order, and timeless serenity of Leonardo's *Saint Anne, the Virgin and Child* with the emotional and dynamic effect of Nicolas Poussin's *Rape of the Sabine Women*. In the latter, note that a split-second in time is being portrayed, as if the scene were but one frame of a motion picture. Similar comparisons can be drawn between Michelangelo's *David* (p. 65) and Bernini's *David Slaying Goliath* (p. 79). The Palace of Versailles (p. 79) is certainly a fine example of "grandiose magnificence," one of the characteristics of the baroque. The ceiling fresco by Giovanni Battista Gaulli and *Adoration of the Magi* by Peter Paul Rubens are other excellent visual examples of baroque style (see color plates).

2. Discuss the importance of music to the nobility in the baroque. By way of illustration, ask how many of the students have their own radios and/or stereo sets (most likely they all do). Do we not use modern sound equipment in a manner similar to the nobility, to provide music for entertainment, relaxation, and dancing? Is not the student with his portable radio like the nobleman with his traveling orchestra? Using Louis XIV as the epitome of the high baroque, discuss life at the Palace of Versailles (p. 79) and other courts. Mention could be made of *Les vingt-quatre violons du roi*, followed by a discussion of the size, instrumentation, and performance practices of the baroque orchestra. Some of the students may even have seen *Tous les matins du monde*, the film dealing with Louis XIV's famous gambist Marin Marais and his teacher, Monsieur de Sainte Colombe.

3. Discuss the life and duties of the court musician, and compare them to those of the town musicians (stadtpfeiffer, waits, etc.). Include the responsibilities of the music director, and compare with similar positions today (Sousa, et al., writing and performing their own music as well as that of others). Stress the constant demand for new music.

4. Discuss the concept of the figured bass, and its similarity to modern lead sheets. If possible, bring a sample to class, and illustrate, or discuss, the manner in which a cocktail pianist or jazz performer chords and improvises on a melody. Explain the importance of the doubling instrument on the bass line, especially considering the low dynamic level of the harpsichord.

5. As an introduction to the complete unit on the baroque, consider showing *New Voices for Man* or *Age of the Composer*, videos in *The Music of Man* series dealing with the baroque period, or a filmstrip, such as *Music and Art in the Baroque* (EAV).

6. In approaching a new period, it is suggested that representative excerpts of both the old and new styles be compared, and the Student Workbook has a worksheet for that purpose. Josquin's *Ave Maria*, for example, could be compared to the opening of Bach's *Wachet Auf*, or Gabrieli's Ricercare to the Fifth *Brandenburg*. Be sure to identify the compositions after discussion, in the hope the students will wish to hear more, and also as preparation for when they study the compositions later in the course.

QUESTIONS AND TOPICS

1. How does the use of recurrent motivic development in the baroque compare with the melodic style of contemporary jazz improvisation?

2. Describe some  conventions adopted by baroque composers in setting words to music.

3. Describe the elements that comprise figured bass.

4. The growth of the violin family during the baroque period.

5. The development of the orchestra and orchestration during the baroque period.

## III-2. THE CONCERTO GROSSO AND RITORNELLO FORM

OBJECTIVES

This section defines the elements that comprise the multimovement concerto grosso. The role of tutti and soloists are described, and the ritornello form is explained and illustrated by the first movement of Bach's Fifth *Brandenburg* Concerto, for which a Listening Outline is provided.

SUGGESTIONS

1. Review the concept of terraced dynamics, and the baroque principle of contrast between loud and soft sounds. Define the concerto grosso, and introduce ritornello form.

2. Review any previous discussions about Bach. Review also the use of the Listening Outlines, and then play the ritornello theme (in brief and basic sets, 9:43). Once the students can recognize the theme, proceed into the first movement. Because of the present decibel level of much popular music, it will probably all sound soft, and it may take several hearings before they are able to hear dynamic and instrumental contrasts. When they can distinguish tutti from ripieno passages, continue into the movement, stressing especially the great (and unusual) harpsichord solo. Mention might be made of the difference in baroque terminology in that flute meant recorder, while the German flute was the modern flute. If possible, contrast two recordings of the same work, one in which the recorder takes the place of the flute as a solo instrument.

3. Volume III/2 of the *Neue Bach Ausgabe* contains the six *Brandenburg* concertos along with three facsimiles of the composer's manuscript. The second and third of the facsimiles should prove particularly interesting to the student: the second shows the opening of the Fifth Concerto, while the third contains a copy of the continuo part, with the figures placed above the bass line.

4. Some mention should be made of the other five concertos in the *Brandenburg* set. If time is insufficient to play any portions, at least discuss the varied instrumentations with the aim of whetting the appetites of any performers in the class. Certainly flutists should be interested in numbers 4 and 5, trumpeters in number 2, horn players in number 1, and so forth. Note that the Student Workbook has a page for them to complete while listening to one of the other concertos.

QUESTIONS AND TOPICS

1. Describe the use of the ritornello in the concerto grosso.

2. Describe the use of tutti versus soloists in the concerto grosso.

3. Describe the circumstances surrounding the composition of Bach's *Brandenburg* Concertos.
4. Bach in Cöthen.
5. The use of soloists in Bach's six *Brandenburg* concertos.

## III-3. THE FUGUE

### OBJECTIVES

In this section a general definition of fugue is presented, the makeup of the fugal exposition explained, and the form of the fugue as a whole discussed. The following terms, relating to fugal procedures, are defined: subject, answer, countersubject, episode, stretto, pedal (or organ) point, inversion, retrograde, augmentation, and diminution. Bach's *Little* Fugue in G Minor for organ is analyzed, complete with Listening Outline.

### SUGGESTIONS

1. Discuss the form of the fugue, the various terms involved, and ways in which the subject can be varied. Show how the fugue is one more resolution to the artistic challenge of providing unity as well as variety. Play or sing the subject of Bach's *Little* Fugue as many times as necessary for the students to be able to sing along (in brief and basic sets, 4:04; score in NS). In some classes just the first two bars may have to suffice for the subject. When the students are sure about the subject, challenge them to count how many complete statements of the subject they hear in the work. You might help them with the first two or three, especially if you have diagrammed the exposition on the board. The Workbook has a listening exercise that can be used to sketch the entrances of the subject and to indicate episodes. After listening, ask for a show of hands for how many heard four complete statements, five, etc., as high as you feel necessary. The usual variety of showings will prove to them how skillful Bach was in presenting the subject, and since the answer is in the text, will also give you an indication of who reads the assignments.

2. Discuss the question of transcriptions, comparing them to the original (see the Research Project in the Student Workbook). In addition to the standard orchestral transcriptions, you might consider a symphonic band transcription (Col M-31126), an arrangement for wind quintet, or even a transcription for koto, shakuhachi, guitar, bass, and drums (RCA VICS-1458).

3. As another example of a fugue, consider the prelude and fugue in C minor from Bach's *Well-Tempered Clavier*, book 1. Comparison can be made between the harpsichord, piano, clavichord (Archive 2708006), Swingle Singers (Phillips PHM 200-097), and synthesizer (Col MS-7194) versions. In each case ask the students to give reasons for their preferences.

### QUESTIONS AND TOPICS

1. Describe the ways in which a fugue subject can be varied.
2. Define and illustrate inversion, retrograde, augmentation, and diminution.
3. Bach's organ fugues.
4. Bach's *Well-Tempered Clavier*.
5. Bach's own precedent for musical transcriptions.

## III-4. THE ELEMENTS OF OPERA

### OBJECTIVES

Since opera originated in the baroque period, this section is designed to introduce the student to the various conventions of opera as a prelude to the discussion of Monteverdi's *Orfeo*.

The text describes the function of all those involved in an opera production: singers, orchestral players, conductor, chorus, dancers, supernumeraries, technicians, stagehands, vocal coaches, and prompters. Also discussed are the relationship between composer and librettist, the characteristics of serious as opposed to comic opera, and the enormous range of characters to be found on the musical stage. The basic voice categories are explained, as are the various types of musical numbers to be found in opera, including the aria, the recitative, and the various types of vocal ensembles. Also included is a discussion of the functions of the operatic chorus and the prelude or overture.

SUGGESTIONS

1. Through informal discussion in class, determine the general attitude toward opera. Why is it that so many of our students have negative opinions? An open discussion should bring out many valuable points, both from those who have had good as well as bad experiences. (How can an unprepared visit to the local opera house or traveling troupe by a grade school class possibly have favorable results?) While the terms are important, they should be secondary to the aim of exciting and preparing the students for an actual performance.

2. Begin with a dramatic play: are not certain conventions accepted, such as the passage of time, differences of place, and the invisible fourth wall? In opera the audience is simply asked to accept one more convention: the characters sing their emotions, rather than "emote" them. As for the claim that all operas are tragic, note that there are a number of comic ones, but note also that any list of academy award nominations will have a great number of tragedies represented. Is tragedy more noble, or more worthy perhaps, of artistic effort than comedy?

3. Present "a visit to the opera house" by starting at whatever level you feel your students are. You may have to begin by telling them where operas are given in your area, how to get there, where to buy tickets, how the prices compare with movie or theater tickets, how to dress (some may still have the mistaken notion that all patrons of the Metropolitan Opera wear white tie and tails), the ushers, the program, and finally the seat. Hopefully the above can all be dispensed with in many classes, but if the students have never seen anything live except a rock or rap concert, they may need some guidance. Once in their hypothetical seats, discuss the overture or prelude, the aria, ensemble, chorus, when to applaud, etc. Note that the Student Workbook has a page devoted to preparing for a visit to the opera in the hope of making such a trip a more pleasurable experience.

4. To add a note of humor, especially if the class is already familiar with opera and most of the terms covered, you may wish to read excerpts from the commentaries on opera by Joseph Addison and Benedetto Marcello reprinted in SSR. Although these essays were inspired by opera as it existed in the eighteenth century, much of their content can apply to opera in any era, including our own.

QUESTIONS AND TOPICS

1. Describe some of the performers involved in the making of opera.
2. Describe some of the various voice categories used in opera.
3. Discuss the controversy surrounding the translation of opera and the use of supertitles.
4. Describe some of the uses of the operatic ensemble.
5. Opera: its prehistory.
6. The economics of opera, past and present.
7. The opera audience, past and present.
8. Ballet in opera.

## III-5. OPERA IN THE BAROQUE ERA

OBJECTIVES

The origins of opera in the Florentine Camerata are explained, and the early efforts of Peri and Monteverdi described. The influence of Greek mythology and ancient history on these early operas is shown. The rise of the virtuoso singer, the castrato, and the form of the da capo aria are covered. The career of Claudio Monteverdi is briefly traced and his contributions to the development of opera described. The plot of *Orfeo* is outlined, and the recitative *Tu se' morta* is discussed in detail, complete with text and translation.

SUGGESTIONS

1. Review the Renaissance madrigal, especially with regard to its polyphonic treatment of the text. Then discuss the Florentine Camerata and their desire to have a single vocal line follow the rhythms and pitch fluctuations of speech. In order to illustrate, ask the class to read any sentence in the text, using different voice inflections to change meanings. How would they set the sentence to music?

2. The aims and ideals of the Camerata are expressed in the writings of Pietro de'Bardi, Ottavio Rinuccini, Giulio Caccini, and Jacopo Peri, all to be found in SSR. You may wish to scan these pertinent writings quickly for passages to be read and discussed in class. See also *The Earliest Operas* in MWW.

3. Discuss the Orpheus legend, and its importance throughout history even up to modern times (perhaps some of the students have seen the Cocteau film.). Review the Florentine Camerata, and the elements of baroque opera. Review, if necessary, Italian pronunciation, and set the scene before playing the recitative *Tu se' morta*. The text mentions three climaxes; discuss and see if the students can hear them in context. (Recording in brief and basic sets, 2:21)

4. The revolutionary aspect of the early baroque can be discussed by reference to the violent attack on Monteverdi by Artusi, and the reply by Monteverdi's brother, both found in SSR. See also *The "Second Practice"* in MWW.

QUESTIONS AND TOPICS

1. Discuss the aims and ideals of the Florentine Camerata.
2. Describe those factors that made Venetian opera a great tourist attraction.
3. Describe the form and function of the recitative and da capo aria combination.
4. Stage machinery in the baroque era and the contemporary opera house.
5. The castrato as a sociomusical phenomenon.
6. Trace the career of Monteverdi, and explain his importance in the history of music.
7. Monteverdi and the development of the orchestra.
8. The Orpheus legend as treated by Peri, Monteverdi, Rossi, Gluck, Pergolesi, Krenek, and Stravinsky.

## III-6. THE BAROQUE SONATA

OBJECTIVES

In this brief section the sonata is defined as "a composition in several movements for one to eight instruments." The trio sonata is defined, with Arcangelo Corelli's Trio Sonata in E minor, Op. 3, no. 7 discussed as an example.

SUGGESTIONS

1. Review the concept of basso continuo, and the practice of having an instrument double the bass line of the organ or harpsichord. Remind students of the sound of the harpsichord, as in the *Brandenburg* concerto covered previously. Discuss also the baroque practice of interchangeability between upper voices, such as the text's reference to violins, flutes or oboes.

2. You may wish to review the origin of the sonata by referring back to Gabrieli's Ricercar in the Twelfth Mode discussed earlier. Its multisectional form is a step toward the multi-movement baroque sonata.

3. Discuss the development of the violin family, and how it differs from the viol. Place Corelli's position in the development of violin technique, the importance of chords and double stops, and the "golden age of strings." The major violin makers, such as Nicolò Amati, Antonio Stradivarius, and Andrea Guarnerius, might also be mentioned at this time.

4. Discuss Corelli's Sonata Op. 3, no. 7, which the text describes as "a fine example of the baroque trio sonata." (Recording in supplementary sets) Note that Parrish and Ohl refer to this work as "a typical sonata da chiesa," and you may wish to introduce the differencs between the sonata da chiesa and da camera.

QUESTIONS AND TOPICS

1. Describe the overall construction of the baroque sonata.
2. Discuss the instrumental makeup of the trio sonata.
3. Distinguish between the sonatas da camera and da chiesa.
4. The origins of the baroque sonata.
5. The baroque sonata in England, France and Germany.
6. Discuss Corelli's role in the expansion of violin technique.
7. Describe Corelli's compositional output.
8. Discuss the overall formal plan of Corelli's Trio Sonata in E minor, Op. 3, no. 7.

# III-7. ANTONIO VIVALDI

OBJECTIVES

The career of Antonio Vivaldi is discussed in this section, including his work at the Pietà. The *Spring* Concerto from *The Four Seasons* is analyzed as representative of his output. A Listening Outline is provided for the first movement.

SUGGESTIONS

1. Review the discussion on Corelli, and the rise of the violin family. Discuss the work of Vivaldi in Venice with relationship to the development of string technique, and also the great variety of instrumental combinations. The text mentions the revival of his music in the 1950s, and a look at the number of his concertos listed in the latest Schwann *Opus* will quickly bear that out.

2. Discuss the concerto analyzed in the text, first within the context of the complete *Four Seasons,* and then as the opening work in the set. Be sure to read the translation of the sonnet which inspired Vivaldi, resulting in works the text refers to as predecessors of romantic program music. (The original Italian text, and the florid dedication to Count Venceslao Marzin, are included in the Eulenburg edition (1220/3) of the score). As with the Bach discussed earlier, it might prove beneficial to play the ritornello theme first, then discuss tone painting, finally playing through the complete movement. A Listening Outline is provided for the first movement, and it is included in the brief and basic sets (3:15; score in NS). The second and third movements are included in the supplementary sets.

3. There are several recordings of this work using original instruments (Col. Odyssey Y 35930, for example). Without going too deeply into the arguments pro and con the use of original instruments, a comparison of the two interpretations could result in a lively and thought-provoking discussion.

QUESTIONS AND TOPICS

    1. Describe Vivaldi's career and his subsequent position in music history.
    2. Describe the concerts of the Pietà.
    3. Discuss the overall form and general character of Vivaldi's *Spring* Concerto.
    4. The Vivaldi revival in the 1950s.
    5. Vivaldi's music for unusual instruments and combinations.
    6. Vivaldi's concerti grossi: one concerto 300 times?

## III-8. JOHANN SEBASTIAN BACH

OBJECTIVES

    Bach's career is traced from his birth into a musical family in 1685, through the various positions he held throughout Germany, to the final years at St. Thomas Church in Leipzig. The richness of his harmony and contrapuntal inventiveness are described, as are the rhythmic propulsion and the rich symbolism that characterize his output.

SUGGESTIONS

    1. The main biographical details of Bach's life are presented in this section, so it would be worth a few minutes to discuss his place in music history in his own time, and contrast it to his position at present (a page is provided in the Student Workbook for the biographical details). Some mention might also be made of his successful sons, and how they overshadowed him near the end of his life. You might also mention Anna Magdalena, who with four young children to take care of (from Bach's previous wife) still had to learn to play the harpsichord, resulting in the delightful *Notebook*, which should be recommended to any pianists in the class.
    2. Review the works already discussed, and place them within the chronology outlined in the text. Following sections may be introduced at this time, such as the baroque suite (III-9) and the chorale and church cantata (III-10), both of which include music by Bach as examples.

QUESTIONS AND TOPICS

    1. Describe the elements of Bach's style.
    2. Trace Bach's career from birth until 1723, the year he accepted the position in Leipzig.
    3. Describe Bach's duties in Leipzig.
    4. The Bach family.
    5. Bach's contemporaries, with special reference to the career of Georg Philipp Telemann.

## III-9. THE BAROQUE SUITE

OBJECTIVES

    The national origins of the various dances that make up the baroque suite are explained, as are the character of each dance and the binary form which they share. Also covered is the non-dance movement that frequently opens the suite: the French overture. Bach's Suite no. 3 in D major is examined in detail.

SUGGESTIONS

1. Discuss the importance of dancing to the nobility, and that at least one hour per day would be spent with the dancing master. Stress the significance of couple dancing in the evening, and that the ability to dance was one sign of a gentleman or lady. Discuss also the desire of the common people to emulate as best they could the actions of the nobility, including dancing, though on a lower and less sophisticated level.

2. Discuss the early history and development of the dance suite, and the work of Froberger in establishing the general sequence of allemande, courante, sarabande, and gigue. Froberger's Suite in E minor (MM no. 35) may be used to illustrate the development of the suite before Bach.

3. Discuss Bach's keyboard works, such as the English and French Suites, and the Partitas. Show how they continue the development of the suite from Froberger, and how Bach has added other dances, such as the gavotte, passepied, loure, and anglaise, and non-dance sections such as the prelude and air. The Student Workbook has a listening exercise for comparing two baroque suites.

4. Discuss Bach's orchestral suites, especially with regard to differences from the keyboard suites: the French overture, and the "modern" dances instead of some of the earlier forms.

5. Discuss Bach's Suite (Overture) No. 3, pointing out similarities and differences to the keyboard suites. If possible, play two different versions of one of the movements and compare with regard to the performance of the dotted rhythms (double dotted performance?), tempo, suitability for dancing, and effective use of instrumentation. In this regard it would be interesting to compare recordings of modern and period instruments (Air, Bourrée, and Gigue in basic sets, 4:42, 1:10, and 2:48; music in NS)

QUESTIONS AND TOPICS

1. Discuss the characteristic formal structure of the dances that form the baroque suite.

2. Describe the component parts and stylistic characteristics of the French overture.

3. Discuss the characteristics of each of the three dances in Bach's Suite in D major: gavotte, bourrée, and gigue.

4. The paired dances of the Renaissance as predecessor of the baroque suite.

5. The origins of the sarabande.

# III-10. THE CHORALE AND CHURCH CANTATA

OBJECTIVES

The place of music in the Lutheran service is described in this section, and the nature of the Lutheran chorale and the chorale prelude defined. The church cantata designed for the Lutheran service in Bach's time is singled out for special attention, after which a detailed study of three of the seven movements of Bach's Cantata no. 140, *Wachet Auf, Ruft Uns Die Stimme*, is presented. Texts and translations for the three movements are included, the first with annotations.

SUGGESTIONS

1. Discuss briefly the state of music in the Catholic church at the time (as covered in earlier classes), and the importance of congregational singing in the Protestant church, especially Lutheran services. You may even wish to have the class sing a hymn, unless you can assume all are familiar with the practice.

2. Discuss and define the chorale, using *Wachet Auf* as an example (text, p. 105). Help the students sing the chorale, so they will be better able to recognize it when listening to the cantata.

(If you wish them to sing it with the German text, help them first with the language; otherwise use "la"s)

3. To help students recognize the chorale in contrapuntal settings, and also demonstrate the form, play (live or on record) the chorale prelude based on *Wachet Auf*. (See for example Chapuis, 2-Tel. 2635077)

4. Discuss the form of the cantata, using *Wachet Auf* as an example. Unless you feel the students are fully familiar with the chorale (as a result of the above suggestions), play the seventh movement first. Following that, discuss the parable as a whole, and then each movement, both text and musical setting (fourth and seventh movements in brief and basic sets, 3:57, 1:44; first movement in basic sets, 8:02).

QUESTIONS AND TOPICS

1. Discuss the functions of the chorale and chorale prelude in the Lutheran church service.
2. Explain how the chorale melody is used in Bach's Cantata no. 140.
3. Cite examples of word-painting or musical symbolism in Bach's Cantata no. 140.
4. The Lutheran chorale and the Catholic hymn.
5. Folk songs as a source of the Lutheran chorale.
6. The chorale prelude: a study in textural variety.
7. Bach's cantatas: an overview.

# III-11. THE ORATORIO

OBJECTIVES

This section is intended mainly as a concise introduction to the term "oratorio." The oratorio is traced to its origin in early seventeenth-century Italy, and its characteristics are contrasted with those large-scale baroque vocal genres already discussed, the opera and the cantata.

SUGGESTIONS

1. Discuss the development of oratorio, comparing it to the opera. You may wish to speculate on the characteristics that make a given story suitable for treatment as an oratorio instead of an opera, considering the roles of the narrator, the chorus as commentators on and participants in the drama, and the orchestral accompaniment.

2. As examples of early oratorios you may consider Carissimi's *Jonas* (HAM, 207) or *Judicium Salomonis* (MM, 32). Both examples have texts and recordings. An even earlier example, though not as dramatic as the Solomon excerpt, is Cavalieri's *Rappresentazione di anima e di corpo* (HAM, 183). In all cases the text should be projected or made available through duplication.

QUESTIONS AND TOPICS

1. Compare and contrast the oratorio, opera, and the church cantata.
2. Discuss the roles of the narrator and the chorus in the oratorio.
3. Liturgical drama and the mystery play as forerunners of the oratorio.
4. The Passion oratorio.
5. The oratorio in France: Marc-Antoine Charpentier.

## III-12. GEORGE FRIDERIC HANDEL

OBJECTIVES

Handel's life is traced from his early years as a student of both music and law to his apprenticeship in Hamburg's opera house and his three-year sojourn in Italy. After a brief stay in Hanover, he established himself in London as the leading English composer of the time. His contributions to both opera and oratorio are explained, as are his tribulations as an entrepreneur. The bulk of the section is devoted to three selections from his oratorio *Messiah*.

SUGGESTIONS

1. Discuss briefly the biographical details of Handel's life, his success as an opera composer and impresario, his response to the failure of opera in England through the oratorio, and his stature with Bach as the greatest composers of the late baroque. (The Student Workbook has a worksheet to help with the biographical details.) If time permits, some examples of his instrumental works might be discussed and illustrated.

2. Review Italian opera, especially in its English environment. Suggestions made previously in the discussion of opera (III-4 and III-5 above) may also be considered at this time: readings from Joseph Addison's critique of Italian opera in England (SSR no. 61), and playing "Cara sposa" from *Rinaldo*, the reason for of Handel's first visit to England (MN no. 44).

3. Review the development of oratorio, and the circumstances that prompted Handel to leave opera for this form. With *Messiah* as an example, introduce the opening tenor aria, noting especially the word painting (brief and basic sets, 3:26). Comment briefly on the use of the chorus, and present "For unto us a child is born" (basic sets, 4:17). Be sure to leave sufficient time for the "Hallelujah" chorus, noting the annotated text on page 115. Take a moment to discuss the annotations to the text of the "Hallelujah" chorus before playing, as some students might confuse the actual text with the description (brief and basic sets, 3:49). If sufficient vocal scores are available for distribution, explain the piano reduction, and the possibility that solos heard in the recording may differ from the page due to improvisational embellishments.

4. In these days of informality when gentlemen seldom rise as a lady enters the room (although GIs may remember that they had to jump to attention when an officer entered the room), it may be worth taking a moment to discuss the tradition of rising for the "Hallelujah" chorus. Some feel that audiences still stand today simply because of the king's rising then, rather than as a tribute to the genius of the composer and his composition.

5. There is a very effective video cassette available, which should be considered either for classroom use or outside assignment. The Foundling Hospital version of 1754 was recorded in Westminster Abbey by Christopher Hogwood, the Westminster Abbey Choir, and the Academy of Ancient Music.

QUESTIONS AND TOPICS

1. Discuss Handel's career up to his departure for London in 1712.
2. Describe Handel's approach to the elements of opera.
3. Describe Handel's approach to the elements of oratorio.
4. The effect of *The Beggar's Opera* on Italian opera in England.
5. Opera in England during the first half of the eighteenth century.
6. Handel's instrumental music.

# IV. THE CLASSICAL PERIOD

## IV-1. THE CLASSICAL STYLE (1750-1820)

### OBJECTIVES

This section opens with a general survey of some nonmusical aspects of the classical period. The work of some great figures of the "age of enlightenment" is discussed, as well as the subsequent effect of these men on this age of revolution. Bach's sons are mentioned as representatives of the "gallant style," and their work related to that of the rococo artists. The problematical term "classical" is defined, and the remainder of the section seeks to define (often in comparison with the baroque) the various elements of classical style: contrast of mood, flexible rhythm, homophonic texture, melody, dynamics and the piano, the end of the basso continuo, the classical orchestra, and a general statement on classical forms.

### SUGGESTIONS

1. This section is designed as a general introduction to the classical period, and as such is quite self-sufficient. An exercise for comparing this period with the previous one may be found in the Student Workbook, and it is suggested that this be discussed either in class or as an assignment.

2. The Student Workbook also has a listening exercise to aid in comparing three works stylistically. It is suggested that you play portions of three works in class, permitting sufficient time for the students to fill in the blanks while listening. Space is available for them to write in their decision as to which period they feel it should be, and for them to write in the title and composer (once you've told them), should they wish to hear more on their own. You might compare, for example, the fast section of the French overture from the Bach Suite with the allegro from Haydn's *Surprise* Symphony. You may wish to consider having a baroque, classical, and "style gallant" work, but then the chart would have to be modified through your own discussion.

3. The status of the musician as a high-class servant can be discussed, using the situations of Haydn, Mozart, and Beethoven as examples (see, for example, "Haydn's Duties in the Service of Prince Esterházy," MWW 81). A discussion of the rise of the middle class in this period can concern the question of musical tastes and fashion. For example, the middle class consciously attended public concerts and operas, and provided their children with music lessons to fit them for society. Ask the students how many of them have had music lessons (assuming most of them consider themselves as "middle-class"), and how many public concerts and/or operas they have attended in the past year. Further, you may wish to question if, as a result of this class, they intend to provide such lessons for themselves or their children in the future. (A good time for another commercial, if you have classes available for them to take, and opportunities for instrumental and vocal music making either through community choruses, bands, or orchestras, or through classes.)

4. In discussing some of the political events of the time, you may wish to refer to the illustration of Goya's *The Third of May, 1808*, included in the color plates. Though painted in the classical period, the work has all the characteristics of romanticism. The subjective treatment of the scene puts the viewer squarely on the side of the peasants, even though this was a revolt against established authority and order as understood by the aristocracy at the time. The use of the lantern as a spotlight dramatically highlights the central figures: a person in an obvious martyr pose and a simple cleric, clearly indicating that the common levels of the church (as opposed to the aristocratic bishops and princes) are on the side of the rebellion, and these are

martyrs for a cause. Comparing this work with the *Death of Socrates* by David (color plate) will visually show the differences between the classic and romantic spirits.

5. If you wish to discuss the "style gallant," you might compare one of the compositions of J. C. or K. P. E. Bach to Fragonard's *The Pursuit* (p. 119) and Boucher's *The Interrupted Sleep* (color plate). The same pleasant salon style should be recognizable in both, and therein lay their charm. More important, in a course where virtually all works discussed are masterpieces, one needs the valleys to show off the mountains. Listening to this light unpretentious music, one develops a more genuine appreciation for Mozart. One could also mention that the "style gallant" was the popular movement at the time of the founding of our nation.

6. Should you wish to quote some writings from the period, the two excerpts from J. F. Reichardt (SSR nos. 75, 77) give fascinating insights into the musical life of Vienna and the major figures on the scene. See also "Vienna, 1800," MWW 90.

QUESTIONS AND TOPICS
1. Describe the intellectual climate of the "age of enlightenment."
2. Discuss some of the political events and sociological factors that made the classical period such a time of violent upheaval.
3. Discuss the role of the middle class in the musical life of the classical period.
4. Discuss the principal movements in the visual arts that spanned the period between the baroque and classical periods in music.
5. Discuss the diverse meanings attached to the term "classical."
6. Discuss the characteristics of the so-called "style gallant."
7. Discuss some of the respects in which classical music differed from the music of the baroque.
8. The development of the orchestra during the classical period.

# IV-2. SONATA FORM

OBJECTIVES
A clear distinction is made between the sonata and sonata form (or sonata-allegro form). Sonata form is then divided into its three main components, exposition, development, and recapitulation, and the characteristic properties of each section are analyzed. The optional slow introduction and coda are also discussed. The section concludes with a discussion of the first movement of Mozart's Symphony no. 40 in G Minor, for which a Listening Outline is provided.

SUGGESTIONS
1. It might be helpful to the students if you outlined sonata form on the board, indicating the tonal plan as you do so (since the material is already in the text, this should be done quickly, as the students will not need to copy from the board). Later, while playing the movement, you can silently point to the various sections as they occur, without causing the mood to be broken.

2. In discussing the Mozart movement, you may wish to raise some of the following questions: can examples of sequence be detected in the bridge? What element of the first theme is present in the closing theme? How does insistent repetition contribute to the "closing" quality of this theme? How does the harmony contribute to the "closing" quality of this theme? Are there examples of sequence in the development? Where?

3. It is recommended that multiple copies of the miniature score of the G Minor Symphony be available, and after discussion using the text and chalkboard, students be permitted to follow the score (with as much help as you feel the class needs, by circulating around the room helping

students who might be lost, by calling out rehearsal numbers from time to time, or by pointing to the major sections outlined on the board.) For home listening, draw attention to the Listening Outline in the text (recording in brief and basic sets, 8:16).

QUESTIONS AND TOPICS

1. Identify those movements of a multimovement work that are likely to be in sonata form.

2. Compare and contrast the exposition and recapitulation of a movement in sonata form.

3. Describe the nature of the development section of a movement in sonata form, and discuss the musical techniques that are likely to be found therein.

4. Describe the role of the optional introduction and coda often found with sonata form.

5. Thematic development in sonata form.

## IV-3. THEME AND VARIATIONS

OBJECTIVES

This section presents theme and variations form, and discusses some techniques by which a composer can vary musical ideas. The example given, complete with Listening Outline, is the second movement of Haydn's Symphony no. 94 (*Surprise*).

SUGGESTIONS

1. Depending upon the sophistication of your class, you may or may not wish to tell the old legend about the reason for the "surprise." Do cover the Listening Outline, the basic techniques for providing variation, and the specific means by which Haydn provides variety yet maintains unity (recording in brief and basic sets, 6:12).

2. You may wish to include Mozart's variations on *Ah, vous dirai-je, maman* (probably better known to the students as *Twinkle, Twinkle, Little Star*), K. 265, mentioned on page 122 of the text. Several recordings are listed in the latest Schwann catalog, and the music is easily available.

3. If you wish to pursue the matter even further, the brief and basic sets include the theme and variations on "Simple Gifts" segment of Copland's *Appalachian Spring*, which could be used as an additional example (see Section VI-13 below).

QUESTIONS AND TOPICS

1. Discuss some procedures available to the composer of theme and variations.

2. Thematic variation in improvised jazz.

3. Theme and variations: its prehistory.

## IV-4. MINUET AND TRIO

OBJECTIVES

The purpose of this section is to explain the minuet-trio-minuet form and the internal structure of these larger sections. The Beethovenian transformation of this dance movement into the scherzo is discussed, and the section ends with a discussion of the minuet from Mozart's *Eine Kleine Nachtmusik*, for which a Listening Outline is supplied.

SUGGESTIONS

1. The text states "the minuet was a stately, dignified dance in which the dancing couple exchanged curtsies and bows." Perhaps visions of a room full of ornately dressed gentlemen and

ladies bowing and scraping in three-quarter time fills the head of the student, with even a vague recollection that the Father of our Country was known to have danced the minuet. A few minutes spent in correcting these misconceptions may well give a better appreciation for the importance of dancing, the reason for the minuet's inclusion in symphonic forms even after it lost its popularity as a dance, and of the period as a whole.

It is impossible to have a feeling of baroque and classical style without some appreciation for the importance of the dance. Further information and practical suggestions may be found in Wendy Hilton's *Dance of Court & Theater* (Princeton Book Publishers, 1981). Even selected readings will bring rewarding insights and pleasures to anyone exploring the subject, and the minuet figures quite prominently.

The minuet was a product of the court of Louis XIV, and reflects its stylization and refinement. Classical ballet today is also an outgrowth of that court, and the five basic positions were first outlined by Louis's dancing master. (Perhaps one of your students with ballet experience could quickly demonstrate these positions?) The minuet was normally danced by one couple, while the others observed, flirted, or carried on conversations. The couple would first bow/curtsy to the presence (Louis, or the highest ranking nobleman present) and then to each other. They would then commence an intricate series of steps, tracing patterns with their feet on the floor that would frequently cover the full dancing area. The giving of hands while turning gracefully, and the beautifully embellished "Z" figures can make this a most sensuous dance, far from the common misperception. Steps were small, and the movements clear and economical, full of dignity and poise. The pattern consisted of four steps in six beats, or two measures of music (an important point for conductors and performers to remember so that the music does not become a *1-2-3* waltz). The couple would end facing the presence, and pay their respects again (the "curtsy" by the ladies consisted of a demi-plié).

To give some feeling of the difficulty of this dance, you might ask the class to stand comfortably in place. (Just notice the usual mixture of bad postures!) Now assume the first position (heels together, 45 degree angle), with chest and head up, stomach in (not so easy for some of us!), full of poise, dignity, and noble bearing. Assume that we are dressed in a beautifully ornamented costume, tightly laced or corseted for the ladies and quite heavy for the men. Men would also be expected to have a hat, usually quite ornate and quite heavy. Now try doing a demi-plié followed by a relevé a few times *gracefully*. One will begin to understand why the dancing master and daily practice were so important, and why, as with ballet dancers today, it took years of practice to become a good dancer.

Illustrations of the bow and hand gestures may be found in Hilton's book, and in Pierre Rameau's *The Dancing Master*. Note especially figure 20, "The King's Grand Ball," which illustrates the dance environment described above. Some intricate patterns are illustrated in E. Pemberton's *An Essay for the Improvement of Dancing*. (Both works are available in modern reprints, and the chances are that your library has them in its dance collection.) Musical examples may easily be found in the works of Jean-Philippe Rameau (no relation to Pierre). MHS 4002, besides a pair of minuets from his *Les Indes Galantes*, also contains examples of other dance types of the period. A recording mentioned previously (Section II-2 above), *French Dances of the Renaissance* (Nonesuch H-71036) also contains what Joshua Rifkin calls the perfect model of the "classical" minuet, a work by A. J. Exaudet. This recording is also interesting because the minuet is performed in a period arrangement for viola d'amore and harpsichord, thereby illustrating the sound of that once-popular instrument.

2. Unfortunately, many teachers will feel embarrassed about the above suggestions, and will go directly on to the minuet from Mozart's *Eine Kleine Nachtmusik*. A Listening Outline is available in the text, and of course the form should be discussed before playing. Note that the minuet by

this time is no longer intended for dancing, but rather for pleasant listening, as befits a serenade (recording in brief and basic sets, 2:01).

QUESTIONS AND TOPICS

1. Discuss the character and origins of the minuet as a dance.
2. Diagram the general and internal structures of the minuet movement of the classical symphony.
3. Beauchamp and the origins of classical ballet.
4. The minuet at the court of Louis XIV.
5. From minuet to scherzo: a study of Beethoven's third movements.
6. The serenade in the classical period.

## IV-5. RONDO

OBJECTIVES

This section explains the characteristics of rondo and sonata-rondo form. A Listening Outline is provided for the fourth movement of Beethoven's String Quartet in C minor, Op. 18, no. 4.

SUGGESTIONS

1. Another means of solving the artistic question of achieving variety and yet maintaining unity, the rondo is an important form worthy of discussion. The text uses for its example the last movement of Beethoven's Op. 18 no. 4 to focus on the medium of the string quartet at the same time. If multiple copies of the score are available, they could be used in class, and the Listening Outline used for home study. Both the medium of the string quartet and the form of the rondo should be discussed and illustrated (recording in brief and basic sets, 4:14).

2. You may wish to include the rondo of Beethoven's Piano Sonata in G minor, Op. 13 (*Pathétique*) in your discussion, since it is also contained in the basic set (3:46). A discussion of the first movement of the sonata may be found in Section IV-11 below, and the complete sonata is discussed in the fifth edition of the text, pages 271-74.

QUESTIONS AND TOPICS

1. Describe the principle that underlies rondo form.
2. Diagram two variants of rondo form.
3. Explain sonata-rondo form.
4. The *rondeau* of the French clavecinists: precursor of the classical rondo?
5. The independent rondos of Mozart and Beethoven.

## IV-6. THE CLASSICAL SYMPHONY

OBJECTIVES

The importance of the symphony as the great contribution of the classical period is explained. The symphonic output of Haydn, Mozart, and Beethoven is surveyed, and the characteristic content of each of the four movements of the classical symphony explored.

SUGGESTIONS

1. The basic component parts of the symphony have been discussed in earlier sections: sonata form, theme and variations, minuet and trio, and rondo. It is now time to put all the "trees" into the "forest" and show their context in a complete work. You may wish to cover this material very quickly and go on to the next section, perhaps give a short quiz on the materials covered so far in the classical period, or review the various component parts at this time.

2. If you wish additional materials for discussion in this connection, note that the basic set contains not only the works discussed so far (Haydn's *Surprise* Symphony, II, and Mozart's G minor, I), but the complete Mozart G Minor and Beethoven's Fifth Symphony. The supplementary set includes the first, third, and fourth movements of Haydn's *Surprise* Symphony.

3. Should you wish to discuss a symphony not covered in the text, please note there is a research project for this purpose in the Student Workbook. This would be particularly appropriate, for example, in preparing the students for a live performance they may be expected to attend.

QUESTIONS AND TOPICS

1. Describe the characteristic formal plans and content usually found in a classical symphony.

2. Explain how the various movements of a symphony are unified, balanced, and complemented.

3. Origins of the classical symphony.

4. Haydn's early symphonies.

5. The significance of the Mannheim school in the development of the symphony.

# IV-7. THE CLASSICAL CONCERTO

OBJECTIVES

The importance of the concerto in the classical era is explained and its dramatic nature defined. The classical concerto's three-movement form and double exposition in the first movement are discussed, and this procedure is contrasted with the standard sonata form. The nature and role of the cadenza are also treated.

SUGGESTIONS

1. This section is designed as a brief introduction to the classical concerto. Because the prehistory of the classical concerto has been adequately delineated by previous studies of the baroque concerto grosso and solo concerto, further study of the classical concerto may be deferred until Section IV-9 below, where Haydn's Trumpet Concerto is discussed, or IV-10, where the first movement of Mozart's Piano Concerto No. 23 is discussed.

2. You may wish to explore the form of the double exposition before moving on. The first movement of Mozart's Piano Concerto No. 23, discussed in Section IV-10 below, is a fine example. After discussion, see if the students can recognize variations: Beethoven's Fourth Piano Concerto begins with a brief statement of the theme by the piano soloist, after which the orchestra takes over and presents the material of the first exposition. Beethoven's Fifth (*Emperor*) Concerto begins with an extended cadenza for the pianist—with chordal punctuation by the orchestra—before the orchestra presents the first exposition. Play both opening sections and see if your class can spot these obvious departures from normal procedure in a classical concerto. What effect must these openings have had at the first performance of the works? How is the sense of improvisation generated in the opening of the *Emperor* concerto?

QUESTIONS AND TOPICS
1. Define the roles of soloist and orchestra in a classical concerto.
2. Define the nature and function of the cadenza in a classical concerto.
3. Compare and contrast the first movements of a classical concerto and symphony.
4. Concertos for solo brass and woodwind instruments in the classical period.
5. The cadenza in the classical period: notated or improvised?

## IV-8. CLASSICAL CHAMBER MUSIC

OBJECTIVES
Chamber music is defined in this section as music written for two to nine musicians, with one player to a part. The intimate character of chamber music is stressed, and the problems in playing small ensemble music explained. The string quartet is singled out for special consideration, although other common combinations are mentioned.

SUGGESTIONS
1. The rondo from Beethoven's String Quartet in C minor, Op. 18, no. 4, was studied in Section IV-5 above. Some time should be given to the importance of the string quartet in the development of chamber music, and the reasons for its preeminence as the major form in the genre. One can cite the sheer number and quality of quartets by the "masters," such as Haydn's 68, Beethoven's 16, and the many quartets by Mozart, Schubert, Mendelssohn, Dvořák, Bartók, and others. The supplementary set includes the first movement of Beethoven's Op. 18, no. 1 quartet, and could be compared with one of his later quartets, such as Op. 131 or the *Grosse Fuge*.

2. Discuss and provide examples of other standard forms of chamber music, including woodwind and brass combinations. Chamber music for a group of instruments with piano could well be placed in its own special category, since the piano is generally pitted against the other members of the ensemble. Compare, for example, the Beethoven quartet movement with Schubert's *Trout* Quintet (fourth movement in the basic set) to note the role of the piano when linked with a few other instruments in a chamber music setting. Consider the piano trio, quartet, and quintet combinations. Contrast the two versions of Beethoven's Opus 16, one for piano and winds, the other arranged for piano and strings.

3. The text describes how chamber music during the classical period was often played by well-to-do amateurs or by professional musicians hired to entertain guests after dinner. Have these traditions been entirely lost in our times? Have your students heard any music for small ensembles under these circumstances? A string quartet at a wedding, perhaps? Have they ever sat in on a jam session?

QUESTIONS AND TOPICS
1. Discuss the composition of the classical string quartet.
2. Discuss the nature of chamber music and its performance problems.
3. Discuss the social milieu in which chamber music was performed in the classical period.
4. Haydn's early String quartets: the divertimento.
5. The piano quartet in the classical period.
6. The violin and piano sonatas of Mozart and Beethoven: a comparison.
7. The development of the wind quintet in the classical period.
8. *Harmoniemusik* in the classical period.

## IV-9. JOSEPH HAYDN

OBJECTIVES

Haydn's career is traced from his birth in the Austrian village of Rohrau, through his early childhood years, to his service at Esterháza and his two triumphant visits to London. The features of his musical style are analyzed, and his enormous output is surveyed. The section ends with a description of and Listening Outline for the third movement, sonata-rondo, of his Trumpet Concerto in Eb Major.

SUGGESTIONS

1. Reference has previously been made to some of the biographical details of Haydn in relationship to the status of the composer and musician to the aristocracy and the middle class musical environment, and this would be a good time for review (reference was made to "Haydn's Duties in the Service of Prince Esterházy," MWW 81, in Section IV-1 above). There is a biograp.hical sketch worksheet in the Student Workbook to help with this discussion.

2. Since the supplementary set has the other three movements of the *Surprise* Symphony, this may be a good time to present the complete work. This will not only review the theme-and-variations movement, but place it in context and provide a complete example of a classical symphony.

3. Since the text stresses the importance of Haydn's sixty-eight authentic string quartets and his historical position as (possibly) the innovator of the form, it seems appropriate to discuss some of the major works in this genre. You may wish, for example, to compare the variations movement of the *Emperor* quartet (Op. 76 No. 3) with the variations movement of the *Surprise* Symphony discussed under Section IV-3 above. Considering the text's reference to the "folk flavor" in many of Haydn's themes, how do they compare to the melody *God Save the Emperor* used in the quartet?

4. In discussing the classical orchestra (IV-1 above), the text states that "horns and trumpets brought power to loud passages and filled out the harmony, but they did not usually play the main melody." Reminding the students of the limitations of the natural horns and trumpets to the overtone series, review some orchestral works played in class, or have the students sing a familiar bugle call such as *Taps*. With this background they can then appreciate the great technical improvement introduced by Anton Weidinger, Prince Esterházy's court trumpeter, for whom Haydn wrote the concerto. The change from a simple "filler" role to one of being able to play a sustained melody was unprecedented.

The work is played today on the modern valve trumpet, and has achieved new notoriety with Wynton Marsalis's recording. While not the first to win awards for both "classical" and "jazz" recordings, he is more relevant to most of the students, and a few moments exploring his background before playing the movement should be in order. From a musical family, Marsalis did not begin serious study of the trumpet until he was twelve. As he stated, he wanted to prove a point: that black artists could succeed in fields other than jazz and rock. Performing solos with the New Orleans Philharmonic (his hometown) at the age of fourteen and sixteen, he later studied at Juilliard. A brief selection from one of his jazz records could be used to stimulate student interest before introducing the Haydn, just as, in days past, teachers played recordings of Benny Goodman's swing before discussing his recording of the Mozart Clarinet Concerto. A Listening Outline for the third movement of the Haydn concerto is provided, and the recording is in the basic set (4:26).

5. Since so many of Haydn's works have nicknames, the Student Workbook asks the student to investigate some factors that caused such associations, and you may wish to go over some of the more famous ones in class.

QUESTIONS AND TOPICS
1. Describe the elements of Haydn's musical style.
2. Folk song and peasant dance in the music of Haydn.
3. Discuss the advantages and disadvantages to Haydn from his employment at Esterháza.
4. Haydn's London triumphs.
5. The wind music of Haydn.
6. Haydn's operas and masses.
7. Haydn and the string quartet: the development of a form.

# IV-10. WOLFGANG AMADEUS MOZART

OBJECTIVES
This section surveys Mozart's career from the prodigious early years, through the unhappy Salzburg period, to the final tragedy in Vienna. Mozart's style and his enormous output in all the major forms are described. The section concludes with a detailed discussion of three representative examples of his output, an opera, a symphony, and a concerto. From *Don Giovanni* there are discussions of the opening scene and the *Catalog* Aria from Act I, complete with recitative, annotations, Italian libretto, and English translations. The complete Symphony no. 40 in G minor, K. 550, is discussed (a Listening Outline for the first movement was included in section IV-2 above). The first movement of the Piano Concerto No. 23 in A Major, K. 488, is discussed, and a Listening Outline provided.

SUGGESTIONS
1. Where does one start with Mozart? The whole semester could be spent on this man's work alone, and yet in an introductory course that is neither possible nor practical. The text has singled out three major works as representative, but you may wish to add your personal favorites, and leave the text discussions for the students to do as additional listening at home. In any case, certainly some biographical details of this troubled giant should be discussed (please note the worksheet in the Student Workbook for this purpose). Someone once defined "genius" as a child with a grandmother. You might spend a few minutes discussing why Mozart is generally considered an incomparable genius.

2. Depending on the amount of material covered previously in discussing baroque opera, the student should be made aware of the importance of opera in the classical period. *Don Giovanni* can then be introduced, and the excerpts played in class. If Italian pronunciation was not reviewed previously, the students may need some help at this time. Filmstrips showing the stage settings, scenes, and costumes are available, and would help visualize the plot (both filmstrip and teacher's guide available from MOG). There are several video cassettes of the opera available, some with English subtitles. The text states that Mozart's characters are "individual human beings who think and feel." You might therefore ask several students to act/read through the opening scene, analyzing each person's social position, attitude, and motivation. What is the dramatic function of Leporello's *Catalog* aria? What is Don Giovanni's attitude to life? In his refusal to repent, is it similar to Mussolini's statement "Better to live one hour as a lion, than a hundred years as a lamb." Much can be done with these few excerpts, and all should be aimed at making

the students anxious to see and hear a live performance (the brief set has the Act 1 Introduction, 5:39; the basic set has the Introduction, *Catalog* aria, and the duet *Là ci darem la mano*; vocal score in NS).

3. The first movement of the G minor symphony was discussed in Section IV-2 above. The text now discusses the complete work, with themes. Use multiple copies of the score in the classroom, if possible, so you can help the students keep their place (the brief set has the first movement, 8:16, and the basic set has the complete symphony).

4. The section ends with a discussion of the first movement of the Piano Concerto No. 23 in A Major, K. 488. A Listening Outline is provided, and the movement is included in the basic set (the second and third movements are included in the supplementary set). The recording features the fortepiano, and, beyond discussing Mozart's work, this would be a logical place to discuss the original instruments movement. If not discussed previously, this is a fine place to illustrate the concerto's double exposition. Concerning the popularity of Mozart's piano concertos, you might mention the recent commercial success of the "Theme from Elvira Madigan," which in small print shows it to be the second movement of Mozart's Piano Concerto in C major, K. 467.

5. In view of the text's anecdote concerning its mysterious commissioning, you may wish to include some excerpts from the Requiem. With a view to the coming stylistic period, you may wish to consider the *Dies irae* and *Tuba mirum* sections. A comparison of Mozart's setting with either Berlioz's or Verdi's settings of the same text will clearly demonstrate differences between the classical and romantic viewpoints. The *Dies irae* is included in the basic set (1:44).

QUESTIONS AND TOPICS
1. Describe Mozart's career in Salzburg and Vienna.
2. Discuss the principal influences on the development of Mozart's musical style.
3. Summarize the libretto of *Don Giovanni*.
4. Compare and contrast Mozart's style with that of Haydn.
5. Mozart's letters.
6. Mozart's concertos for solo instruments.
7. Mozart's German operas.
8. Mozart and Freemasonry: *The Magic Flute*.
9. Mozart's music for winds: the divertimenti, cassations, and serenades.

## IV-11. LUDWIG VAN BEETHOVEN

OBJECTIVES
This section opens with a discussion of Beethoven's childhood, his early musical training, and the triumphant early years in Vienna. The deterioration of his hearing and the effect of this affliction on his career is also treated. Beethoven's style, style periods, and his enormous effect on the history of music are described. Two works are discussed in detail: the first movement of the Piano Sonata in C minor, Op. 13 (*Pathétique*), and the complete Fifth Symphony. A Listening Outline is provided for the first movement of the symphony.

SUGGESTIONS
1. The text quietly begins "For many people, Ludwig van Beethoven represents the highest level of musical genius." Can we imagine the course of musical history without Beethoven? What would be the reputations today of Hummel, Clementi, and Pleyel, among others, had there been no Beethoven? As with Mozart, where can one begin? The text, and accompanying record sets,

limit themselves to but four masterpieces: the *Pathétique* Sonata, the C minor symphony, and movements from two of the Opus 18 string quartets. Again you may wish to include your own favorites, leaving these four works for the students to study at home, since Listening Outlines are provided. Again, a worksheet is provided in the Student Workbook to help with the biographical details of Beethoven's life.

2. As a general introduction, consider the film *Beethoven: Ordeal and Triumph* (McGraw-Hill Book Co., 1967, 52 min.) The work deals with his early personal life, his oncoming deafness, and the Heiligenstadt testament (the complete testament is included in MWW, 91). His triumph over despair is illustrated by the Third Symphony, whose themes had already been presented in the country dance and Prometheus Ballet settings.

3. It may be appropriate at this time to take a few moments to discuss the development of the piano and its literature. The harpsichord, the early pianoforte (leather-covered hammers, etc.) and the modern piano should be discussed before introducing the Beethoven sonata. Mention has already been made of the recordings in the brief and basic sets of Mozart's Piano Concerto No. 23 performed on the pianoforte, and it may be compared to the later sounds and effects of the romantic concert grand. Beethoven's *Pathétique* Sonata can then be placed in context. The text provides a detailed analysis of the first movement, and the complete work is included in the basic set (6:01, 4:43, and 3:46; score in NS).

4. The Fifth Symphony is the example chosen to represent Beethoven's orchestral output, and a Listening Outline is provided for the first movement, with a detailed discussion of the complete work. The complete symphony is included in the basic set, and the first movement is included in the brief set (7:35). As mentioned before, you may wish to discuss the Listening Outline quickly in class to prepare the students for home listening, and then use multiple copies of the score in class where you can guide them successfully through it with minimal frustration. There are several fine video performances of the symphony available. If your class is already familiar with the work, you may wish to consider Professor Peter Schikele's sportscaster analysis of the first movement on his *P.D.Q.Bach on the Air* (Vanguard VSD-79268). For a different interpretation, see The Walter Murphy Band's recording *A Fifth of Beethoven* (PS 2015).

5. Remind the students who may have seen Walt Disney's *Fantasia* that Beethoven's sixth symphony was used for one of the sequences. It has been released on video, and you might wish to go into further detail regarding some of the other works in the film.

6. Beethoven's string quartets are considered to be among the greatest in the entire literature—so much so that they simultaneously intimidated and inspired such composers as Schubert, Brahms, and Bartók. The fourth movement of Beethoven's String Quartet Op. 18 no. 4 was discussed in the section on rondo form (IV-5). That section includes a Listening Outline, and the movement is included in the brief and basic sets (4:14). The supplementary set includes the first movement of the first quartet from the set of six comprising Opus 18, composed between 1798 and 1800. A comparison of one of these early movements with the Opus 133 Grosse Fuge would clearly illustrate the text's statement "the sublime works of the late period often contain fugues as well as passages that sound surprisingly harsh and 'modern'."

7. You might also wish to discuss Beethoven's only opera, *Fidelio*. Typical of the many nineteenth-century "rescue" operas, it amply demonstrates Beethoven's genius in taking a form and raising it to heights never before achieved. A filmstrip is available to set the scene, and perhaps the plot can be illustrated with one or more arias and/or choruses.

8. We cannot leave the subject of Beethoven without at least suggesting that some consideration be given to granting your students the opportunity of hearing Schiller's *Ode to Joy* and the magnificent Ninth Symphony. The text, with translation, should be duplicated so that the students may understand the poem. You might mention the rock adaptation (?!) of the

brotherhood theme issued under the title *Song of Joy* some years back, in case any of the students may still remember it, and compare it to the original (actually, no comparison!) More important than the rock version, however, is the current movement in Europe where the brotherhood theme is assuming the status of an unofficial anthem. *Le Drapeau de l'Europe (The Flag of Europe)*, by which this hymn is known, expresses the hope for a peaceful, harmonious European community.

QUESTIONS AND TOPICS

    1. Describe Beethoven's childhood and early musical training.

    2. Describe the sources of Beethoven's income during his Viennese period.

    3. Describe the manner in which Beethoven unified the contrasting movements in his works.

    4. Divide Beethoven's output into periods, and define the characteristics of each phase of his development.

    5. *Fidelio*: opera or staged oratorio?

    6. The Heiligenstadt testament: triumph of genius?

# V. THE ROMANTIC PERIOD

## V-1. ROMANTICISM IN MUSIC (1820-1900)

OBJECTIVES

In the first part of this section, the characteristics of romanticism in the visual arts and literature are described and the achievements of representative artists and writers summarized. In the rest of the section, the following characteristics of romantic music are defined, often in relation to their manifestations in the classical period: individuality of style, expressive aims and subjects, nationalism and exoticism, program music, expressive tone color, colorful harmony, expanded range of dynamics, pitch, and tempo, and form (miniature and monumental).

SUGGESTIONS

1. The Student Workbook contains a self-test to compare the general characteristics of the romantic and classical periods. It can be used in preparation for or discussion in class. If you believe in mnemonics, you may wish to help the students with the following comparison:

| ROMANTICISM | CLASSICISM |
|---|---|
| **S**ubjectivity | **O**bjectivity |
| **I**ndividualism | **T**raditionalism |
| **N**ationalism | **A**ristocracy |
| **E**motionalism | **E**motional restraint |
| **S**upernaturalism | **R**ealism |

Further explanation of these terms may be found in the text and the student worksheet.

2. In discussing the general characteristics of the period, you may wish to refer to some illustrations in the text:

John Constable (1776-1837). One of the major artists of the English landscape tradition, Constable imparts a poetic melancholy and wistfulness to his works while portraying the beauty of his homeland. *The Hay Wain* (1821, p. 178) has this naturalistic romanticism, and anticipates the attitudes and methods of the later impressionists.

Honoré Daumier (1808-79). A biting political cartoonist, Daumier painted aspects of everyday urban life in a dignified and sympathetic manner. *The Third-Class Carriage* (1863-65, color plate) can be compared to the *verismo* movement in opera: the realistic portrayal of ordinary people of the working class, subjects considered dangerous and unsuitable for artistic representation by the middle-class public. H. W. Janson states "In *The Third-Class Carriage* [Daumier] has captured a peculiarly modern human condition, 'the lonely crowd': these people have in common only that they are traveling together in one railway car. Though they are physically crowded, they take no notice of one another—each is alone with his own thoughts." (*History of Art*, Prentice-Hall, 1966, p. 483.)

Eugène Delacroix (1798-1863). The romanticists were interested in the political forces surrounding them, and frequently depicted scenes of emotional turbulence. *Liberty Leading the People* (1830, color plate), however, is more an allegory than a specific event in the Parisian revolution of 1830 that overthrew the Bourbon monarchy and placed the "citizen-king" Louis Philippe on the throne of France. The brilliant colors make the painting highly emotional and sensual. The romantic's interest in the supernatural comes through in the black and white reproduction of Delacroix's *The Bark of Dante* (1822, also known as *Dante and Virgil in the Inferno*,

p. 177), but the rich intensity of color and the contrasts of light and dark are missing. Dante and Virgil are being steered across the lake surrounding the walls of the infernal city of Dis (Roman for Pluto, the god of Hades) while sinners cling to the boat or try to climb in.

Caspar David Friedrich (1774-1840). *The Large Enclosure Near Dresden* (1832, color plate) is typical of Friedrich's delight in the vastness of nature. He loved to portray romantic moods such as meditation, melancholy, or solitude. Friedrich believed that art should be the true language of our emotions, even our piety and our prayers. He defended the uniqueness and vulnerability of the artist's creative subjectivity, and insisted that the artist be complete within himself, a "temple of individuality."

Théodore Géricault (1791-1824). Géricault's most ambitious work was *The Raft of the Medusa*, which created a sensation when first exhibited. Géricault went to great pains to depict the horrible tragedy as realistically as possible, even to the extent of studying corpses in the morgue. Fascinated by the destructiveness of nature and mental aberrations, he made studies of the inmates of mental institutions. Sharing this emotional subjectivity, *Portrait of a Young Man in an Artist's Studio* (1819, p. 174) was formerly attributed to Géricault. The anonymous painting depicts the artist's suffering and isolation, and sympathetically portrays the subject as a human being, not as an object of mythology or allegory.

Joseph Mallord Turner (1775-1851). Turner first gave *The Slave Ship* (1839; color plate) the title *Slavers Throwing Overboard the Dead and Dying—Typhoon Coming On*. It was inspired partly by an incident Turner had read about: the captain of a slave ship had jettisoned his human cargo during an epidemic because he was insured against the loss of slaves at sea, but not by disease. The forces of nature are most effectively used to highlight this emotional and poignant drama.

3. Again, as a general introduction to the period as a whole, you may wish to consider a film or filmstrip. EAV, for example, has both *Romanticism in Art and Music* and, as part of its History of Music series, *Early Romanticism*. Program 1, part 3, in the Music of Man video series, *Age of the Individual,* includes music by Chopin, Liszt, Verdi, Brahms, Wagner, and Tchaikovsky.

4. In presenting musical examples, please note that the Student Workbook contains a Listening Exercise for comparing two or three compositions of differing styles. It is suggested that you choose any three contrasting works, and see if the students can correctly identify their stylistic periods. Room is provided on the sheet for the titles and composers, in the hope that the students may wish to hear more of the works played.

QUESTIONS AND TOPICS

1. What were the political and social conditions that caused the romantic movement?
2. How did the music of the nineteenth century reflect the romantic composer's desire for a closer union between music and the other arts?
3. Discuss some characteristics of romantic literature and painting.
4. Give some examples of musical nationalism and exoticism.
5. Describe some devices that made romantic harmony so colorful.
6. The expansion of the orchestra during the romantic period.
7. The origins of program music.
8. The "union of the arts" in the romantic period.

# V-2. THE ART SONG

OBJECTIVES

The nature of the art song is described in this section, and some principal composers and poets who contributed to the development of the genre are mentioned. The function of the piano accompaniment is explained, and the terms strophic, through-composed, modified strophic, and song cycle defined.

SUGGESTIONS

1. If not already discussed during the elements unit, this would be an opportune time to compare folk songs with art songs. Trained vs. untrained voices, art (piano) vs. folk instruments for accompaniment, range, poetic expression, and craftsmanship are just a few of the aspects that can be considered. Following that, the art song can be discussed, and the reasons for its early nineteenth-century flowering in Germany. Moritz von Schwind's depiction of a "Schubertiad" (p. 179) can be used to illustrate many important points of middle-class music-making.

2. Since the next section contains an example of a through-composed song, you may wish to move right on to Schubert. If time permits, however, you may wish to discuss the illustrative powers of the keyboard as an accompanying instrument. The movement of water, for example, a favorite image of the romantic composer, is suggested by the piano figuration in Schubert's *Die Forelle* and *Auf dem Wasser zu singen*. In *Die Stadt*, no. 11 in Schubert's *Schwanengesang*, the opening figure in the piano part suggests swirling fog and mist. In the sixteenth song of Schubert's *Winterreise, Letzte Hoffnung*, the opening figure of the accompaniment portrays leaves falling from a tree in winter. All these examples, of course, depict various natural phenomena, and this can serve to illustrate the romantic composer's preoccupation with nature, a salient point of the text. In each case, play the example without introduction, and see if the students can identify the tone image correctly. Play the example again after identification to help those who may have had difficulty. Some additional insights may be gained from Gerald Moore's charming record *The Unashamed Accompanist* (Angel 60017), where he discusses and illustrates his craft in a most instructive and humorous manner.

3. If you discuss the famous song cycles mentioned on page 185, don't forget to include *Sgt. Pepper's Lonely Hearts Club Band*, "a landmark of rock music" (p. 339) and a unified song cycle.

QUESTIONS AND TOPICS

1. Define the three major types of musical settings found in art songs.
2. Describe the types of texts used by romantic composers.
3. Describe the function of the piano in the art song.
4. Goethe and the lied.
5. The romantic art song in France.
6. The song cycle in the romantic period.

# V-3. FRANZ SCHUBERT

OBJECTIVES

Schubert's early years as a student are described in the first part of this section, as are his first attempts at composition and his experience as a teacher in his father's school. Following the account of his impoverished adulthood in Vienna, the "Schubertiads," and his untimely death at the age of thirty-one, his output and the characteristics of his style are surveyed. *Erlkönig* is discussed with themes, German text, and annotated translation as an example of a through-composed song.

SUGGESTIONS

1. It is hard to believe that Schubert could compose a work like *Erlkönig* at the age of eighteen, and pointing out that most of the students in the class are probably past that age may

give some appreciation for his genius. Follow this with a discussion of the art song and its forms, if not already done in the previous section. Help the students with the German, and point out some of the romantic traits in the text. When the form and language pose no problems, play *Erlkönig* once through for effect (recording in brief and basic sets, 4:08; score in NS). Depending on how much time you wish to spend on the poem, you might go over it quickly, pointing out the various characteristics of the vocal line and piano accompaniment. You might, however, consider the roles of each of the characters in Goethe's poem. The poem could easily be made into a drama with three players and a narrator to set the scene. Require each student playing a part to analyze the role and react accordingly. Why does the father, for example, not see death? How does the father rationalize each of the boy's fears? What does the Erlking offer each time, until finally making an offer, in the words of the Godfather, the boy "can't refuse"? Having analyzed the poem, one can appreciate the skills required for one performer to interpret the four characters in the story. There are many fine recordings available, and it is suggested that two different interpretations be presented, even contrasting sexes. In this way you can discuss the question of gender in art and popular songs: here the sex of the storyteller is irrelevant, but if a man were to sing a sentimental ballad "He's gone and left me . . . " The recording in the sets is the interpretation by Dietrich Fischer-Diskau. His use of head-tones for the child, chest tones for the father, and *sotto voce* for the Erlking make it a brilliantly effective example to use in class following analysis. Settings of *Erlkönig* by Schubert, Carl Loewe, and Johann Reichardt are included in the *Videodisc Music Series* edited by Fred Hofstetter, issued by the University of Delaware.

2. If you wish to include an example of modified strophic form, note that the basic set includes Schubert's *Die Forelle*. In helping the students with the German, you may wish to point out some romantic traits in the text. Using the mnemonic presented in section V-1 above (SINES), in what way is the text subjective in approach? Do words like "thief," "slyly," and "betrayed" make us sympathize with (feel for?) the fish? Do fish swim? (personification, a part of supernaturalism) One fisherman and one fish, out of many (individualism). You may not wish to spend so much time on the text, but some characteristics of romanticism should be included, followed by a discussion of the role of the accompaniment in fostering these feelings. Being less than two minutes in length, the song could easily bear repetition following discussion.

3. Having discussed *Die Forelle*, you can then lead logically into Schubert's instrumental music with the fourth movement of the Piano Quintet as an example. The 5th edition of the text contains a Listening Outline, and the movement is included in the basic set (8:12).

QUESTIONS AND TOPICS
    1. Discuss the principal stages of Schubert's career.
    2. Discuss Schubert's ability to portray and develop character in his songs.
    3. Describe the function of the accompanist in Schubert's songs.
    4. Schubert's Symphony no. 8 in B minor: unfinished?
    5. Schubert and the "Schubertiads."
    6. Schubert's operas: undeserved neglect?
    7. Schubert's *Schöne Müllerin*: Goethe's *Sorrows of Young Werther* in song?

# V-4. ROBERT SCHUMANN

OBJECTIVES
    This section opens with a brief biography of Robert Schumann that traces the literary influences on his life, his law studies, his attempt to become a virtuoso, and his love for, and eventual marriage to, Clara Wieck. His career as a critic and musical administrator and his

eventual confinement in a mental institution are also discussed. The characteristics of his musical style are defined, and he is represented by a song, *Im wunderschönen Monat Mai* from *Dichterliebe*.

### SUGGESTIONS

1. The text states "Robert Schumann in many ways embodied musical romanticism." In the struggle to get to the twentieth century before the term ends, there may be a tendency to skip Schumann. Since the next section deals with his wife, however, it is hoped that both will be considered on their merits, and for their contribution to the music of the romantic period. The fifth edition of the text discusses *Aufschwung (Soaring)* from his *Fantasiestücke* and it can be used to represent Schumann's piano compositions (in basic set, 2:53).

2. The song cycle was defined in Section V-2 above, and *Dichterliebe* was mentioned as one of the examples. Not mentioned then, but coming up in Section VI-18, is another song cycle that many students will be familiar with: *Sgt. Pepper's Lonely Hearts Club Band.* A discussion of Schumann's *Im wunderschönen Monat Mai* at this time will put the later work in perspective. Schumann's song can, of course, stand on its own and is well worth the few minutes it takes to discuss. The text has the German poem with English translation, and it is contained in the basic set (1:27).

### QUESTIONS AND TOPICS

1. Discuss the characteristics of Robert Schumann's musical style.
2. Describe the contents and purpose of Schumann's *New Journal of Music*
3. Schumann as critic and proponent of "new music."
4. The Schumanns and Brahms.
5. Robert Schumann and the piano miniature.

## V-5. CLARA WIECK SCHUMANN

### OBJECTIVES

This important section describes the life and work of one of the leading concert pianists of the nineteenth century, Clara Schumann. Her life is outlined in brief: her early training by her father, her concertizing throughout Europe, her marriage to Robert Schumann, her friendships with Johannes Brahms and Joseph Joachim, and her important work as performer, editor, and teacher following the death of her husband. The section ends with a discussion of her Romance in G minor for Violin and Piano, complete with Listening Outline.

### SUGGESTIONS

1. Having been in her husband's shadow for so long, it is encouraging to see that Clara Schumann finally receives the attention she deserves. It is hoped that this section will *not* be skipped, for it will provide an opportunity to discuss the many contributions of women in general as well as Clara Schumann. Marcia Citron discusses some composers in her article "Women and the Lied, 1775-1850" (WMM, pp. 224-48), and states "the advent of the nineteenth century witnessed a marked increase in the number of female musicians who utilized their creative talents, with a parallel rise in recognition from contemporary musicians, journalists, and audiences." Compositions by Maria Szymanowska, Josephine Lang, Fanny Mendelssohn Hensel, Louise Ferrenc, and Pauline Viardot-Garcia may be found in HAMW, in addition to three works by Clara Schumann.

2. Following a brief discussion of the opportunities for women performers and creative artists in Europe in the romantic period, Clara Schumann should be presented as a major figure.

As a champion of the music of Brahms, earlier composers, and especially her husband Robert, as a teacher of great influence, as editor of her husband's works, and as a role model for other women struggling for recognition, she was, as Nancy Reich states in "Clara Schumann" (WMM, pp. 249-81), "no ordinary person." The Romance for Violin and Piano is included in the brief and basic sets (2:46), and the text contains a Listening Outline. Her Piano Trio, which many consider one of her finest works, has been recorded and one movement is included in HAMW.

QUESTIONS AND TOPICS
1. Discuss Clara Schumann's compositions and their acceptance in a male-dominated society.
2. Consider the opportunities for women in music in the romantic period.
3. Juggling home and career: Clara Schumann as performer and wife/mother.
4. Women composers in the romantic period.

# V-6. FRÉDÉRIC CHOPIN

OBJECTIVES
This section traces Chopin's life from the early years to his prolonged stay in Paris. The brilliance of the artistic and intellectual milieu of the French capital is described, along with Chopin's place in it and his liaison with George Sand. The style of Chopin's piano music is described, and the section concludes with a discussion of and Listening Outline for the Nocturne in Eb major, Op. 9 no. 2, and brief discussions of the Étude in C minor, Op. 10, no. 12 (*Revolutionary*), and the Polonaise in Ab major, Op. 53.

SUGGESTIONS
1. Only the Nocturne is included in the brief set, but the basic set includes four of Chopin's works: the Preludes in E and C minor, Op. 28, nos. 4 and 20 (1:51, 1:32), the Polonaise in Ab major, Op. 53 (6:17), and the Nocturne in Eb major, Op. 9, no. 2. The Étude in C minor, Op. 10, no. 12 (*Revolutionary*) is contained in the supplementary set (2:43). The two preludes can be mentioned in passing as other examples from the "Poet of the Piano," and to discuss briefly whether any piano student's education can be considered complete without studying the music of Chopin.
2. The Harvard Dictionary defines a nocturne as "a lyrical melody accompanied by broken chords pedaled to collect the harmonies." If not already discussed in previous sections, this would be an opportune time to demonstrate the use of the piano's three pedals. The opening of Chopin's Nocturne in Eb major is given in the text, with the pedals clearly marked. Does this technique give a feeling of overall calm? The text refers to this work as an "intimate composition . . . tinged with sweet melancholy." In what way is it intimate? Melancholic? Could the nocturne be as effective in a meter other than 12/8? The melody, its repetition in varied form (given in the text), and the ornamentation should be briefly discussed. It would be most helpful if multiple copies of the music were available. (Recording in brief and basic sets, 4:05)
3. In discussing the *Revolutionary* Étude, first describe the purpose of an étude. You might ask the students to try the old trick of patting one's head while rubbing one's stomach. How can one develop such a technique? Similarly, how can one play a smooth legato run in the left hand while playing block chords in the right, both compounded by the furious tempo? Ask the students, for example, to try making a smooth run with their left hands on their desks (the first five fingers are fine, but then what?). If possible, have multiple copies of the work available for classroom use. You may wish to pose some of the following questions regarding the work's ABA form: what signals the return of the A section? Are there examples of sequential repetition in the

B section? Can changes of key be heard in the B section? How is the octave theme of the A section varied in the return of A? The text mentions that the tension of the étude momentarily subsides just before the final outburst. By what musical means is this relaxation of tension achieved? (In supplementary set, 2:43).

4. The text discusses the Polonaise in Ab major, Op. 53. Again, it would be helpful if the students could use multiple copies of the music in class. If so, be sure to point out the long introduction and the place where the main theme appears. Should anyone comment on the meter as appropriate for a stately processional, remember that the ceremonial measured step in the British Army is still done to a 3/8 or 3/4 meter.

QUESTIONS AND TOPICS

1. Describe the intellectual and cultural world of the Paris in which Chopin lived.
2. Describe the elements of Chopin's piano style.
3. Chopin and George Sand.
4. Nationalism and Chopin: the mazurkas and polonaises.
5. George Sand and Feminism.

## V-7. FRANZ LISZT

OBJECTIVES

This section opens with an account of Liszt's glamorous and multifaceted career. We read of his activities as virtuoso pianist, composer, conductor, writer on music, and finally abbé. Liszt's style, his invention of the symphonic poem, his use of thematic transformation, and the influence of the works of Goethe upon him are also discussed. The section closes with a discussion of one of his *Transcendental Études*, no. 10 in F minor, with Listening Outline.

SUGGESTIONS

1. Spend a little time discussing the rise of the virtuoso performer, especially in view of Liszt's role. Compare Liszt as a solo performer, for example, with Bach or Haydn, and stylistic differences will inevitably result.

2. Some mention should be made of Liszt's orchestral works, such as *Les Préludes* (do any of the older students remember this was the theme for the Lone Ranger?) and the Second Hungarian Rhapsody (anyone remember the old cartoon?). His importance as the creator of the symphonic poem, his use of thematic transformation, his championing of contemporary music, his many important piano transcriptions of orchestral works, and his promoting the folk music of his many ethnic interests all bear discussion.

3. Liszt's piano music is represented by his *Transcendental Étude* no. 10 in F minor. If not already covered under Chopin, the purpose of an étude should be explained, and then related specifically to Liszt. The text has a Listening Outline, and the work is included in the brief and basic sets (4:42).

QUESTIONS AND TOPICS

1. Describe Liszt's activities at Weimar.
2. Describe the symphonic poem, and explain the process of thematic transformation.
3. Describe the elements of Liszt's writing for the keyboard.
4. Liszt as showman and virtuoso pianist.
5. Liszt as the champion of new music.
6. Liszt's "Hungarian" music.

## V-8. FELIX MENDELSSOHN

OBJECTIVES

The first portion of this section discusses the precociousness of the young Mendelssohn, his influence as a conductor of Bach, and his personality. Also discussed is the phenomenal success of his oratorio *Elijah* in Birmingham, England. Important aspects of his style are described, and some of his best-known compositions are listed. The section ends with a discussion of the first movement of his Violin Concerto in E minor.

SUGGESTIONS

1. It would be interesting to ask the students how many compositions by Mendelssohn they can name. Very frequently music that is used for functional purposes loses its association with the mainstream of musical performance. Did anyone remember to name the recessional so frequently used at weddings? While on the subject, you may wish to play part of the suite's Overture, which he wrote at the age of seventeen (score in NS). Can the students identify the "elfin quality" of the light and transparent orchestral texture mentioned in the text?

2. If this is the only solo concerto discussed in the course, some time should be taken to cover basic terminology. The basic set includes the first movement (12:01, score in NS). Multiple copies of the score should be provided, if possible, but you might consider using the violin and piano arrangement. Not only is it cheaper in price, it shows what a student would use to learn the work. Further, it might be easier for some to follow the piano reduction, if they are not quite ready to handle a full score. The inserted violin part can be discussed in the light of performance practices: this is the part that the soloist must memorize before appearing in any serious performance with an orchestra. Just looking at the part in that light may impress on the students what is involved in being a soloist. After listening to the music, you may wish to pose some questions: in the development section of the first movement, what material from the exposition is chosen for development, and what developmental procedures are adopted? How does tempo contribute to the approach to the coda of this movement? Upon what thematic material is this coda based?

3. If time permits, go on to the other movements, following the score. Some questions to consider: the allegretto non troppo that serves as an introduction to the finale is based on music heard previously; what is the source of this material? As with the first movement, ask the students to identify the sources of the thematic material of the development section of the Finale and to describe the developmental processes at work. These movements may be found in the supplementary set (7:28, 6:07).

4. There being so few original band works available from this period, you may wish to include that medium by discussing the Overture for Band he wrote when just fifteen years old. Your library may have the old Goldman Band recording *Band Masterpieces* (Decca DL-78633), or perhaps a tape of your college band in performance. The work is charming, and represents an important phase in the evolution of band repertoire.

5. *Elijah* is not as popular as it once was, but you might still wish to play some portions in class. The scene where Elijah challenges the prophets of Baal and then brings on the rain can be quite effective, especially with a few judicious cuts.

QUESTIONS AND TOPICS

1. Discuss Mendelssohn's influence as a conductor.
2. Describe Mendelssohn's musical style.
3. Discuss how Mendelssohn's Violin Concerto deviates from the classical concerto.

4. Mendelssohn and the Bach revival.
5. Mendelssohn in Leipzig: the Gewandhaus Orchestra and the Conservatory.
6. Mendelssohn and Shakespeare's *Midsummer Night's Dream*.
7. Mendelssohn and the oratorio.

# V-9. PROGRAM MUSIC

## OBJECTIVES

This section covers the nature of program music and its popularity during the romantic period. A distinction is drawn between program and absolute music, and four categories of program music are established: program symphony, concert overture, symphonic poem (or tone poem), and incidental music.

## SUGGESTIONS

1. A few questions asked of the class will quickly let you know their feelings toward program music. Thinking back to their days in elementary or junior high school, do they remember compositions played in their music classes, or in their art classes to evoke visual responses? Some may think of the many programmatic works in Walt Disney's film *Fantasia*. To highlight the text's statement that music alone can make no definite reference to ideas, emotions, or objects, play two contrasting selections and ask the students to write down on a piece of scrap paper (or in the Workbook) what they believe is happening. What mood is the composer trying to evoke? Are there examples of sound effects? What images come to mind? What actions, if any, are being portrayed in the music? A particular favorite that never fails to evoke interesting responses is Prokofieff's *Scythian Suite*. The second and third movements ("Chuzhbog and the dance of the evil spirits" and "Night") usually are identified as some form of argument followed by repose, but the range of who is doing what to whom is quite varied. Be sure to identify the work after the discussion, in the hope they may wish to hear the complete suite.

2. Now that *Fantasia* is available on video cassette, you may wish to illustrate the effectiveness of program music by playing one of the programmatic selections. Dukas' *Sorcerer's Apprentice*, starring Mickey Mouse, is most memorable and engrossing.

3. Regarding the text's comment that "musicians and audiences in the romantic era liked to read stories into all music, whether intended by the composer or not," you might mention the "Fate knocking at the door" or "V for Victory" aspects of Beethoven's Fifth Symphony. Similarly, *Peter and the Wolf* was interpreted as a moralistic story during World War II (the text specifies audiences of the romantic period, but here it appears in recent memory). The wolf was interpreted as the Axis powers, the duck (swallowed alive) France, with Peter, the bird, and the cat being the Allied powers. You can most likely think of other examples, and you may wish to raise the question of the value of program music in the first place.

4. The following three sections have examples of program music that you may wish to mention at this time. Section V-10 deals with Hector Berlioz and the *Fantastic Symphony*. The brief and basic sets contain Smetana's *Moldau*, discussed in Section V-11. Tchaikovsky's *Romeo and Juliet* Overture is discussed in Section V-12, and is included in the basic set (18:40). You may wish to include other personal favorites, in which case please note the research projects provided in the Student Workbook designed for use in class or for assigned listening either in this section or at other times in the course. These pages concern the four main forms of orchestral program music. In each case the student is asked to list some representative examples, and then listen to one, identify the form, briefly summarize the plot, and name those musical techniques that evoke literary or pictorial ideas. You may wish to help the students with some examples, or suggest they

consult standard concert guides in the library. Along with the works already mentioned in the text, here are a few suggestions just to get started:

a. the program symphony: *Romeo and Juliet, Harold in Italy* (Berlioz), *Ilya Mouromptz* (Glière), *Faust, Dante* (Liszt), *Scheherazade* (Rimsky-Korsakov), *Alpine* and *Domestic* Symphonies (Strauss), *The Ornithological Combat of Kings* (Heinrich), and *Through the Looking Glass* (Taylor);

b. the concert overture: *Tragic, Academic Festival* (Brahms), *Rob Roy, King Lear,* and *Waverley* (Berlioz), *Cockaigne* (Elgar), *Russian Easter* (Rimsky-Korsakov), and *Faust* (Wagner);

c. the symphonic poem: too numerous to mention, but consider Debussy, d'Indy, Franck, Gershwin, Griffes, Honegger, Ives, Mussorgsky, Respighi, Saint-Saëns, Sibelius, and Villa-Lobos as well as Liszt and Strauss.

d. incidental music: there are many overtures intended for dramatic plays (Beethoven, Mendelssohn, Paine, and Vaughan Williams) but suites from plays are less frequent. *Peer Gynt* (Grieg) is a classic, and a portion of *L'Arlésienne* (Bizet) was discussed in the unit on elements under texture (see I-8). Since the text also mentions movie scores, you might include some examples. The London Symphony Orchestra's recording of the music from *Star Wars* (20th Cent. C-2541) may come as a complete surprise to both those who have seen the film and those who have not. For those who have, you might ask if they can now listen to the music without the visual image running through their minds.

QUESTIONS AND TOPICS

1. Give some examples of the suggestive power of music.
2. Discuss the function of incidental music.
3. Compare and contrast the concert overture and the symphonic poem.
4. Forerunners of romantic program music.

## V-10. HECTOR BERLIOZ

OBJECTIVES

Berlioz's musical education, his infatuation with the Shakespearean actress Harriet Smithson, and the circumstances surrounding the composition of the *Fantastic Symphony* are covered in this section. Berlioz's success in winning the Prix de Rome is contrasted with his later alienation from the Parisian public and his success as composer-conductor outside France. The brilliance of Berlioz's orchestration and other elements of his musical style are described. The section ends with a discussion of the fourth and fifth movements of the *Fantastic Symphony*, with a Listening Outline for the fifth.

SUGGESTIONS,

1. Looking at the Schwann catalog, it is hard to believe that just a few years ago a society had to be formed to promote Berlioz's music. Whether the society can take all the credit or not, there obviously has been a great increase in the popularity of his music. *The Trojans* in Boston and on national television, the *Childhood of Christ* as a regular Christmas feature in New York, and numerous interpretations of the *Fantastic Symphony* currently available on record all attest to this popularity. This first French romantic composer and "daring creator of new orchestral sounds" should be included in any introductory course, even if only briefly in passing.

2. A typical example of French romanticism is Rouget de Lisle's *La Marseillaise*. In Berlioz's arrangement for soloists, double chorus, and full orchestra, it becomes a crystallization of the romantic spirit. If you cannot fit anything else in, at least try this (Angel S-26518).

3. It was suggested in the discussion on musical style (1-10 above) that the *Dies Irae* and *Tuba Mirum* sections of two Requiems be compared. While the stereo recording of Berlioz's setting will not equal the quadruphonic sound of the original brass bands reverberating throughout a massive cathedral, the effect can still be quite impressive.

4. A brief look at Berlioz's four symphonies will bear out the text's remarks concerning his great originality and emphasis on new and imaginative tone colors: the *Fantastic Symphony* (discussed below), *Harold in Italy* for solo viola and orchestra, *Roméo et Juliette* for solo voices, chorus, and orchestra, and finally the *Grande Symphonie Funèbre et Triomphale* for large wind band with six-part chorus in the last movement. All deserve some consideration, but as the last one is another of the very few examples of authentic band music of the period, an excerpt could demonstrate the sound of that medium to the students. At the same time, remind them there were original works for band being composed and not just transcriptions. Instead of an "orchestral" recording, it is suggested that the version by the Musique des Gardiens de la Paix de Paris (MHS 1276 or Nonesuch 71368) be considered since it is performed by a true symphonic band, the medium Berlioz intended.

5. The text discusses the *idée fixe*, and the fourth and fifth movements of the *Fantastic Symphony*. The fifth movement is included in the brief set (9:51), and the basic set includes both movements (6:48, 9:57). The supplementary set contains the *idée fixe* (0:30). For a very interesting discussion of this work, see Leonard Bernstein's "Berlioz Takes a Trip," included as a 7-inch disk along with his recording of the work (Col. MS-7278). Each movement is discussed, and the themes are illustrated by the orchestra, an advantage we do not usually have in the classroom. Andre Previn also gives a very interesting talk on this symphony, complete with many fascinating illustrations of the people involved, in his video cassette for Home Vision. Among the many elements to be discussed in this symphony, you may like to point out that the second movement is a waltz, the most popular dance of the romantic era. The 3/8 time signature may confuse students who think the waltz must be in 3/4, but that came later. It is interesting to note that this symphony was written in the same year that Johann Strauss Senior obtained his first important position (the *Sperl*), from where his fame began to spread, and while his more famous son was just five years old. If you intend to discuss the final movement, be sure to play the original chant of the *Dies Irae* for background. One recording presently available is the *Missa pro Defunctis* (MHS 915; score in NS).

6. The Student Workbook contains a research project to illustrate the changes that have taken place in the symphony orchestra. The students are asked to compare, and place in a seating plan, the instrumentalists called for in Bach's *Brandenburg* Concerto No. 5, Haydn's *Surprise* Symphony, and this symphony by Berlioz. Please help the students, if necessary, but this project should help them visualize the tremendous changes that have taken place, and define the continuous growth in personnel and instrumentation from the baroque through romanticism.

QUESTIONS AND TOPICS
1. Discuss the circumstances surrounding the composition of the *Fantastic Symphony*.
2. Discuss the use of the *idée fixe* in the *Fantastic Symphony*.
3. Discuss unusual features of the orchestration of the *Fantastic Symphony*.
4. Berlioz's *Treatise on Instrumentation and Orchestration*.
5. Berlioz the critic.
6. Berlioz and the French musical establishment.
7. Quadruphonic sound in the nineteenth century: the Berlioz Requiem.
8. Berlioz and Shakespeare.

# V-11. NATIONALISM IN NINETEENTH-CENTURY MUSIC

## OBJECTIVES

The rise of nationalism in Europe and how it led to the unification of some countries is discussed in this section. Those countries whose musical heritage had been dominated by the music of Italy, France, Germany, or Austria, particularly Russia, Poland, Bohemia and the Scandinavian countries, felt the strongest impact of nationalism. Major nationalistic composers, including the "Russian five," are mentioned. The text then focuses on one famous nationalistic work, Smetana's *The Moldau*, for which a Listening Outline is provided.

## SUGGESTIONS

1. Nationalism was a major characteristic of the nineteenth century, and indeed the present strife in Africa, Ireland, and the former Yugoslavia are but three examples of many of this movement continuing into the twentieth century. You may wish to discuss the meaning of "nation," for many students consider it is a political unit. How then does one feel allegiance to a political unit, especially if it has little or no relevance to you? Perhaps if we substitute "ethnic group" for "nation" it will become more meaningful. We can then discuss the factors that comprise an ethnic group: common language, religion, race, folk traditions, costume, legends, dances, art, and music. It proceeds logically that nationalistic music contains these same elements: the dances, rhythms, timbres, melodies, language, legends, and heroes of the ethnic group ("folk"). You may wish to discuss at this time differences between nineteenth- and twentieth- -century approaches to folk music: forcing the music into established traditional molds (major and minor, regular rhythms, etc.) versus the music conforming to its own patterns despite "irregularities." The Workbook has two small research projects, Nationalism in Music and Nationalist Composers, to help with the discussion.

2. Using Smetana as an example of a nationalistic composer, discuss his role in the nationalistic movement of his native land, with his musical output as the logical result. *The Moldau* is the second of six poems from his cycle *Má Vlast (My Country)*, all of which contain detailed programs supplied by the composer. All six are available on record, and if time does not allow the playing of another of these tone poems (the first, *Vysehrad*, has become quite popular, with good cause), it would be helpful to discuss the general nature of the programs with your class. *The Moldau* is included in the brief and basic sets (11:53; score in NS), and there is a Listening Outline in the text. You might therefore consider using a filmstrip in class for the overall visual and aural effect (the one available from EAV has proven quite effective), with the Listening Outline and recordings for home study.

3. Two of the works mentioned in the text are included in the supplementary set: the "Coronation Scene" from Modest Mussorgsky's *Boris Godunov* and Antonin Dvořák's Symphony *From the New World*.

The *Boris* excerpt (8:26) is presented as an example of musical nationalism in general, of the "Russian five," and specifically of Mussorgsky's creative output. The fifth edition of the text contains a transliteration of the Russian text with an English translation. You may wish to show a filmstrip (available from MOG) to set the scene and give some idea of the magnificent stage settings and costumes before giving the plot of the work. A video cassette of a live performance by the Bolshoi Opera in Rimsky-Korsakov's revision is available from Kultur. In discussing specific Russian characteristics, reference can be made to the folk song included in the text. What are the modal elements in this tune? Are there other examples of modality in this scene? Are there any examples of asymmetric meters? Mussorgsky's aim was to reflect the rhythms of Russian speech in his musical settings; is there anything specifically Russian in the composer's setting of the text?

Dvořák seems to be having a great revival, especially with celebrations of the centenary of his American sojourn. An interesting analysis of the *New World* Symphony may be found in Leonard Bernstein's *The Infinite Variety of Music* (Simon and Schuster, 1962), which you may wish to scan before presenting this work. In discussing the symphony, help the students identify the syncopations and the pentatonic and modal scales cited in the text as sources for the popular character of the work. Another interesting exercise would be to locate the examples of thematic recall and motivic development discussed in the text. For example, how does the "ominous" bass motive of the introduction foreshadow the opening theme of the first movement? In the development of the first movement, precisely how are the first and third themes combined and varied? In the bridge of the slow movement, which motives from the first movement are used, and how is the "climactic" quality of the quotation achieved? In the scherzo, which motives from the first movement are recalled in the bridge to the trio and in the coda, and how are they manipulated? Make sure that all quotations from previous movements that appear in the development section of the Finale are identified and the processes of development and variation that they undergo are understood. The complete symphony is contained in the supplementary set (9:19, 11:48, 7:52, 11:44). Before leaving this symphony, you may wish to discuss Dvořák's attitude to American music. Folk songs have frequently been incorporated into symphonic music, but it is very seldom that the reverse is true. For that reason, it would be interesting to play *Goin' Home*, the "spiritual" derived from the addition of words to Dvořák's original melody of the second movement. The rendition by Paul Robeson is most effective (2-Van. T-57/8).

QUESTIONS AND TOPICS

1. How did nineteenth-century music reflect the political currents and aspirations toward freedom by the European nations?
2. Describe some characteristics of folk music.
3. Describe how a composer can express nationalism in music.
4. Describe some nonmusical aspects of nationalism in the romantic period.
5. Romantic nationalism in Scandinavia.
6. Discuss the form of *The Moldau*.
7. Smetana's patriotic operas.
8. Rimsky-Korsakov and his "corrections" of Mussorgsky's *Boris Godunov*.
9. Discuss Dvořák's use of thematic recall in the *New World* Symphony.
10. Discuss the folk elements present in Dvořák's *New World* Symphony.
11. Dvořák in America.

# V-12. PETER ILYICH TCHAIKOVSKY

OBJECTIVES

Tchaikovsky's musical career is examined from its late inception at the age of twenty-one through the early years of intense productivity, a disastrous marriage, and his subsidy by Madame von Meck. The successes of his mature years are described and his works surveyed. The characteristics of his musical style are discussed, and the section ends with a discussion of his overture-fantasy *Romeo and Juliet*.

SUGGESTIONS

1. The text mentions several of Tchaikovsky's most popular compositions, and a few moments could be devoted to reviewing them and any possible performances seen by the students. Several companies have been presenting the ballets, and *The Nutcracker* has been

televised over PBS, as has the opera *Pique Dame*. The *Overture 1812* is one of those gigantic productions, frequently done with cannon and even fireworks in gala performances. The symphonies, even the earlier ones, are available in many recorded interpretations. Because so much of his music is so well known, it is difficult to pick any one work for supplemental listening, so you might consider playing small excerpts. Note that both sets include the *Dance of the Reed Pipes* from *The Nutcracker* (2:30; discussed in section I-9 above).

2. The *Romeo and Juliet* overture is included in the basic set (18:40). Discuss the plot of the story first, and then ask the students which elements they would choose if they were to write an orchestral work. How would they depict these elements? Following this discussion, present Tchaikovsky's solution to these same problems. It is again recommended that multiple copies of the score be made available for classroom listening and discussion. Some additional questions you may wish to consider regarding this work: what are the factors that make the Friar Laurence theme hymnlike? The love theme, on its initial appearance, is scored for solo english horn (*mf*, *espr.*) doubled by muted violas (*dolce*), and accompanied by cellos and basses (*pizz.*) and horns (*p*). There is no dynamic marking for the violas. Obviously, the conductor must decide the relative strength of the english horn versus the muted viola sound. In the recording you use, which sound predominates? If possible, tape two or more recordings of this passage, and ask the students to compare the balances achieved by different conductors.

3. Concerning Tchaikovsky's musical style, please note there is a research project in the Student Workbook that asks the student to distinguish national from international characteristics in the three ballets. Brief plot summaries are also requested, in the hope that the students will become interested in and familiar with these works, which, as the text states, contain some of his best music.

QUESTIONS AND TOPICS
1. Describe the elements of Tchaikovsky's musical style.
2. Summarize the program of the *Romeo and Juliet* overture.
3. Discuss the tragic aspects of Tchaikovsky's life.
4. Tchaikovsky and the Russian ballet.
5. Tchaikovsky's operas.
6. Tchaikovsky and Shakespeare.
7. Tchaikovsky's American voyage.

# V-13. JOHANNES BRAHMS

OBJECTIVES
The biographical section discusses Brahms's early years in Hamburg, his discovery by Robert Schumann, and his lifelong association with the composer and his wife Clara. Brahms's life and activities as conductor and musical scholar in Vienna are described, as are his relentless self-criticism and his gruff personality. The characteristics of his musical style are analyzed, and the section concludes with a discussion of his Symphony No. 4 in E minor, with a Listening Outline provided for the fourth movement.

SUGGESTIONS
1. The text begins the section on Brahms's music with the statement that he "created masterpieces in all the traditional forms (except opera)." If he was such a traditionalist, a characteristic discussed previously as "classical," how then can he be considered a romantic composer? How exactly did he reinterpret classical forms? As for the number of masterpieces, one

could discuss his relatively small output in comparison to earlier composers (only four symphonies, when Beethoven, Schubert, Dvořák, Spohr, and Bruckner each composed nine, etc.) in the light of his high standards and extreme self-criticism. The question of which of these masterpieces to present to the class will depend on your own preferences, for all are worthy of consideration. The pianist will have his/her favorites, certainly among them the two Rhapsodies. The symphonist will not only push for the four symphonies, but the concertos and double concerto as well. The chamber music enthusiast will insist that nowhere in the nineteenth century is there such a wealth of material, each a gem: the three string quartets, the two string quintets and two sextets, the cello sonatas, the clarinet sonatas and quintet, and the horn trio. Then there are the lieder, which compare favorably with the masterpieces of Schubert and Schumann. The Student Workbook has posed a challenge to the students to explore some of these areas.

2. The form of theme and variations was presented in the unit on classical music, section IV-3 above. With that experience in mind, especially Haydn's lengthy AB theme for the *Surprise* Symphony, the text's reference to the thirty variations on a theme in the fourth movement of Brahms's Fourth Symphony may seem frighteningly endless. Stress the brevity of the theme and the rich variety of the variations. (You may even consider playing the movement once through before any technical discussion to see how many students actually recognized the form.) The work is contained in both sets (10:13), and there is a Listening Outline in the text. If you prefer, Home Vision has a video with Andre Previn conducting the Royal Philharmonic Orchestra.

3. If your students are familiar with the popular rock group Yes, you may consider the old educational adage of reaching them through works with which they are already familiar (starting where they are). Yes's recording *Fragile* (Atlantic SD 19132) contains a track called *Cans and Brahms*. Did you know that Brahms, according to the record jacket, is "traditional"? Quoting further from the liner notes, "'Cans and Brahms' is an adaptation [extracts from the third movement of Brahms' 4th Symphony in E minor] by Rick Wakeman on which he plays electric piano taking the part of the strings, grand piano taking the part of the woodwind, organ taking the brass, electric harpsichord taking reeds, and synthesizer taking contra bassoon." Amazing how Wakeman can distill this magnificent movement into one minute and thirty-five seconds, and all by himself! Perhaps a moment could be spent on clarifying the matter, and even playing the original third movement as a prelude to your discussion of the fourth. Brahms certainly deserves better! "Traditional," indeed!

QUESTIONS AND TOPICS
1. Describe Brahms's early years as a student in Hamburg.
2. Describe the elements of Brahms's musical style.
3. Describe Brahms's relations with the Schumann family.
4. The chamber music of Brahms.
5. Brahms as musicologist.
6. Brahms and the Bible: the *Four Serious Songs*, and the *German Requiem*.
7. Brahms and the techniques of thematic variation.

# V-14. GIUSEPPE VERDI

OBJECTIVES
The biographical portion of this section takes Verdi from his impoverished youth through his musical studies in Milan to the production of his first opera, *Oberto*, at La Scala. We learn of the tragic loss of his wife and two children and of the instantaneous success of *Nabucco*, with its strong political overtones. The operas of Verdi's middle years are discussed, as are the

masterpieces of his old age. The characteristics of Verdi's operatic style are defined, with particular attention to the later works. The section closes with a discussion of *La donna è mobile* from Act III of *Rigoletto*.

SUGGESTIONS

1. Many students have the mistaken notion that opera is the pleasure and pastime of the wealthy few, the initiates, and the oddballs. How refreshing to find the text state that Verdi composed "not for the musical elite but for a mass public whose main entertainment was opera." If the students are first generation Americans, ask them to query their grandparents about opera "in the old country" if it is in Western Europe. The scene for *I Pagliacci* would sound very familiar to them, for many learned to love opera by means of traveling companies (the tables seem to have reversed somewhat: ballet has become an American phenomenon, while in Europe it was the pleasure of the elite). How then to prove that Verdi's music appealed to all? Perhaps the melodramatic aspects will cause a smile these days, but can *Star Wars* be called anything but a melodramatic medieval romance set in the future? Let us not try to make Verdi's operas other than what they are, melodramas (for the most part); therein lie their passionate appeal and timelessness. For an overview of Verdi's life and works, consider Kultur's video cassette with Sherrill Milnes, *Homage to Verdi*.

2. The text and translation, with musical annotations, of the great aria *La donna è mobile* from *Rigoletto* are given in the text, and this may be a good place to start with any discussion of Verdi. To place the aria in context, review the plot up to this point. Again, a filmstrip would be helpful in setting the scene and illustrating the stage settings and costumes (recording in basic set, with the Quartet, 8:07; filmstrip and teachers guide available from MOG).

3. To encourage the students to become familiar with other Verdi operas, the Student Workbook has a research project devoted to "My Favorite Verdi Opera." This can be discussed in class or used as an outside assignment. It would be particularly appropriate if used in preparation for a local or televised performance.

QUESTIONS AND TOPICS

1. Explain the significance of the cry *Viva Verdi*.
2. Describe the characteristics of Verdi's early and middle period operas.
3. Describe the characteristics of Verdi's late operas.
4. Verdi and Italian unification.
5. Verdi and the plays of Shakespeare.
6. Continuity in Verdi's late operas.

# V-15. GIACOMO PUCCINI

OBJECTIVES

Puccini's rise to fame, from his days as an impoverished student in Milan to the position of Italy's leading opera composer just before the turn of the century, is the subject of the first part of this section. His musical style is described, and his output surveyed. The section concludes with the scene between Mimi and Rodolfo in the first act of *La Bohème*, for which the libretto and an English translation are provided.

SUGGESTIONS

1. The text deals very briefly with *verismo*, but you may wish to explore further into this aspect of Italian opera. Reference was made to Honoré Daumier's *Third-Class Carriage* in Section

V-1 above as a visual representation of the same realistic style as that promoted by the operatic composers. The Prologue to Leoncavallo's *I Pagliacci* expresses the romantic composer's desire for "true to life" scenes, and has many good points for discussion. Contrast, for example, the image of Leoncavallo with the tears streaming down his face, sobbing as he writes, with Mozart developing a complete symphony in his mind before writing anything on paper. Contrast *uno squarcio di vita* with stories of kings and queens, Orfeo and legends, or Nordic mythology. Remembering that Leoncavallo's father was the presiding judge at the trial of the unfortunate "Canio," or that Puccini read the autobiography of the child resulting from Madame Butterfly's marriage, the aims of the *veristi* become more personal. If time permits, the complete second act of *I Pagliacci* never fails to evoke enthusiastic student response. A fine video with Placido Domingo is available, or a filmstrip from MOG can be used to set the scene and outline the plot.

2. In presenting *La Bohème*, invoke student responses with a comparison to their own life styles. How many of them know what a cold-water flat is, for example? What do the terms Latin Quarter, garret, tubercular, and consumption mean? Discuss the characters of the opera as real people. Just how good, for example, is Rodolfo's love life? Mimi's? Is the love duet too much too soon? Are they not two of a kind, dreamers, ready for a romantic involvement? If you have some students act out the scene before listening, they will find that the sentiments may be expressed in different words today, but the meaning is usually the same. As an example, couldn't we translate *c'è freddo fuori* as "Baby, it's cold outside!"? The brief set and text include the scene from Mimi's entrance through the conclusion of her aria (14:04), and the basic set has the scene through the end of Act I (19:01). The text has the Italian libretto with annotated English translation. There is a filmstrip and teacher's guide available from MOG, and there are several fine video cassettes of the complete opera with English subtitles..

3. As in the section on Verdi, the Student Workbook has a research project devoted to "My Favorite Puccini Opera." Please note that the Workbook also has a blank "biographical sketch" page that could be used for any of the major operatic composers discussed, or with student projects.

QUESTIONS AND TOPICS
1. Describe Puccini's operatic style.
2. Summarize the plot of *La Bohème*.
3. Discuss the characteristics of *verismo* opera.
4. *Tosca* as an example of *verismo* style.
5. Thematic recall in the operas of Puccini.

# V-16 RICHARD WAGNER

OBJECTIVES
In this section, the details of Wagner's biography are woven into the account of his development as a composer and conductor, political revolutionary and exile, and musical essayist. His relationship to King Ludwig of Bavaria and the construction of the Wagner theater in Bayreuth are also discussed. Wagner's style and his system of leitmotifs are described, and the plot line of the Ring cycle summarized. The section concludes with a discussion of the "Love Scene" from Act I of *Die Walküre*, for which an annotated libretto and English translation are provided.

SUGGESTIONS

1. The Prelude to Act III of *Lohengrin* was presented in the very first unit (I-1), and could be reviewed at this time (Listening Outline, p. 6). You might also mention the famous wedding march from this opera as an example of music that everyone would recognize, even if they don't realize it is by Wagner.

2. Since the example presented in the text, the "Love Scene" from *Die Walküre*, is a high point in the *Ring* cycle, some explanation of the plot is necessary, although it can become quite confusing if done in too much detail. Both the Metropolitan Opera's PBS broadcast and the Bayreuth production of the complete cycle have been released on video cassette (the Met also on laser disc) and should be considered. There is a filmstrip available from MOG that can be used to illustrate scenic designs and costumes, and help visualize the characters and their intricately involved relationships. The outline as given in the text will help, especially if assigned as reading before class. Discuss the various leitmotifs, and illustrate them either through taped excerpts or on the piano. The text has the original German and annotated translation of the conclusion of the love duet, and it is included in the brief and basic sets (7:58). The Student Workbook has a research project to help in outlining the essentials of the plot, and to list some of the more famous excerpts from each of the four operas. You might wish to help the students with these, drawing heavily on the works performed at orchestral concerts.

3. If your class is already familiar with the *Ring* cycle, and it happens to be around April 1, you might wish to play Anna Russell's very interesting (and humorous, of course) analysis of *The Ring of the Nibelungs* (Col. MG-31199). This version does not appear on the record sets!

QUESTIONS AND TOPICS

1. Describe Wagner's character and personality.
2. Discuss Wagner's operatic innovations.
3. Summarize the plot of *The Ring of the Nibelung.*
4. The treatment of leitmotifs in *Die Walküre.*
5. Wagner's *Gesamtkunstwerk* and his theories of music and drama.
6. Wagner as a critic of nineteenth-century society.

# VI. THE TWENTIETH CENTURY

## VI-1. MUSICAL STYLES: 1900-1950

OBJECTIVES

This section contains a survey of the principal technical developments in music during the first half of the century. After a brief discussion of parallel changes in the arts and sciences of the early twentieth century, the influences of folk and popular music, Asian and African music, and European art music from the Middle Ages through the nineteenth century are traced. The main body of the section considers the principal parameters of music—tone color, harmony, tonality, rhythm, and melody—in relation to the music of earlier periods. Among the topics considered are the prominence of the percussion section in twentieth-century music, new ways of playing conventional instruments, polychords, fourth chords, tone clusters, polytonality, bitonality and atonality, and polyrhythms. Reference is made to a wide variety of music.

SUGGESTIONS

1. A brief discussion of the radical changes that have taken place in the first half of the twentieth century is in order. The Student Workbook has an exercise that you may wish to use in class or assign for outside exploration. Placed in the broader context, the students should be able to appreciate that changes in music are no more radical than those in other areas.

2. In discussing the general characteristics of the period, consider other aspects of our society such as literature, costume, manners and mores, as well as art. The illustrations in the text should prove helpful in relating music to the other arts:

Alexander Calder (1898-1976). While perhaps best known for his mobiles, or sculptures in continuous and unmotorized motion, Calder also produced a number of stabiles, or stationary sculptures. *The Hundred Yard Dash* (1969, color plate) is typical of his later style.

Marc Chagall (1887-1985). Chagall's style, while reflecting cubist, surrealist, and expressionist affinities, is distinctly personal. In 1941, at the invitation of the Museum of Modern Art, Chagall and his wife came to New York. "At first Chagall felt rejuvenated by the new environment, and in 1943 he painted *The Juggler*, whose main figure is half bird and half man. Painted in lush colors, the picture is full of symbols of the artist's childhood memories—of circuses, of his house in Vitebsk, of his Uncle Nench playing the fiddle, and of the big clock which hung in the Chagall home." (Claude Marks, *World Artists 1950-1980*, p. 149).

Helen Frankenthaler (b. 1928) *Flood* (1967, color plate) seems to present the forces of nature, and a sense of unleashed power, in an atmospheric and dramatic abstraction.

David Hockney (b. 1937). *Thrusting Rocks* (1990, color plate) is an example of the work of the British painter, graphic artist, photographer, and stage designer who has spent many years working in America.

Wassily Kandinsky (1866-1944). Kandinsky was a leading member of the second major group of expressionist artists to arise in Germany, *Der Blaue Reiter (The Blue Rider)*. It has been suggested that the four panels Kandinsky designed in 1914 for an American collector's dining room represent the four seasons. (See for example *Kandinsky: the Development of an Abstract Style* by Rose-Carol Long). Winter has been suggested as the mood for *Painting No. 198*, with summer as the stimulus for *No. 200* (color plates). Since Kandinsky never identified the works as such, however, it would be more important to emphasize his aim of charging form and color with a purely spiritual meaning by eliminating all resemblance to the physical world.

Ernst Ludwig Kirchner (1880-1938). Informal leader of a group of expressionist artists known as *Die Brücke (The Bridge)*, Kirchner revolted against traditional academic standards and sought to establish a new unity of nature and emotion. In *Street Scene, Dresden* (1907, color plate) Kirchner uses distortion of form, color, and shape to symbolize our unhappily anonymous existence.

Claude Monet (1840-1926). The Impressionists were interested in capturing the effect of light and atmospheric conditions on their subjects. The text explains the origin of the word, and Monet's *Impression, Sunrise* (1872, exhibited 1874) is included among the color plates. The text also includes a black and white reproduction of *La Grenouillère* (1869, p. 260), a popular summer resort area. It would be most helpful if color reproductions or slides of this work and the identical scene by Renoir could be obtained, as they would clearly illustrate the techniques and aims of the movement.

Pablo Picasso (1881-1973). *Three Musicians* (1921, p. 251) is an early example of collage Cubism in which the figures are reduced to essentially geometrical equivalents, each separate viewpoint "pasted" over the others to form a single perspective. "The broken shapes, filled with flat, bright color against dark tonal variations, move with a syncopated rhythm and vivid dissonance analogous to those of modern music." (*Gardner's Art Through the Ages*, 5th ed., p. 701) The bright colors are missing in the black and white reproduction, so it is hoped you can find a color print to do justice to the work. If you discussed Leoncavallo's *I Pagliacci* in class, do your students recognize that Picasso's "three musicians" are Pagliaccio/Pulcinello, Arlequino, and Dr. Graziano from the *Commedia dell'Arte*? Picasso's *Girl Before a Mirror* (1932, color plate) is considered one of his finest canvases, and was inspired by one of his romantic liaisons. The surrealistic qualities of deformation and fanciful imagery come through effectively with the brilliant colors in the reproduction.

Andy Warhol (1929-1987). *Marilyn*, from *Ten Marilyns* (1967, color plate) is an example of Pop art, a controversial though highly influential avant-garde movement in the 1960s. A reaction against the abstract expressionists, it is characteristic of his work, and is one of a series of representations of famous personalities.

2. The text refers to many musical examples with the great variety of topics discussed. Though all the material will be elaborated on later, you may wish to treat some topics in detail now. A stylistic comparison listening exercise may be found in the Student Workbook. Space is provided for comparing four different compositions. You might wish to contrast styles in this introduction to the twentieth century by including impressionist, expressionist, and neoclassical works as well as earlier periods. Integrate concepts presented in this section, if possible, in choosing these examples. A few moments from Stravinsky's *Les Noces*, for example, can demonstrate the importance of the percussion section, Milhaud's *The Creation of the World* can serve as a quick introduction to the use of jazz in the art music of Europe, and Prokofiev's *Classical* Symphony can very quickly demonstrate the revival of an old style to serve contemporary interests. Be sure to provide composers and titles in the hope the students will wish to hear more of the selections chosen.

3. If time permits, you may wish to contrast Stravinsky's *Pulcinella* with the Pergolesi work that inspired it. Whether the Pergolesi Trio Sonata is spurious or not should have no relevance to Stravinsky's treatment of the material.

QUESTIONS AND TOPICS

1. Discuss some developments in the visual arts and science that paralleled the rise of the new music.

2. Discuss the influence of jazz on twentieth-century music.

3. Discuss new harmonic devices and approaches to tonality in the twentieth century.

4. Discuss some of the new rhythmic procedures of twentieth-century music.

5. Discuss the new attitudes toward dissonance that arose during the twentieth century.

6. The Paris International Exhibition of 1889 and its influence on music.

7. Music for percussion ensemble in the twentieth century.

8. The rise of ethnomusicology as a discipline, and its influence on the music of the twentieth century.

# VI-2. IMPRESSIONISM AND SYMBOLISM

OBJECTIVES

This section provides background information on two artistic movements that were to have their musical counterparts in the work of Claude Debussy: impressionist painting and symbolist poetry. The painters Monet, Renoir, and Pissarro represent the impressionist movement in painting. Symbolist poetry is represented by Mallarmé, Verlaine, and Rimbaud.

SUGGESTIONS

1. As a general introduction to the topic, the filmstrip *Impressionism in Art and Music* (EAV) is to be highly recommended. The first of the two filmstrips in the set deals with Monet and Debussy, and reinforces the materials in the text (the second deals with other painters and musicians). Just to see the impressionist works in color is worth the time and effort involved. If that is not possible, at least take a few moments to discuss the Monet painting that gave its name to the movement and is included among the color plates in the text.

2. Since this section is designed as a prelude to the section on Debussy, you may choose to go to it directly. Time can be taken to play Debussy's *Reflets dans l'eau*, the first number from book 1 of his *Images* for piano. This marvelously evocative "water music" is of direct relevance to the text's remarks about the impressionist painters' obsession with water: "Using light, pastel colors, they depicted the ripples and waves of the ocean and the river Seine." Debussy's great masterpiece, *La Mer*, is even more useful for this demonstration, but is a much longer work. Compare Debussy's interpretation with another example of "water music" discussed earlier in the course, Smetana's *The Moldau* (V-11). Although the students have not yet been formally introduced to the details of Debussy's style, they may still be able to make some interesting observations regarding differences between Debussy's language and that of Smetana. When playing the Debussy work, ask the students to describe examples of aquatic action that seem to be implied by the music.

QUESTIONS AND TOPICS

1. Explain the origin of the term "impressionism."

2. Describe the work of the impressionist painters.

3. Describe the nature of symbolist poetry.

4. The "sounds" of symbolist poetry.

5. Debussy's songs on texts by Verlaine.

6. Water as subject for impressionist painting and music.

## VI-3. CLAUDE DEBUSSY

OBJECTIVES

Debussy's career is traced from his entrance into the Paris Conservatory at the age of ten, to the summers spent as a pianist in Russia, and his winning of the Prix de Rome. The influences of Wagner and Asian music on the young French composer are discussed, along with the artistic successes and personal tragedies that marked his life. The elements of his musical style are described, and the section ends with a discussion of the *Prelude to "The Afternoon of a Faun,"* for which a Listening Outline is provided.

SUGGESTIONS

1. Some of the various influences on Debussy and his musical style should be discussed. If you like memory aids, you might treat them in the following order: the church modes, the whole-tone scale, and the pentatonic scale. The text mentions Debussy's use of jazz elements (p. 252), but occasions are infrequent. In your summary of his techniques to "drown the sense of tonality" you can then modify the old rhyme used by brides as they dress on their wedding day: "something old, something new, something borrowed, but seldom something blue." Childish, perhaps, but it does help some students remember. Following that, the main problem should be to locate examples of Debussy's innovative procedures as outlined in the text and to be heard in the *Prelude to "The Afternoon of a Faun"* and other works. Search for examples of modal, pentatonic and whole-tone scales, streams of parallel chords, and (in piano pieces) the characteristic uses of the damper pedal. As with all projects of this sort, it will be helpful if the examples are transferred to cassette before class.

2. As an example of a Debussy piece based on a whole-tone scale, you might play *Voiles* from the *Préludes*, book 1 (see excerpt, p. 264; recording in supplementary set, 4:25). Note how pedal points contribute to the static quality of the piece, and how there are no dominant-tonic cadences, even at the end. Debussy achieves some contrast by shifting to a pentatonic scale in bars 42-47 (beginning *En animant*). In addition to *Voiles*, sections of *La Mer* might be played to demonstrate Debussy's later orchestral style.

3. The Listening Outline provided for the *Prelude to "The Afternoon of a Faun"* may be used for analysis in class, and then assigned for home listening (in brief and basic sets, 10:21; score in NS). In that way you can use class time to follow the score where you can help the students. They will soon agree with the text that "the pulse in Debussy's music is sometimes as vague as the tonality." If they have been following scores of the major works to date, they will no doubt realize how difficult it is to follow Debussy in comparison to the classical composers (they also should realize that difficulty in following the score has no relationship to the quality). In discussing *The Afternoon of a Faun* you might be interested in Leonard Bernstein's analysis, including a complete performance of the work, contained in "The Delight and Dangers of Ambiguity," fourth in his series of Norton Lectures (Col. M3X-33024). The work is also included in the *Videodisc Music Series* edited by Fred Hofstetter (University of Delaware). If you are daring, consider showing Nijinsky's choreography, now available on cassette.

4. If you wish to discuss Debussy's views on nationalism, his self-description as *musicien français*, and his vocal music, consider *Noël des enfants qui n'ont plus de maisons*. While nationalistic in intent, it nevertheless is truly impressionist.

QUESTIONS AND TOPICS

1. Describe Debussy's innovations in harmony.
2. Analyze Debussy's orchestral techniques.

3. Describe the elements of Debussy's piano style.
4. Debussy's chamber music.
5. The style of Debussy's *Pelléas et Mélisande*.
6. Exoticism in the music of Debussy.

# VI-4. NEOCLASSICISM

### OBJECTIVES

Neoclassicism is described as an artistic movement that emphasizes emotional restraint, balance, and clarity. Neoclassical composers used musical forms and stylistic elements of earlier periods, particularly of the eighteenth century. Neoclassicism is described as a reaction to romanticism and impressionism. The section ends with a reference to neoclassicism in the poems of T. S. Eliot and the paintings of Pablo Picasso.

### SUGGESTIONS

1. The basic set includes the first movement of Stravinsky's *Symphony of Psalms* (3:21; score in NS), representative of his work in this style. Stravinsky's unusual orchestration should be noted: since the violin was the center of the classical orchestra, you may ask the students to comment on their omission in this "deliberate evocation of the past." You may wish to supplement this discussion by showing slides or color reproductions of neoclassical paintings by Picasso. Consider the subject matter of the paintings shown, and ask the students to identify those features that seem neoclassical.

2. If time permits, you may wish to discuss the work of the other neoclassical composer mentioned in the text, Paul Hindemith. Other than these few references, his work is not discussed. Considering any instrumentalists in the class, for example, you might discuss his theories of *Gebrauchsmusik*, and the importance of his sonatas for various instruments, mainstays of senior recitals.

3. In connection with the "Back to Bach" slogan, you may wish to discuss the views expressed by Benny Goodman in his article "Learn Bach before Bop" included in *Perspectives in Music Education: Source Book III* (MENC, 1966). His choice of composer is significant, as well as sonorous.

### QUESTIONS AND TOPICS

1. Describe the characteristics of neoclassical music.
2. Neoclassicism in the works of Stravinsky and Picasso.
3. Quotation in the poetry of T. S. Eliot.
4. Neoclassicism as a reaction to romanticism and impressionism.
5. Hindemith and *Gebrauchsmusik*.

# VI-5. IGOR STRAVINSKY

### OBJECTIVES

Stravinsky's career is traced from his early years in St. Petersburg, his studies under Rimsky-Korsakov, to his discovery by Sergei Diaghilev. The impact of the Ballet Russe on the entire cultural scene in Europe from 1909 to 1929, the success of Stravinsky's three "Russian" ballets, including the famous 1913 riot, and his emergence as the twentieth century's most celebrated composer are discussed. The elements of Stravinsky's various changes of style are described, and a brief survey made of his output. The unit ends with a discussion of four sections of *The Rite of Spring*. A Listening Outline is provided for the opening section.

SUGGESTIONS

1. In discussing the biographical details of Stravinsky's life, note there is a page in the Student Workbook for this purpose. There is also a research project devoted to his music, with the students being asked to listen to and compare representative works from each of his three major periods. A biography of Stravinsky on video cassette, *Once at a Border . . . Aspects of Stravinsky*, is available from Kultur.

2. The third of Stravinsky's "Russian" ballets needs little introduction to the musically knowledgeable, but will be a new and exciting experience for those who have not heard it before, provided it is not just "dropped" on them. You might begin with a brief discussion of primitivism and African influences on the arts. Even in the black and white reproduction in the text one can see these influences reflected in Picasso's *Les Demoiselles d'Avignon* (p. 270). Three of the heads are adaptations of African masks, even though the "Avignon" of the title refers to Barcelona's red-light district (one writer interprets the two figures on the right as sailors making their choices from the ladies of the establishment). This work caused quite a sensation when first exhibited, and was a major step toward Cubism. Compare the primitivism of Picasso's painting with Stravinsky's rhythms in the *Rite of Spring*. A brief excerpt was used previously in discussing rhythm in the twentieth century (p. 258); if not done then, ask the class to count the beats, with accents, as suggested (music majors can go directly to the musical notation). After accomplishing it successfully in a slow or moderate tempo, ask them to do it again as close to the original tempo as possible. The passage from the *Dances of the Youth and Maidens* can be done similarly, and hopefully the students will recognize the passages when they hear them in the performance. For those capable of reading music, the use of multiple copies of the score will be most rewarding and informative. The instruments of the orchestra should be discussed first, especially with regard to the many performers who are expected to double (bass clarinets, contrabassoons, Wagner tubas, etc.). The brief set includes the first three sections discussed (7:35). The basic set contains part II, the *Sacrificial Dance* (4:38). The work is also available on CD-ROM.

3. Jazz elements are another facet of Stravinsky's creativity not fully discussed in the text. Consider his *Piano Rag Music* and *Ebony Concerto*, as well as *The Soldier's Tale* mentioned in the text. There is a video cartoon of the latter which is most interesting, but the visual effects may detract from the aural.

QUESTIONS AND TOPICS

1. Discuss Stravinsky's rhythmic innovations.
2. Discuss Stravinsky's relationship with the Russian Ballet.
3. Stravinsky and Picasso.
4. Stravinsky's works for the ballet after Paris.
5. Stravinsky and Balanchine.
6. Stravinsky's serialism.

# VI-6. EXPRESSIONISM

OBJECTIVES

Expressionism is defined as an artistic movement "which stressed intense, subjective emotion." The section concludes with a brief summary of the characteristics of expressionist art and music.

SUGGESTIONS

1. Designed as a brief overview, this section is best supplemented by showing slides of various expressionist painters, including the self-portraits by Arnold Schoenberg. The text centers on the expressionist movement in Germany and Austria from 1905 to 1925. The first major group of expressionist artists was *Die Brücke (The Bridge)*, whose informal leader was Ernst Ludwig Kirchner. His *Street Scene, Dresden* was discussed in Section VI-1 above, and is included among the color plates. Wassily Kandinsky, mentioned in the text as an example of creativity in several areas, was the leader of the second major group of expressionist artists, *Der Blaue Reiter (The Blue Rider)*. His *Painting No. 198* and *No. 200*, included in the color plates, were discussed in Section VI-1 above. In discussing the subject matter of the various paintings that you use, try to determine how their parameters—color, line, brushstroke, foreshortening, points of entry, etc.—contribute to the "intense, subjective emotion" of the pictures.

Expressionism has been described as "The Shriek of the Inner Soul." A most fitting illustration is Edvard Munch's *The Scream* (p. 276). Helen Gardner described the work as "a quite disturbing vision of neurotic panic breaking forth in a dreadful but silent scream, the scream heard within the mind cracking under prolonged anxiety." (*Art Through the Ages*, 5th ed., p. 681). Munch recounted the stimulus for the painting: "One evening I was walking along a path—on one side lay the city and below me the fjord. I was tired and ill—I stopped and looked out across the fjord—the sun was setting—the clouds were dyed red like blood. I felt a scream pass through nature; it seemed to me that I could hear the scream. I painted this picture—painted the clouds as real blood.—The colors were screaming." (Thomas M. Messer, *Edvard Munch*, p. 84). The "jarring colors" are missing from the text's black and white reproduction, so try to borrow a slide or color reproduction from your art department to show the work in all its brilliance.

2. You may wish to discuss some sociological aspects of expressionism. The movement is related to Freud's work with hysteria and the unconscious, and is seen as a German reaction to French impressionism. Germany, having lost World War I, gave rise to the movement. The terrible depression in Germany (your stamp-collecting students may have seen some of the multimillion mark stamps from the 1920s) is only one aspect of the period that eventually prepared the way for Hitler and Nazism.

QUESTIONS AND TOPICS

  1. Describe the emotional content of expressionist art.
  2. Describe the characteristics of expressionist art and literature.
  3. Describe the characteristics of expressionist music.
  4. Expressionism as social protest.

# VI-7. ARNOLD SCHOENBERG

OBJECTIVES

Schoenberg's early years as a musical autodidact are described, as is his artistic progression from the late romantic style of his earliest music through the atonal works to the development of his twelve-tone system. Also discussed are his activities as a private teacher of theory and composition, and his later appointments to academic posts in Berlin and California. An overview of his output is provided, and the characteristics of his music discussed along with explanations of atonality and the twelve-tone system. Detailed descriptions of *Premonitions* from his Five Pieces for Orchestra, Op. 16, and of *A Survivor from Warsaw* are provided.

SUGGESTIONS

1. Schoenberg's atonal and serial works are discussed in the text. To illustrate his early style, you might play *Verklärte Nacht*, written in 1899. The work is available in its original version for string sextet and in a transcription for string orchestra. Because it is too long to be played in its entirety, representative material from each of the work's sections could be taped. The students should be challenged to guess at the nature of the program that inspired the music, followed by a reading of the Dehmel text. You might also mention Anthony Tudor's ballet *Pillar of Fire*, choreographed to this work.

2. *Vorgefühle (Premonitions)*, the first of Schoenberg's Five Pieces for Orchestra, is used as an example of his atonal music. It is included in the basic set (2:01; score in NS).

3. Before discussing *A Survivor from Warsaw*, it is suggested that you discuss another great antiwar protest: Picasso's *Guernica*. There are many similarities in both expressionist works, and having a large illustration of the Picasso (after discussion) in view while listening to the Schoenberg work can provide an uneasy feeling of intense emotion (just what the expressionists wanted!)

4. The text contains the complete narration of *A Survivor from Warsaw*. Before playing the work, study the text with the students and isolate those words that in your students' opinion seem to require particular musical emphasis. Then note what Schoenberg does to enhance words such as "unconscious," "worries," "painful," and "groaning and moaning." By what musical means are these words emphasized? (in brief and basic sets, 5:59)

5. As with Stravinsky, the Student Workbook has a research project devoted to Schoenberg. The students are asked to listen to and compare representative works from each of his three major periods.

QUESTIONS AND TOPICS

1. Describe the characteristics of Schoenberg's atonal music.
2. Discuss the methodology of the twelve-tone system.
3. Schoenberg's *Gurrelieder* compared to *Moses und Aron*.
4. "Air from another planet": Schoenberg's Second String Quartet.

# VI-8. ALBAN BERG

OBJECTIVES

The brief biographical portion of this section notes Berg's relationship to his teacher, Schoenberg, and surveys his output. Berg's opera *Wozzeck* provides the basis for the discussion of his musical style, and the section ends with the last two scenes of the opera, the texts of which are accompanied by English translations.

SUGGESTIONS

1. A few sections back, the text stated "expressionism is an art concerned with social protest." Take a few moments to discuss the societies that saw the birth of Büchner's *Woyzeck* (Hesse, not as yet part of Prussia or Germany, 1830s) and Berg's *Wozzeck* (Germany after World War I). As an example of expressionist social protest, Berg's work is unsurpassed. The text includes a discussion of scenes 4 and 5 of the third act, followed by the libretto and annotated English translation. These scenes, with the long interlude between, are included in the basic set (9:36; vocal score in NS). You might wish to use the filmstrip and teacher's guide available from MOG in discussing the details of the plot. The opera is available on video cassette. If possible, play the complete third act without interruption, as intended by the composer.

2. If you do just the last two scenes, consider playing them for dramatic impact first, and discuss musical techniques later. After all, if the students were to go to the opera to see the work, they would not normally receive a lecture on the musical techniques beforehand. Taking scene 4, for example, did the students notice the use of spoken dialogue? Did the *Sprechstimme* bother them, or make them smirk, as sometimes happens at performances of *Pierrot lunaire*? In scene 5, did they notice that the children were playing a singing game? Or did these techniques of vocal production so naturally fit the drama that they were not noticed? Further, did they remember that by definition an opera is a play sung throughout? What would have been the dramatic effect on the work if all the spoken and *Sprechstimme* parts were to be sung in good nineteenth-century style? What beautiful melodic line could possibly fit the anguished cry *Ich wasche mich mit Blut!*? The text comments "Berg did not intend for the listener to concentrate on or even be aware of these unifying techniques" (the variation procedures in each of the five scenes of Act III). You might, nevertheless, explore the variation process as it is used in the act. Tonality is apparent in sections of the first scene; where may "variations on a theme" be perceived in this scene? Were the students aware of the "variations on a single tone [B]" around which the second scene is organized? What is the rhythmic pattern that forms the basis for the variations in the third scene? How does the variation technique unify the last scene of the opera?

3. Berg's instrumental music may be represented by his *Lyric Suite* for string quartet. Since only two of the six movements of the work (the first and last) are entirely serial, the *Suite* can be used to make the not so surprising point that "atonal" and "serial" music often sound quite similar. The work is also famous for its quotation from Wagner's *Tristan and Isolde* in the last movement, and its autobiographical program. Another of Berg's instrumental compositions that is frequently performed is his Violin Concerto. It is notable for the triadic basis of its tone row, and for its use of a Bach chorale in the second movement, both examples of the composer's eclecticism.

QUESTIONS AND TOPICS
1. Define the traditional and modern elements that coexist in Berg's music.
2. Summarize the plot of *Wozzeck*.
3. Discuss the formal organization and structure of *Wozzeck*.
4. The works of Georg Büchner.
5. *Woyzeck* and *Wozzeck*: a comparison.
6. Berg's *Lulu*.
7. Serialism and atonality in Berg's *Lyric Suite*.

# VI-9. ANTON WEBERN

OBJECTIVES
In this section we learn of Webern's early musical training, his studies in musicology at the University of Vienna, and his private lessons with Arnold Schoenberg. Also discussed are his experiences as conductor, his love of nature, his Christian mysticism, and his tragic death at the hands of an American soldier in the Austrian Alps. The elements of his style are described, and the section ends with a discussion of his Five Pieces for Orchestra, Op. 10. A Listening Outline is provided for the third piece.

SUGGESTIONS
1. The third of the Five Pieces for Orchestra is included in the brief and basic sets (1:28; score in NS), and a Listening Outline is provided in the text. The complete set is so short that you

could perhaps find time for them all. Multiple copies of the miniature score would be helpful, especially if the students had the opportunity of following *The Rite of Spring* several classes back.

2. Since about half of Webern's output consists of songs or choral works, it might be interesting to supplement the above orchestral pieces with a sample of the composer's vocal music. Webern's Op. 15 and Op. 16, the Five Sacred Songs and the Five Canons on Latin Text, can be chosen for discussion not only because of their great beauty but because they reflect the composer's Christian mysticism alluded to in the text. The two groups of songs are accompanied by small chamber groups, the latter with just clarinet and bass clarinet. These songs also contain many instances of canonic writing, a salient feature of Webern's style. Robert Craft, in the liner notes to *The Complete Music of Webern* (Col. CK4L-232) describes the Opus 15 songs as "the first of Webern's incomparable masterpieces." Note that Craft's is not the only complete works on record: Pierre Boulez also recorded the *Complete Works* (4-Col. M4-35193) with favorable acceptance.

3. The Symphony, Op. 21, is recommended as an example of twelve-tone style. The work is scored for small orchestra, and is in sonata form. The first movement is a four-part double canon in contrary motion. The second movement is in variation form, with the first variation a transposition of the row while the accompaniment is a double canon. The orchestration is a perfect example of Webern's development of *Klangfarbenmelodie*.

QUESTIONS AND TOPICS
    1. Describe the elements of Webern's musical style.
    2. Contrast Webern's music with that of Schoenberg and Berg.
    3. Religious mysticism in Webern's vocal works.
    4. Webern's use of unconventional instruments.
    5. Musical pointillism: Webern's use of tone-color melodies.

# VI-10. BÉLA BARTÓK

OBJECTIVES
    Bartók's career is traced from his early years as a piano student of his mother. The text discusses the influence of the Hungarian nationalist movement on the young composer, and his absorption in peasant folk songs. Bartók's successes are discussed, as is his emigration to the United States in 1940 and the commissioning of the Concerto for Orchestra in 1943, two years before his death. The elements of his style are described, and the section ends with a discussion and Listening Outline of the second movement of his Concerto for Orchestra.

SUGGESTIONS
    1. Bartók's developmental and variation procedures are among the most fascinating aspects of the Concerto for Orchestra. It has been said that the introduction to the first movement contains two ideas that grow in intensity as they are varied. Exactly how are they varied, and how is the intensification accomplished? In the allegro vivace that follows, exactly how are the themes fragmented? In the development section, can the imitation of the brass fanfare theme be traced precisely from instrument to instrument? Similar questions can be used regarding development and variation techniques throughout the work. The first movement is included in the basic set (9:00; score in NS), the second in the brief set (6:06). The text has a Listening Outline for the second movement.

    2. There is such a wealth of compositions that could be discussed, if time only permitted. You might consider the Sonata for Two Pianos and Percussion because of its innovative use of

the percussion ensemble, the *Rumanian Folk Dances* or *Hungarian Sketches* to demonstrate the twentieth-century composer's attitude toward folk elements, or one of the string quartets, considered by many to be the finest examples of the genre in this century. Considering there may be some future music or music education majors in class, time should be taken to discuss the importance of Bartók's *Mikrokosmos*. Perhaps some brief examples could be played, especially in discussing polytonality, modality, irregular and changing meters, and tone clusters.

3. One of Bartók's most exciting and colorful works is the *Music for Strings, Percussion, and Celesta*, a composition that very nicely supplements the materials in this section. Of particular interest is the formal plan of the fugue that constitutes the first movement of the work. Its tonal plan, dynamic organization, and use of thematic inversion should be explained and carefully charted on the board. If time pressures do not allow playing the whole work, consider the third movement, Adagio. It is another example of the composer's "night music" and, as such, provides a perfect counterpart to the Elegy of the Concerto for Orchestra.

4. An article by Benny Goodman was mentioned in Section VI-4 above (neoclassicism). You might mention in this connection that Goodman's commitment to contemporary music was quite serious, as shown by his commission to Bartók that resulted in the *Contrasts* for violin, clarinet, and piano in 1938, the same year as Goodman's first Carnegie Hall swing concert. While you are at it, you also might mention Goodman's commissions to Paul Hindemith and Aaron Copland resulting in concertos for the clarinet.

### QUESTIONS AND TOPICS

1. Discuss Bartók's interest in folk music and the influence of folk music on his works.
2. Discuss Bartók's use of traditional forms in the Concerto for Orchestra.
3. Discuss some of Bartók's innovations in the use of orchestral instruments.
4. Bartók as teacher: *Mikrokosmos*.
5. Bartók's six string quartets.

## VI-11. CHARLES IVES

### OBJECTIVES

Charles Ives's career, from his boyhood interests in music through his years at Yale and his eventual emergence as a successful insurance broker, forms the subject matter of the first part of this section. The musical elements that contributed to his original style are described, and the section concludes with a discussion of Ives's *Putnam's Camp, Redding, Connecticut*, from *Three Places in New England*.

### SUGGESTIONS

1. In discussing the biographical details of this interesting American composer, please note there is a page for this purpose in the Student Workbook. The page may be used for Ives, George Gershwin (discussed in the next section), Aaron Copland (VI-13), Duke Ellington (VI-16), or Leonard Bernstein (VI-17). Whomever you feel to be the major and most influential American composer of this century, and all have been seriously advocated, some biographical details of a native composer should be explored to counter the heavily European emphasis of the text. As a general introduction to Ives and his music, the film or video cassette *A Good Dissonance Like a Man* is most highly recommended.

2. The basic set contains the second of Ives's *Three Places in New England*, *Putnam's Camp, Redding, Connecticut* (5:58; score in NS). Reminding the students that it was composed the year after the famous 1913 *Rite of Spring* riot, but not performed until 1930, urge them to listen to the

work with contemporary, not nineteenth-century ears, or, as Ives put it, "get up and use your ears like a man [woman]!" Considering that new Americans will probably not be familiar with "Yankee Doodle," "Columbia, the Gem of the Ocean," or "The British Grenadiers," it would probably be helpful for the class to sing a stanza of each to familiarize themselves with some of the basic materials that Ives uses in this work. If the class is already familiar with these songs, or can learn them easily, divide the students into two or more groups and have them sing the songs polyphonically. Try the same key at first, and, if that succeeds, do it again polytonally. The students will not only have a lot of fun doing this, they will see how challenging twentieth-century techniques can be and have a new understanding and appreciation of the music.

3. An astonishing amount of music by this once-neglected composer is now available on records, although scores may be harder to locate. Among the works that could be sampled, in addition to the complete *Three Places in New England*, are *Central Park in the Dark*, *Symphony Holidays* (which contains the *Fourth of July* movement), and his *Variations on "America"* for organ or in orchestral transcription. All are representative of Ives, and serve to illuminate the text.

4. Some consideration should be given to Ives's choral and vocal music, as well as the above instrumental compositions. Many of the two hundred songs will prove interesting and representative, but a personal favorite is *The Greatest Man*; its one and a half minutes of listening time are well rewarded. Gregg Smith's arrangement of *Romanzo di Central Park* is another delight that always evokes most favorable responses in class. As for choral music, *Psalm 90*, which Ives himself felt to be one of his finest works, is magnificent. Choral parts are quite reasonable for this work, and essential for classroom use.

QUESTIONS AND TOPICS

1. Describe the constituents of Ives's style.
2. Describe the sources of the preexisting material used in *Putnam's Camp, Redding, Connecticut*.
3. Ives as essayist: *Essays before a Sonata*.
4. The *Concord* Sonata.
5. Ives and the insurance business.

## VI-12. GEORGE GERSHWIN

OBJECTIVES

Gershwin's career is traced from his boyhood on the lower east side of New York's Manhattan island, through his discovery and study of music, the days of song plugging, his first Broadway success, to his death at the age of thirty-eight at the height of his fame. Some of his Broadway musicals are mentioned, along with some of the many hit songs. *Porgy and Bess*, "his most extended work," is discussed, as are his active social life and interest in art. The section closes with a discussion of the *Rhapsody in Blue*, for which a Listening Outline is provided.

SUGGESTIONS

1. It was mentioned in the discussion on Charles Ives that Gershwin has been advocated as one of the most influential American composers of the century. Considering that Ives, Aaron Copland, Leonard Bernstein and Duke Ellington are also considered major figures in twentieth-century music, the proposal is open for healthy discussion. In any case, it is recommended that some biographical details be researched on at least one of them, and so a worksheet is provided in the Student Workbook.

2. Gershwin had a tremendous influence on later jazz performers and composers, but this discussion might better be left for the unit on jazz. With his brother Ira, the Gershwins also greatly affected the American musical theater. While revivals are unfortunately infrequent, songs from their many shows do remain current, and bear discussion in class. So too do his orchestral works, such as the ever popular *American in Paris*, the *Cuban* Overture, and the Piano Concerto. The Three Preludes for piano are frequently performed, and even the charming *Lullaby* for string quartet, his first "classical" piece, has been revived with great success. But the songs are to many the most lasting, and should be discussed. For some idea of the scope of Gershwin's creativity, see his works list in the *New Grove Dictionary of American Music*.

3. The text briefly mentions *Porgy and Bess*, and it is strongly recommended that some excerpts be played in class, or assigned for outside listening. It took fifty years for this "folk opera" to become accepted as a true opera in every meaning of the word and to reach the Metropolitan Opera, but it is now generally recognized as a masterpiece. The recording by the Houston Opera, which added many sections omitted from earlier recordings, is highly recommended, and will be a refreshing experience for those who know the work only through the older musical theater (rather than operatic) versions.

4. Before discussing the *Rhapsody in Blue*, especially since jazz will probably not yet have been covered, it would help to place the work in perspective by introducing some basic jazz concepts at this time, especially syncopation and ornamentation. Some discussion of dance bands and their music would be helpful. Louis Armstrong's *Hotter than That* was introduced in the very first section of the text, and a comparison of this work with the *Rhapsody*, written three years earlier, should be most enlightening. It should be noted that Paul Whiteman was not the first to treat jazz seriously in concert form, since James Reese Europe's Clef Club Symphony was active in this area even before World War I. Whiteman, however, being white, had greater success at the time, and did have the foresight to commission Gershwin and others for new works for his Aeolian Hall concert. The complete concert has been reconstructed and recorded in its original form and instrumentation (Musicmasters 7037-2-C), and it is most interesting to see and hear the wide diversity of composers represented. It is also most enlightening to hear the original Grofé orchestration of the *Rhapsody in Blue*. Grofé's later version for full symphony orchestra is included in the supplementary set (15:56; score in NS), and a comparison of the two versions should provoke a lively discussion. A Listening Outline is provided for the symphonic version, so that the original can be discussed and played in class, leaving the later version for outside study and comparison.

QUESTIONS AND TOPICS

1. Describe and illustrate the jazz elements found in Gershwin's *Rhapsody in Blue*.

2. Discuss the contributions of Paul Whiteman and his band to the main stream of American music, and Gershwin's role in that contribution.

3. Compare the original Grofé arrangement of *Rhapsody in Blue* with his later symphonic version.

4. Gershwin and the American musical theater.

5. *Porgy and Bess*: opera, folk opera, operetta, or just another Broadway musical?

6. Jazz elements in Gershwin's "classical" works.

7. Classical elements in Gershwin's "jazz" works.

8. Gershwin's *Rhapsody in Blue*: how rhapsodic, how blue?

## VI-13. AARON COPLAND

OBJECTIVES

In the biographical portion of this section we learn of Copland's early years in Brooklyn, his period of study in France, and his cultivation of the jazz idiom for a few years on his return to the United States. Copland's stylistic changes and his output are surveyed, and the elements of his style defined. The section ends with a discussion of the ballet *Appalachian Spring*, with a Listening Outline provided for the seventh section.

SUGGESTIONS

1. Copland's career is unusual in that, at various times, he has chosen to strike out consciously in new directions. Thus the author has divided his output into works that were jazz-inspired, those in which popular elements predominate, and those—such as the serial pieces—that were aimed at a limited and highly sophisticated audience. *Appalachian Spring* represents Copland's "popular" style. Selected excerpts of his *Music for the Theater* and his Piano Concerto, written shortly after his return to America, can serve to illustrate his brief flirtation with jazz. Copland's adoption of serial procedures is evident in the Piano Quartet (1950), based on an eleven-note row, and in later works such as the Piano Fantasy and *Connotations for Orchestra*. See if the students can define those elements of Copland's style that are common to all phases of his work. Which elements are peculiar only to the jazz works? Only to the serial works?

2. *Appalachian Spring* is fully discussed in the text, but you may wish to discuss Martha Graham and the differences between modern and classical ballet techniques. The music is available on record and film in its original version for chamber orchestra, but the arrangement for full orchestra has become more popular. A filmstrip version that uses the same synopsis as the text is available from EAV. The 1961 production is available in black and white on video cassette in *Martha Graham—An American Original in Performance*. The theme and variations on *Simple Gifts* section of this work is included in the brief and basic sets (2:58). A nice prelude to the performance of the variations would be Copland's setting of *Simple Gifts* for voice and orchestra, and beautifully sung by William Warfield (Col. MS-6497).

3. The text mentions Copland's name as having become synonymous with American music and hopefully this also will be discussed. His ballets, and what makes them "American," could be illustrated briefly. His *Fanfare for the Common Man* can be mentioned as an example of music's use in psychological warfare as well as an example of Copland's skill, for are any of the other nine fanfares commissioned of the great composers of the time ever heard today? Finally, *A Lincoln Portrait* deserves at least mention in class, if time is unavailable for performance.

QUESTIONS AND TOPICS

1. Describe the music of Copland's "jazz period."
2. Describe the music written by Copland in the aftermath of the great depression.
3. Describe Copland's extracompositional musical activities.
4. Copland as film composer.
5. Jazz in the music of Aaron Copland.
6. Copland and serialism.
7. Copland and music for high school ensembles.

## VI-14. MUSICAL STYLES SINCE 1950

OBJECTIVES

This section surveys changes in musical styles since 1950. Among the topics considered are the increased use of the twelve-tone system, serialism and its applications to musical parameters other than pitch, chance music, minimalist music, musical quotation, the return to tonality, electronic music, the "liberation of sound," mixed media, and new concepts of rhythm and form.

SUGGESTIONS

1. This section can be seen as an introduction to the three composers and their works discussed in the next section. It serves the function also of raising some of the many visible and audible trends that have not otherwise been covered in the text. The Student Workbook includes an exercise to help in discussing the ten major developments listed in the text. It is suggested, if you wish to give an overview, that you present examples of each (but not necessarily in the order listed, asking the students to identify the style being played), and then help them identify differences through perceptive questioning.

2. You may wish to discuss the philosophy behind the composition of John Cage's 4'33" or similar works. Regarding his chance music, he explains in his writings (*Silence*, London, 1968) that *Imaginary Landscape No. 4* was composed by following the rules of I-Ching (Book of Changes) in tossing three coins six times. The method is quite complex, and does provide a rationale to chance music that is frequently overlooked or misunderstood.

3. In discussing electronic music, you may wish to consider the text's references to the "humanization" of electronic sounds. While adding live performers to taped sounds may be "humanizing," would we call adding animal sounds to live performers "animalizing"? This was done by Respighi in *The Pines of Rome* (the nightingale in the "Pines of the Janiculum"), and by Hovhaness in *And God Created Great Whales* (if you are inclined to modern causes, you may wish to bring in the "Save the Whales" campaign in connection with the latter).

4. For creative and imaginative sounds from the piano and a new method of notation, consider Henry Cowell's *The Banshee*. Be sure to see his program notes and recorded discussion included in the recording of his piano works (Folkways FM-3349). A copy of the score, with explanation of the symbols, may be found in Joscelyn Godwin's *Schirmer Scores*.

5. A major development since 1950 not singled out in the text, but involving all ten listed, is the evolution of the wind ensemble as a separate medium from the symphonic band. A major work that will illustrate the genre, new methods of notation and sound production, and serve as an example of the composer's work is Penderecki's *Pittsburgh* Overture. Scores are reasonable in price, and recordings are available.

QUESTIONS AND TOPICS
1. Discuss the elements of total serialism.
2. Describe the varieties of chance music.
3. Describe the varieties of electronic music.
4. John Cage's *Silence*.
5. The Columbia-Princeton electronic music center.
6. Rock and electronic music.
7. Electronic music versus electronic amplification.
8. Minimalism in art and music.

## VI-15. MUSIC SINCE 1950: THREE REPRESENTATIVE PIECES

OBJECTIVES

This section presents brief biographical sketches of three important contemporary composers, and a discussion of a representative composition by each. The composers and their works are Edgard Varèse (*Poème électronique*), Ellen Taaffe Zwilich (*Concerto Grosso 1985*), and John Adams (*Nixon in China*). Listening Outlines are provided for the Varèse and Zwilich works.

SUGGESTIONS

1. To cover all three composers would probably require more time than available, but you might spend a few moments on each:

a. Varèse: the text discusses the *Poème électronique*, and has a Listening Outline for the opening section. That excerpt is included in the brief set (2:43), and the basic set has the complete work (8:05). Take a moment to discuss the concept of the exhibition for which the work was intended. Those students who have been to Disneyland or Disney World will recognize the application of Le Corbusier's and Varèse's concepts to several Disney exhibits.

b. Ellen Taaffe [pronounced *Taif*] Zwilich: *Concerto Grosso 1985* is discussed in the text and the first movement included in the brief and basic sets (2:41).

c. Adams: *Nixon in China* is discussed, a libretto for the opening of Act I Scene 2 is provided, and the scene is included in the brief and basic sets (4:13). How do the students react to contemporary figures singing on the stage (or is 1972 already too far removed for them)? Considering that many of the people are still alive, do the students relate more closely to them than the dead characters of the past traditionally found in opera?

2. This section concludes the text's survey of twentieth-century "classical" music. You might pause for a while to take stock of the future. Which of the twentieth-century composers discussed in the text appear to your students to be the most significant? Why? Is it possible to forecast future developments in an art, based on what seems most significant today? A similar question, *Sic Transit Gloria Mundi*, is posed to the students in the Student Workbook, which you may like to use in your discussion. There are also several blank biographical outlines scattered throughout the Workbook that you can use to discuss a specific composer you feel the hope of the future, or one whom the students should explore further.

3. To get the students involved and aware of twentieth century music in their own area, the Student Workbook has a research project that asks them to compile statistics and figure out percentages. Perhaps you can help them locate concert offerings, especially if they are not familiar with the usual means of concert listings.

QUESTIONS AND TOPICS

1. Electronic music: its prehistory.
2. Women and music: feminism in the arts.
3. Trends in contemporary opera.

## VI-16. JAZZ

OBJECTIVES

This section describes jazz as music rooted in improvisation and characterized by syncopated rhythms, a steady beat, and distinctive tone colors and techniques of performance. The West African, European, black, and white American roots of jazz are discussed. Ragtime and the blues are presented as immediate sources of jazz. The elements of tone color, improvisation, rhythm, melody, and harmony are then examined in their relationship to jazz. Jazz styles and their proponents are then briefly discussed: New Orleans style, swing, bebop, cool jazz, free jazz, and jazz rock or fusion.

SUGGESTIONS

1. The text examines some of the roots of jazz, and the Student Workbook has an exercise to help in the discussion. Section VII-2 below, Music in Sub-Saharan Africa, is important for its information on jazz roots. Some interesting examples of prejazz influences and practices may be found in the *Recorded Anthology of American Music* (New World Records) distributed gratis to many educational institutions. Some misconceptions concerning jazz can also be cleared up at this time.

2. Besides *The Smithsonian Collection of Classic Jazz* mentioned in the text there are the *Folkways Jazz Series* (Folkways Records), *History of Classic Jazz* (Riverside Records), and *The Jazz Story* and *Capitol Jazz Classics* (Capitol Records) sets that should be consulted for examples. Choosing representative examples of the eight styles discussed in this section, you can help the students discover those features that identify the work as jazz, and those that separate each substyle from the others. An exercise is provided in the Student Workbook to help with this comparison. You might consider presenting the works in chronological order, or in random fashion, depending on the level of the students.

3. As a general introduction to the subject, you may wish to present the *Listening to Jazz* or *An Audio Visual History of Jazz* videos or filmstrips narrated by Billy Taylor (EAV). You may prefer Leonard Bernstein's recorded discussion *What is Jazz* (Col CL-919), which has a most interesting feature not usually available in other sources: *Empty Bed Blues* sung "straight" (without jazz elements) in contrast to Bessie Smith's classic version.

4. The basic set includes the *Maple Leaf Rag* (3:13), and the work is mentioned in the text. The music of this and many other Joplin rags is available in Vera Brodsky Lawrence's *Collected Piano Works of Scott Joplin* (Dover). As an indication of how ragtime has become respectable, note the many recordings listed under Joplin's name in the "Composer Section" (not the "Current Popular" or "Jazz" sections) of the Schwann catalog. While basically a piano genre, note there are recordings available of instrumental arrangements that could be used in class for discussion as to how and why.

Now that *Treemonisha* is available on record (2-DG 2707083) and the Houston Grand Opera production is available on video cassette (Kultur 1240), you should consider playing some scenes or excerpts from this delightful work. You might ask why a successful ragtime composer would want to write an opera, perhaps comparing it to the same desire in a successful Broadway musical composer a quarter century later (*Porgy and Bess*).

One normally thinks of ragtime as a strictly male domain. How interesting, and enlightening, to see Northeastern's disk *Pickles & Peppers: Rags by Women* (NR 225), which includes ragtime compositions by May Aufderheide, Geraldine Dobyns, Julia Lee Niebergall, Irene Cozad, Adaline Shepherd, and others, all beautifully performed by Virginia Eskin. Shepherd's *Pickles & Peppers* was so popular that it was used in William Jennings Bryan's 1908 presidential campaign, and this was twelve years before women were even allowed to vote!

5. In discussing the blues, play the basic chord progression in simple block chords. Impress on the students that the progression is simple enough for beginners with limited skills, yet allows an infinite number of variations in the hands of skilled performers. The Workbook has an exercise that asks the students to try their hands at writing a few stanzas of blues lyrics, or rhymed couplets in iambic pentameter. You might even set a few student samples to the blues progression, and see if they can compare with the texts known to have been improvised by the

performers at the time. The basic set includes *Lost Your Head Blues* (2:54), and other examples may be found in the record sets mentioned previously.

6. Some attention should be given to New Orleans as the cradle of jazz, along with some of its major figures. The Folkways and Columbia sets mentioned previously each have records devoted to the New Orleans style, and the accompanying commentaries will prove valuable. The commentaries by Martin Williams in the *Smithsonian Collection of Classic Jazz* are also most helpful. The basic set includes King Oliver's *Dippermouth Blues* (2:32). Reference is made in the text to the Listening Outline for Louis Armstrong's *Hotter Than That* (p. 7), which should be reviewed at this time. The Student Workbook has a blank "Biographical Sketch" that can be used to discuss biographical details about Armstrong or any other major figure in jazz or rock.

7. After reviewing New Orleans and Chicago style Dixieland, some attention should be given to the shift in emphasis from collective improvisation by performers to the evolution of set arrangements by specialists before the performance (not forgetting opportunities for solo improvisation). The organization of the swing band and the method of performance should be covered and then illustrated. The basic set includes the Benny Goodman Band's recording of *Blue Skies* (3:19). Perhaps some time could be devoted to the significance of the 1938 Carnegie Hall concert. Significant also is the contribution of Fletcher Henderson, who made this arrangement for the Goodman Band. Perhaps some additional time could be spent on Henderson's role in the development of swing, and other examples of his work presented. That discussion should not diminish the time spent on Benny Goodman: his article "Back to Bach," his commissioning works for the clarinet from Copland, Bartók, Hindemith and other contemporary composers, his role in the period under discussion aptly shown by the title "King of Swing" bestowed on him, and his great work in breaking down racial barriers through his integrated trio, then quartet, at a time when such things were just not done, all attest to his importance.

Textbooks not so long ago considered Stravinsky and Schoenberg as the two major figures of the twentieth century. Then, gradually, it was suggested that the heights be shared by a third, Bartók. Now there are writers who strongly advocate Duke Ellington as a fourth member of that illustrious group. It may seem strange at first, but it does suggest that sufficient time should be spent in class to discuss his accomplishments and compositions. The basic set includes the *Concerto for Cootie* (3:17), and there is a Listening Outline in the fifth edition.

If time permits, some of the other major figures in the swing era could be discussed. You might wish, for example, to tie in Stravinsky's *Ebony Concerto* with Woody Herman's band, for whom it was written.

8. Dizzy Gillespie, Thelonious Monk, and Charlie Parker are mentioned as the major figures in bop style. Parker's *KoKo* (basic set, 2:51) can be used to compare bop to swing and New Orleans style instrumentation and performance practices. The students may need several hearings to be able to recognize the changes, but the work is quite short, and bears repetition.

9. Lester Young, Stan Getz, Lennie Tristano, and Miles Davis are mentioned as important figures in cool jazz, and there are many recordings available. It is hoped that some of the performers using instruments unusual to jazz also be discussed. Herbie Mann, Yusef Lateef, Roland Kirk, and Clark Terry are only a few of the many possible choices, all worthy of investigation.

10. Ornette Coleman and John Coltrane are mentioned as major proponents of free jazz. You might be tempted to discuss the text's statement that free jazz is similar to the chance music of John Cage and his followers, and compare techniques and works. You might also wish to compare free jazz with Schoenberg's atonal period. Has this movement influenced other performers in the field? How, for example, would you classify Miles Davis's *Bitches Brew*, considering that he was just discussed above as a leading proponent of cool jazz?

11. Since rock will be discussed in section VI-18 below, one can use the section on fusion as a logical bridge. Comparison might be made of typical instrumentations, performance techniques, and timbral combinations, among others, of jazz and rock groups, leading to a discovery of the elements that each contributed to the jazz rock style.

QUESTIONS AND TOPICS
    1. Describe the roots of jazz.
    2. Discuss the traditional uses of jazz.
    3. Describe the elements of jazz that make it unique.
    4. Minstrel music as a predecessor of jazz.
    5. Describe the usual form of a ragtime composition.
    6. Discuss the working conditions of the ragtime pianists.
    7. Joplin's "Red Back Book," *Alexander's Ragtime Band*, and instrumental ragtime.
    8. Women ragtime composers and their works.
    9. The role of the piano in the black and white cultures of late nineteenth-century America.
    10. Discuss the subject matter and form of the lyrics used in the blues.
    11. Describe the twelve-bar blues progression.
    12. Define and discuss the "blue" notes used in the blues.
    13. Country, urban, and classic blues.
    14. True-blue and untrue blues.
    15. Blues "royalty": Ma Rainey, Bessie Smith, and Dinah Washington.
    16. Describe the cultural activities of the black and white communities in New Orleans around the turn of the last century.
    17. Buddy, Bunk, the King, the Kid, and Jelly Roll.
    18. The career of Louis Armstrong.
    19. Describe the composition of the typical swing band.
    20. Describe the role of the musical arranger in the swing era.
    21. Discuss Duke Ellington's contributions to the history of jazz.
    22. Swing and New Orleans jazz: a comparison.
    23. The many sides of Benny Goodman.
    24. The career of Edward Kennedy "Duke" Ellington.
    25. Contrast and compare bebop with swing or New Orleans style music.
    26. The career and contribution of Dizzy Gillespie.
    27. Discuss some unusual instruments used in cool jazz.
    28. Discuss the characteristics of free jazz.
    29. Back to Bach: the Modern Jazz Quartet, Swingle Singers, et. al.

# VI-17. THE AMERICAN MUSICAL

OBJECTIVES
    The elements of the American musical are explained, and its development from the operetta, vaudeville, and revue described. The golden era of the American Musical is defined as 1920 to 1960, and many leading composers of the time are mentioned. The musical after 1960, especially the work of Andrew Lloyd Webber and Stephen Sondheim, is briefly discussed. Leonard Bernstein's career is traced from his birth and education to his spectacular debut with the New York Philharmonic. His many compositions are discussed, and *West Side Story* is examined in detail. A Listening Outline is provided for the *Tonight* ensemble from that work.

SUGGESTIONS

1. The text states "the musical is one of the most important American contributions to twentieth-century popular culture." One might question the word "popular" in the statement, since musicals are being performed by trained singers in opera houses as well as on Broadway. However one approaches the subject, it is important and deserves recognition. This section discusses the sources of the musical, its golden era, and new concepts emerging since 1960. The question then of what to cover in the time available must depend on the experiences of the students. Hopefully, many of them will have seen film versions of musicals, in which case the elements and history can be covered quickly. If it turns out that many students have never seen a musical, live or on film, more time should be allowed to make up for this disturbing gap in their education. You can choose your own favorites to develop a brief historical survey or you can consider using *American Musical Theater* and *American Musical Theater: the 1970s*, both available on video or filmstrip from EAV.

2. The best way to understand the musical is to see one. The Student Workbook has a research project designed to prepare the students for a trip to the theater. If there are no live performances available, one can use the project in preparing for a video performance. *An American in Paris*, *Brigadoon*, *Fiddler on the Roof*, *The Sound of Music*, *South Pacific*, *The King and I*, and *West Side Story* are only a few of the many musicals available on video cassette.

3. If the students are already knowledgeable about musicals and have had many pleasurable experiences, discuss and contrast a typical musical of the 1920s, 30s, or 40s with a current show. Is there a plot? How do the music, dancing, and social mores differ? Stephen Sondheim has emerged as one of the most important figures in musical theater. All of his shows have been recorded, several have been performed on PBS, and hopefully video cassettes will be forthcoming. *Sunday in the Park with George* and *Sweeney Todd* are significant works that should be discussed with excerpts.

5. Bernstein has been mentioned several times in earlier sections, such as his discussions of the *Fantastic Symphony* (V-10), the *Prelude to "The Afternoon of a Faun"* (VI-3), and *What is Jazz* (VI-16). He truly, as the text states, "accomplished the difficult feat of bridging the worlds of 'serious' and popular music." To document that statement, one should present excerpts from one of his symphonies or his *Chichester Psalms* as well as his more famous ballets and musicals. The overture to *Candide* has become a staple at concerts, so it would be opportune to present some arias, or even a complete scene, from that work to illustrate his fusion of classical and popular elements.

2. The text concentrates on *West Side Story* as one of the most significant of American musicals. A video cassette is available, and if the students are not already familiar with the work, it is suggested that one or more scenes would be the best way to present the musical. Some discussion of the Shakespeare original may be in order, especially if the students read *Romeo and Juliet* in high school. A Listening Outline is provided for the *Tonight* ensemble, and it is included in the brief and basic sets (3:39). In discussing the work, consider: in what way was *West Side Story* a product of the 1960s? Why does the show still have relevance today? How does the performance by opera singers (on the recordings) differ from the original cast performance? Which do the students prefer, and why? How do we react to trained singers in a "Broadway musical"?

QUESTIONS AND TOPICS

1. Discuss the sources of the American musical.
2. Outline the typical form of a musical comedy song.
3. Describe the differences between operetta, vaudeville, and the revue.
4. The book musical compared to the concept musical.

5. The innovations of Stephen Sondheim.

6. Discuss the contributions of Leonard Bernstein to American music.

7. Trace the emergence of ballet in the American musical with special consideration of the work of Jerome Robbins.

8. Outline the plot and interrelationships, musical and dramatic, found in *West Side Story*.

9. *West Side Story* and *Romeo and Juliet*: similarities and differences.

10. *Candide*: opera, operetta, or Broadway musical?

## VI-18. ROCK

OBJECTIVES

Defined as vocal music with a hard, driving beat often featuring electric guitar accompaniment and heavily amplified sound, rock and roll, later simply rock, evolved from many styles of American popular music. Rhythm and blues, country and western, soul, Motown, disco, funk, punk or new wave, heavy metal, rap, and African popular music are all described through styles and performers. Discussions of rock tone color, rhythm, form, melody, and harmony follow. The section closes with discussion of *Lucy in the Sky with Diamonds* from the Beatles' *Sgt. Pepper's Lonely Hearts Club Band*.

SUGGESTIONS

1. In discussing popular performers and styles, it is always difficult to keep out personal emotions and prejudices, both student and teacher. Some students may refuse to see any connection between rhythm and blues and early rock, for example, insist they are completely different, and feel responsible for the defense of their personal favorites. One must be very sensitive then to any discussion of soul, Motown, Elvis, teenage "rebellion," etc.

2. Many styles are discussed in this section, and you may wish to present an historical survey, or a random selection to see if the students can identify sounds and characteristics. Selective songs from recordings issued before *Sgt. Pepper* could be compared to the one discussed in the text, and again to those from later recordings. The various elements should be discussed and illustrated in the same serious and scholarly manner as any other stylistic period covered (because of audience behavior at rock concerts, students tend to carry on conversations while the music is played, something not tolerated in other styles, and so should not be tolerated here).

3. This section on rock offers a perfect opportunity for student involvement in class presentations or term projects (this is particularly appropriate for teachers who feel uneasy about covering this area). The Workbook proposes two rock research projects that can be used:

a. *The diversity of rock styles—an analysis* asks the student to pick four rock pieces popular today that show definite relationship to other styles of music, and identify those relationships; and

b. *Some popular rock groups today—a comparison* asks the student to investigate the instrumentation, theatrical aspects, and musical characteristics of four popular rock (not disco) groups.

4. The text discusses *Sgt. Pepper* in the light of a song cycle. In what way is it similar to the great cycles of Schubert and Schumann, and in what way different? Is Kamien "leaning over backwards" in giving the recording such an artistic designation? A detailed analysis and outline of *Lucy in the Sky with Diamonds* is given. While discussing, try playing it at different levels of dynamics. Is the effect the same? The words of the song are not included in the text, but may be found on the record jacket.

QUESTIONS AND TOPICS

1. How did rock and roll reflect the needs and fantasies of a segment of the American public during the 1950s?

2. Contrast the image of teenagers in the thirties and forties with their image in the fifties.

3. Describe  the characteristics of rock.

4. Audience behavior at rock concerts.

5. Is popular music today any different in its social applications than the popular music of previous centuries?

6. Rock and roll: a business?

7. Theatrics in the performance of rock.

8. Discuss the evolution of the Beatles.

9. The price of success? Factors in the dissolution of the Beatles.

# VII. NONWESTERN MUSIC

## VII-1. MUSIC IN NONWESTERN CULTURES

OBJECTIVES

While nonwestern music reflects the diversity of the world's social and economic systems, languages, religions, and geographical conditions, there are some features common to most musical traditions. These factors are discussed, as is the influence of Asian and African music on modern composers and performers. A distinction is drawn between the script tradition of European cultures and the oral tradition of nonwestern music, followed by discussions of improvisational traditions and vocal techniques. The various instrumental classifications are described, and regional factors discussed. The importance of melody, rhythm, and texture in contrast to harmony and polyphony is discussed, and the section ends with a brief discussion on the interaction between nonwestern and western music.

SUGGESTIONS

1. Ethnomusicology is a relatively recent field to the recording industry, and so new items are constantly appearing. For that reason it is suggested that catalogs be scanned from time to time. In addition, the many varied selections available from Folkways (available from the Library of Congress) and Nonesuch should prove to be very helpful in demonstrating the wide variety of nonwestern music. See also the discographies found in several of the books listed in Appendix 3 of the text. Just playing portions for the sake of new experiences may be sufficient for some classes, but for others you may wish to ask the students to comment on scale types, tonality, melodic shape, or any of the elements discussed in Part I (Elements) of the text. As suggested in that earlier unit, you might wish to compare an African vocal excerpt with a Japanese work, and then both to traditional western practices.

2. To give some visual experiences, you may wish to consider a video such as *The Quiver of Life: Native Music Making Around the World*, program 1 in *The Music of Man* series (EAV), such as *Music and Culture* (video or filmstrip, EAV) or others on the market.

3. The Student Workbook contains a research project dealing with nonwestern instruments. The listing given there can in no way be considered complete, but can be used as a basic introduction. Presentations by students from these cultures, especially if actual instruments and illustrations are included, would make this a very valuable and meaningful topic. Students could explore one culture, or choose a specific instrumental type and trace it through several cultures (guitarists exploring nonwestern plucked string instruments such as the p'i p'a, shamisen, *etc.*). The following instruments are suggested in the Workbook:

### AFRICA

| | |
|---|---|
| drums | membranophones; many different varieties |
| bimpombu, wana | idiophones; bells in many varieties |
| azibwasi, sakala, towa | idiophones; rattles in many varieties |
| imbila, mbila, ilimba, marimba | idiophones; series of graduated tuned wooden bars |
| mbira, sanza, kalimba | idiophones; sound board with metal or cane tongues |
| kora | chordophone; African harp |
| kerar | chordophone; Ethiopian form of lyre |
| bwanzi, ihango, dorungu, gwanzu | chordophones; African board zithers |

## CARNATIC
### (southern India, Sri Lanka)

| | |
|---|---|
| mridanga | membranophone; two-headed barrel drum |
| vinā | chordophone; fretted long-necked plucked instrument with four melody and three drone strings |
| tamburā | chordophone; long-necked lute with four metal strings used to provide a continuous drone |

## CHINA

| | |
|---|---|
| ch'in | chordophone; seven-stringed zither |
| sheng | aerophone; mouth organ with 12 to 19 bamboo pipes |
| erh hu | chordophone; two-stringed bowed fiddle |
| p'i p'a | chordophone; four-stringed, pear-shaped plucked lute |
| san hsien | chordophone; three-stringed long-necked lute played with a plectrum |
| chang ku | membranophone; hourglass drum |

## HINDUSTANI
### (northern India, Pakistan, Bangladesh)

| | |
|---|---|
| sitār | chordophone; long-necked lute with 7 strings, 9-13 sympathetically vibrating strings, and 19-23 movable frets, |
| tablā | membranophone; pair of single-headed drums |
| sarōd | chordophone; fretless stringed instrument with four or five melody, three drone strings and 8-12 sympatheitc strings |
| tamburā | chordophone; long-necked lute with four metal strings used to provide a continuous drone |

## JAPAN

| | |
|---|---|
| shakuhachi | aerophone; end-blown bamboo flute with five holes |
| shamisen | chordophone; lute similar to the Chinese san hsien |
| koto | chordophone; 13-stringed zither with movable bridges |
| sho | aerophone; mouth organ similar to the Chinese sheng |
| biwa | chordophone; lute similar to the Chinese p'i p'a |
| tsuzumi | membranophone; hourglass drum similar to the Chinese chang ku |

## KOREA

| | |
|---|---|
| komunko, hyon kum | chordophone; 6-stringed zither similar to Chinese ch'in |
| taegūm | aerophone; transverse bamboo flute |
| haegūm | chordophone; two-stringed bowed fiddle |
| chang go | membranophone; hourglass drum similar to the Chinese chang ku |

## NATIVE AMERICAN

| | |
|---|---|
| drums | membranophones; many different varieties |
| bull-roarer | aerophone; wood attached to a string whirled through the air |
| axmāl | idiophones; rattles in many varieties |
| panpipes | aerophone; set of end-blown pipes |
| whistles | aerophones; end-blown flutes in many varieties |

NEAR AND MIDDLE EAST

| | |
|---|---|
| ūd | chordophone; Arabic form of the European lute |
| saz | chordophone; long-necked lute with frets |
| rabāb | chordophone; fiddle with one to four strings |
| zurnā | aerophone; double reed shawm |
| naqqāra | membranophone; pair of small kettledrums |
| dawūl | membranophone; large bass drum |

4. Another research project in the Student Workbook is devoted to the exploration of the musics of other cultures, such as the middle east, India, China, southeast Asia, Inuit, and Native American, which can be used to broaden the scope of the discussions, used for student projects (especially if the student comes from one of those cultures), or as a class project to find new materials.

QUESTIONS AND TOPICS

1. Contrast the method by which western music has been transmitted with that of nonwestern music.
2. Describe some instrument types used in nonwestern music.
3. Describe some vocal techniques used in nonwestern music.
4. The influence of Islamic music on the development of north African music.

# VII-2. MUSIC IN SUB-SAHARAN AFRICA

OBJECTIVES

Dividing the African continent into two large geographical areas, this section focuses on the music of the countries below the Sahara Desert. The place of music in society, permeating virtually all aspects of African life, is briefly discussed. Some of the more important instrument types and ensembles are described, including the *mbira* and "talking drums," and African texture, vocal techniques, and performance practices. Discussions of a call-and-response song from Angola and a dance song from Tanzania conclude the section.

SUGGESTIONS

1. The text states "music permeates virtually every aspect of African life." You may wish to take a few moments to discuss the use of music in our own society, and see if it is not also so permeated. The use of music for ceremonies such as graduations and to welcome visiting dignitaries, for rousing enthusiasm at sports events, to stimulate the spending of money in stores, to promote intoxication or seduction in dimly lit bars, to alleviate anxiety during the takeoff and landing of aircraft, for family and religious holidays; in short, virtually everything we do involves music. How then are the African peoples so different from ourselves?

2. A map of Africa, though politically inaccurate as soon as published due to the constantly changing conditions, may still be of value in helping the students grasp the cultural variety and diversification of the area being discussed. Reference to the African sections of Alex Haley's *Roots* may invoke responses in some students who saw the television series or read the book.

3. As with any form of music, seeing and hearing a live performance far surpasses any discussion. There may be a local group or student club willing to perform and demonstrate in class, whose performance can be attended by the class, or a class demonstration by one of the performers followed by attendance at the full performance. If that is not possible, you might be able to locate some authentic instruments at a local museum.

4. The recordings contain the two examples discussed in the text: Song from Angola (1:25), and *Mitamba Yalagala Kumchuzi* (1:31). Additional examples may be found in the Folkways catalog, or the recommended anthology *Africa South of the Sahara* (Ethnic Folkways Library FE-4506). You may wish to compare American "African" recordings of "talking drums" with Folkways *African Drums* (Folkways 4502AB).

QUESTIONS AND TOPICS
1. Describe the use of music in sub-Saharan societies.
2. Describe the importance of drums in African societies.
3. Describe the basic construction of the *mbira*.
4. Vocal techniques used in sub-Saharan Africa.
5. The human body as a percussion instrument.
6. The relationship of "talking drums" to "tone languages."

# VII-3. KOTO MUSIC OF JAPAN

OBJECTIVES
The music of Japan is represented by focusing on the koto: its performance techniques, its origins, and two of its tuning systems. Some basic forms of koto music, whether for solo, duet, vocal accompaniment, or in combination with the shakuhachi and shamisen, are described. A duet for two kotos, *Godan-Ginuta*, is discussed as a representative example of the classical music of Japan.

SUGGESTIONS
1. Once again the suggestion is made that the possibility of a live performance on authentic instruments or a visit to a local museum or musical instrument collection be explored. If that is impossible, check with your audio-visual department to see if there is a videotape available on inter-library loan that would help bring the discussion to life. *Japanese Music & Musical Instruments* by William P. Malm (Rutland, Vermont: Charles E. Tuttle Company, 1959, paperback 1990) is an excellent survey and contains many illustrations and diagrams.

2. The text discusses Mitsuzaki Kengyō's *Godan-Ginuta*. After explaining the instruments and techniques involved, the meaning of "kengyō" as a rank bestowed upon masters, and some historical details of koto playing, play the recording (in sets, 2:56). Ask the students to describe the various musical elements and timbres, comparing them to western traditions, but remembering which came first.

3. Some additional recordings you might consider are *Koto: 18th Century Traditional Music of Japan* (Everest 3306), *Classical Japanese Koto Music* (Everest 3206), and *Japanese Koto Classics* (Nonesuch H-72008). You also may wish to consider some twentieth-century works that feature traditional Japanese instruments, such as Toru Takemitsu's *November Steps* for biwa, shakuhachi, and orchestra (RCA LSC-7051).

4. The Student Workbook has a research project for students to explore the music of another nonwestern culture. This could be done as an outside assignment, especially if there are students from cultures other than the two discussed in the text. If time permits, this would be a wonderful opportunity for class projects and oral presentations.

5. Mention has already been made of traditional Japanese instruments being used in performances of western music, such as the Bach transcriptions for koto, shakuhachi, guitar, bass and drums (III-3 above). Another example is the New Koto Ensemble of Tokyo's recording of

Mozart's Symphony no. 40 in G minor, and *Eine Kleine Nachtmusik* performed on eight kotos (Angel S-37553).

QUESTIONS AND TOPICS
1. Discuss the two most common systems of koto tuning.
2. Describe the method of playing koto.
3. The origins of the koto.
4. The koto ensemble.
5. The use of music in the Japanese theater.
6. The shakuhachi and the shamisen.

# CODETTA

Some end-of-term suggestions you may wish to consider, based on the materials found at the rear of the Student Workbook:

1. *Going to a Concert*, some practical hints that can be discussed in class or assigned for outside reading.

2. *Concert Reports*, some pre-concert suggestions, hints on writing the concert report, and three concert report forms for your convenience in verifying attendance at live performances.

3. A *Post-Course Listening Analysis*, similar to the Pre-Course Listening Analysis given at the beginning of the course (see this Manual, p. 3, suggestion 1.d). It is to be hoped that the students themselves will realize how much they have accomplished in the course by being able to express themselves musically in an intelligent and knowledgeable manner.

4. A *Post-Course Evaluation* that you can use for an anonymous evaluation of the course, its aims and accomplishments.

5. An *Answer Key* for the many self-help questions in the Student Workbook.

The answers for the *Unit Quizzes*, however, are *not* included in the Student Workbook, but at the end of this manual so you may duplicate the pages for the students if you decide not to use them as true examinations.

# Part 2

# Test Bank

# I. ELEMENTS

*Please note:* questions 1-20 are suggestions for testing student listening skills. (see p. xii)

1. The dynamics of the excerpt may be described as
   a. pianissimo       b. piano          c. forte          d. fortissimo

2. The excerpt is being performed by a
   a. string quartet   b. woodwind quintet   c. brass quintet   d. piano trio

3. In the string quartet excerpt, the instruments are being played
   a. col legno        b. legato         c. pizzicato      d. staccato

4. The solo woodwind instrument in the excerpt is a
   a. flute            b. oboe           c. clarinet       d. bassoon

5. The brass instruments in the excerpt are being played
   a. open             b. muted          c. pizzicato

6. The solo instrument in the excerpt is a
   a. xylophone        b. vibraphone     c. glockenspiel   d. set of chimes

7. The excerpt is in _____ meter.
   a. duple            b. triple         c. quadruple      d. quintuple

8. The tempo of the excerpt may be described as
   a. adagio           b. andante        c. allegro        d. presto

9. The melody of the excerpt is relatively
   a. conjunct         b. disjunct

10. The excerpt is a
    a. trill           b. scale          c. sequence       d. chord

11. The harmony of the excerpt is relatively
    a. consonant       b. dissonant

12. The harmony of the excerpt is basically
    a. diatonic (major or minor)         b. chromatic

13. The harmony of the excerpt is basically
    a. major           b. minor

14. The texture of the excerpt is
    a. monophonic      b. polyphonic     c. homophonic

15. The excerpt
    a. begins like a fugue               c. is homophonic in texture
    b. is polyphonic, but not a fugue

16. This composition is an example of _____ form.
    a. AB               b. ABA               c. AABA               d. theme and variations

17. The excerpt was composed during the _____ period.
    a. Renaissance      b. baroque           c. classical          d. romantic

18. The instrumental excerpt is an example of a
    a. symphony         b. concerto          c. sonata             d. string quartet

19. The vocal excerpt is an example of
    a. recitative       b. an aria           c. an art song        d. a folk song

20. The song being performed is in _____ form.
    a. strophic         b. modified strophic   c. throughcomposed   d. free form

21. Music can be defined as _____.                                                Ans. c
    a. sounds produced by musical instruments                                            p. 2
    b. sounds that are pleasing, as opposed to noise                                     SG
    c. an art based on the organization of sounds in time
    d. a system of symbols that performers learn to read

22. The four main properties of musical sounds are pitch, dynamics, tone color, and      Ans. a
    a. duration         b. rhythm            c. melody             d. medium             p. 2

23. The relative highness or lowness of a sound is called                                Ans. b
    a. timbre                              c. dynamics                                    p. 2
    b. pitch                               d. octave                                      SG

24. Pitch is defined as                                                                  Ans. c
    a. degrees of loudness or softness in music                                          p. 2
    b. the quality that distinguishes musical sounds
    c. the relative highness or lowness that we hear in a sound
    d. leaning on a musical note

25. The pitch of a sound is decided by the _____ of its vibrations.               Ans. c
    a. amplitude                           c. frequency                                  p. 2
    b. timbre                              d. dynamics                                    SG

26. The _____ of a sound is decided by the frequency of its vibrations.                  Ans. b
    a. dynamics         b. pitch           c. timbre             d. amplitude            p. 2

27. The frequency of vibrations is measured in                                           Ans. b
    a. cycles per minute                   c. dynamic levels                             p. 2
    b. cycles per second                   d. Italian words                              SG

28. In general, the smaller the vibrating element, the _____ its pitch.             Ans. a
    a. higher                              c. lower                                      p. 3
    b. softer                              d. louder                                     SG

29. In music, a sound that has a definite pitch is called a
   a. noise
   b. dynamic accent
   c. sound
   d. tone

   Ans. d
   p. 3
   SG

30. A *tone* in music is a sound that
   a. is pleasing to the ear
   b. is produced by irregular vibrations
   c. has an indefinite pitch
   d. has a definite pitch

   Ans. d
   p. 3

31. The distance in pitch between any two tones is called
   a. duration
   b. dynamic accent
   c. timbre
   d. an interval

   Ans. d
   p. 3
   SG

32. If a pitch vibrates at 880 cycles, the octave below would vibrate at ____ cycles.
   a. 220          b. 440          c. 660          d. 1760

   Ans. b
   p. 3

33. When two different tones blend so well when sounded together that they almost seem to merge into one tone, the interval is called a(n)
   a. dynamic accent     b. octave          c. pitch range          d. interval

   Ans. b
   p. 3
   SG

34. When tones are separated by the interval called a(n) _____, they sound very much alike
   a. pitch range     b. diad          c. octave          d. cycle

   Ans. c
   p. 3

35. The distance between the lowest and highest tones that a voice or instrument can produce is called
   a. pitch range
   b. an octave
   c. timbre
   d. dynamic accent

   Ans. a
   p. 3
   SG

36. Dynamics in music refers to
   a. the quality that distinguishes musical sounds
   b. the relative highness or lowness we hear in a sound
   c. an exemplary performance
   d. degrees of loudness and softness

   Ans. d
   p. 4

37. Degrees of loudness and softness in music are called
   a. dynamics
   b. pitches
   c. notes
   d. tone colors

   Ans. a
   p. 4
   SG

38. A dynamic accent occurs in music when a performer
   a. emphasizes a tone by playing it more loudly than the tones around it
   b. plays all the notes loudly
   c. stamps his or her foot on the floor
   d. begins speeding up the music

   Ans. a
   p. 4
   SG

39. When a performer emphasizes a tone by playing it more loudly than the tones around it, it is called a
   a. blooper
   b. dynamic accent
   c. crescendo
   d. pianissimo

   Ans. b
   p. 4

40. The Italian dynamic markings traditionally used to indicate very soft, soft, and very loud are respectively
    a. piano, mezzo forte, forte
    b. mezzo piano, forte, fortissimo
    c. pianissimo, piano, fortissimo
    d. pianissimo, forte, fortissimo

    Ans. c
    p. 4

41. The Italian dynamic markings traditionally used to indicate very soft, loud, and very loud are respectively
    a. piano, mezzo forte, forte
    b. mezzo piano, forte, fortissimo
    c. pianissimo, piano, forte
    d. pianissimo, forte, fortissimo

    Ans. d
    p. 4
    SG

42. A gradual increase in loudness is known as a
    a. decrescendo
    b. crescendo
    c. fortissimo
    d. diminuendo

    Ans. b
    p. 4
    SG

43. A gradual decrease in loudness is known as a
    a. ritardando
    b. crescendo
    c. fortissimo
    d. diminuendo

    Ans. d
    p. 4

44. *Timbre* is synonymous with
    a. sound
    b. vibrations
    c. tone color
    d. dynamic accent

    Ans. c
    p. 5
    SG

45. *Tone color* is synonymous with
    a. sound
    b. amplitude
    c. timbre
    d. dynamic accent

    Ans. c
    p. 5

46. It is difficult to sing well because _____ than in speaking.
    a. singing demands a greater supply and control of breath
    b. vowel sounds are held longer
    c. wider ranges of pitch and volume are used
    d. all of the above

    Ans. d
    p. 7
    SG

47. The range of a singer's voice depends on
    a. training
    b. physical makeup
    c. training and physical makeup
    d. which microphone the singer uses

    Ans. c
    p. 8

48. While professional singers can command a pitch range of two octaves or more, an untrained voice is usually limited to about
    a. half an octave
    b. one octave
    c. an octave and a half
    d. two octaves

    Ans. c
    p. 8

49. Which of the following is *not* a normal classification of male voice ranges?
    a. contralto
    b. baritone
    c. tenor
    d. bass

    Ans. a
    p. 8

50. Symphonic bands differ from symphonic orchestras in that they
    a. are smaller
    b. have a drum major instead of a conductor
    c. play only marches
    d. do not contain a string section

    Ans. d
    p. 8
    SG

51. A symphonic band
    a. is another term for symphonic orchestra
    b. consists mainly of brass and percussion instruments
    c. uses a drum-major instead of a conductor
    d. consists mainly of brass, woodwind, and percussion instruments

Ans. d
p. 8

52. *Register* refers to
    a. part of an instrument's total range
    b. playing two or more notes at the same time
    c. the instrument manufacturer's brand name
    d. the number of reeds an instrument uses

Ans. a
p. 8

53. A part of an instrument's total range is called a
    a. mute                          c. pizzicato
    b. register                      d. range

Ans. b
p. 8
SG

54. The bow that string players usually use to produce sound on their instruments
    is a slightly curved stick strung with
    a. catgut          b. horsehair          c. string          d. flax

Ans. b
p. 10
SG

55. The strings of a violin are tuned
    a. by tightening or loosening the pegs      c. by moving the bridge
    b. by putting on new strings                d. at the factory

Ans. a
p. 11
SG

56. Plucking the string with the finger instead of using a bow is called
    a. tremolo                       c. vibrato
    b. pizzicato                     d. pluckato

Ans. b
p. 13
SG

57. *Pizzicato* is an indication to the performer to
    a. draw the bow across two strings at the same time
    b. repeat tones by quick up-and-down strokes of the bow
    c. veil or muffle the tone by fitting a clamp onto the bridge
    d. pluck the string with the finger instead of using the bow

Ans. d
p. 13

58. When the string player causes small pitch fluctuations
    by rocking the left hand, it is called
    a. vibrato          b. pizzicato          c. tremolo          d. nervoso

Ans. a
p. 13

59. If a string player uses vibrato—rocking of the left hand to produce small pitch
    fluctuations—it is because
    a. the performer is unsure of the correct pitch
    b. the performer is nervous
    c. using vibrato is easier than not using it, and no one can hear the fluctuations anyway
    d. using vibrato makes the tone warmer and more expressive

Ans. d
p. 13
SG

60. The very high-pitched tones that are produced when a string player
    lightly touches certain points on a string are called
    a. harmonics          b. vibrato          c. pizzicato          d. tremolo

Ans. a
p. 13
SG

61. Rapidly repeating tones by quick up-and-down strokes of                    Ans. a
    the bow is a string technique known as                                      p. 13
    a. tremolo                              c. vibrato
    b. pizzicato                            d. portamento

62. Woodwind instruments are so named because they                             Ans. d
    a. are made of wood                     c. have wooden key mechanisms       p. 13
    b. use a wooden reed                    d. were originally made of wood     SG

63. The highest woodwind instrument in the orchestra is the                    Ans. a
    a. piccolo                              c. oboe                             p. 13
    b. flute                                d. clarinet                         SG

64. The lowest instrument in the orchestra is the                              Ans. d
    a. piccolo                              c. double bass                      p. 13
    b. tuba                                 d. contrabassoon                    SG

65. Flute and piccolo players                                                  Ans. a
    a. blow across the edge of a mouth hole   c. use a single reed             p. 13
    b. blow through a "whistle" mouthpiece    d. use a double reed

66. A thin piece of cane, used singly or in pairs by woodwind players, is called a    Ans. a
    a. reed                                 c. double stop                      p. 13
    b. mute                                 d. mouthpiece                       SG

67. The english horn is neither English nor a horn, but a(n)                   Ans. d
    a. form of bugle                        c. percussion instrument            p. 15
    b. piece of cane used by woodwind players   d. alto oboe

68. The saxophone is                                                           Ans. b
    a. a double reed woodwind instrument    c. a brass instrument               p. 16
    b. a single reed woodwind instrument    d. not a true musical instrument

69. Which of the following is *not* a double reed instrument?                  Ans. b
    a. oboe                                 c. bassoon                          p. 16
    b. clarinet                             d. english horn

70. Which of the following is *not* a brass instrument?                        Ans. d
    a. cornet                               c. euphonium                        p. 16
    b. french horn                          d. english horn

71. Brass instruments did not acquire valves until _____ century.         Ans. c
    a. the middle of the eighteenth         c. the middle of the nineteenth     p. 17
    b. the end of the eighteenth            d. the end of the nineteenth

72. The vibrations of brass instruments come from                              Ans. d
    a. a column of air in a metal tube      c. a double reed                    p. 17
    b. a single reed                        d. the musician's lips

73. A hollow, funnel-shaped piece of wood or plastic that brass
    players use to alter the tone of their instruments is called a
    a. tailpiece         b. crook              c. mute              d. reed

Ans. c
p. 17
SG

74. The _____ are the only orchestral drums of definite pitch.
    a. snare drums                    c. timpani
    b. bass drums                     d. tambourines

Ans. c
p. 17

75. Which of the following is *not* a percussion instrument of definite pitch?
    a. tambourine        b. timpani            c. xylophone         d. chimes

Ans. a
p. 18

76. The xylophone consists of a set of _____ bars that are played with mallets.
    a. metal                          c. plastic
    b. wooden                         d. glass

Ans. b
p. 19

77. The piano has _____ keys, spanning more than 7 octaves.
    a. 47                             c. 66
    b. 56                             d. 88

Ans. d
p. 23

78. The ____ has strings that are plucked by a set of plastic, leather, or quill wedges.
    a. piano                          c. harpsichord
    b. organ                          d. accordion

Ans. c
p. 23

79. The main tool of composers of electronic music during the 1950s was the
    a. synthesizer                    c. piano
    b. tape studio                    d. sampler

Ans. b
p. 24
SG

80. The _____ has many sets of pipes controlled from several keyboards,
    including a pedal keyboard.
    a. piano                          c. harpsichord
    b. organ                          d. accordion

Ans. b
p. 24

81. The _____ is a keyboard instrument that uses vibrating
    air columns to produce sound.
    a. piano             b. organ             c. harpsichord        d. accordion

Ans. b
p. 24

82. Various sets of pipes on an organ are brought into play by pulling knobs called
    a. keys                           c. stops
    b. pedals                         d. gos

Ans. c
p. 24

83. Electronic systems that can generate, modify, and control sounds are called
    a. amplifiers                     c. synthesizers
    b. computers                      d. stereo sets

Ans. c
p. 24
SG

84. A technology based on placing brief digital recordings of live sounds under
    the control of a synthesizer keyboard is known as
    a. sampling                       c. analog synthesis
    b. digital frequency modulation synthesis    d. MIDI

Ans. a
p. 25

85. Synthesizers                                                                    Ans. d
   a. can usually be played by means of a keyboard                                  p. 24
   b. allow the composer complete control over pitch, tone  color, dynamics, and duration
   c. can generate a practically limitless variety of sounds and noises
   d. all of the above

86. Analog synthesis refers to a technology based on                                Ans. a
   a.  representing data in terms of measurable physical quantities                 p. 24
   b. placing brief digital recordings of live sounds under the control of a synthesizer
       keyboard
   c. representing physical quantitites as numbers
   d. interfacing synthesizer equipment

87. Digital frequency modulation synthesis refers to a technology based on          Ans. c
   a. placing brief digital recordings of live sounds under the control             p. 25
       of a synthesizer keyboard
   b. representing data in terms of measurable physical quantities
   c. representing physical quantitites as numbers
   d. interfacing synthesizer equipment

88. MIDI is a                                                                       Ans. c
   a. technology based on placing brief digital recordings of live sounds under     p. 25
       the control of a synthesizer keyboard
   b. technology based on representing data in terms of measurable physical quantities
   c. standard adopted by manufacturers for interfacing synthesizer equipment
   d. technology based on representing physical quantitites as numbers

89. _____ is a standard adopted by manufacturers for interfacing                Ans. d
   synthesizer equipment                                                            p. 25
   a. sampling                               c. analog synthesis
   b. digital synthesis                      d. MIDI

90. The _____ is a regular, recurrent pulsation that divides                     Ans. a
   music into equal units of time                                                   p. 27
   a. beat                                   c. tempo
   b. syncopation                            d. rhythm

91. The element of music defined as the ordered flow of music through time, or more  Ans. c
   specifically, the particular arrangement of note lengths in a piece of music, is  p. 27
   a. beat                                   c. rhythm
   b. tempo                                  d. meter

92. The organization of beats into regular groupings is called                      Ans. a
   a. meter                                  c. tempo                                p. 28
   b. syncopation                            d. dynamics

93. The first, or stressed, beat of a measure is known as the                       Ans. b
   a. upbeat          b. downbeat          c. head          d. intro                p. 28

94. When an accent occurs on an unexpected beat, the effect is known as
    a. an error                              c. expiation
    b. syncopation                      d. pizzicato
Ans. b
p. 29

95. Which of the following is the slowest tempo indication?
    a. adagio                              c. allegro
    b. andante                         d. vivace
Ans. a
p. 29

96. _____ is defined as putting an accent in music where it would not normally be expected.
    a. meter                              c. tempo
    b. syncopation                      d. dynamics
Ans. b
p. 29

97. The term _____ refers to the rate of speed of the beat of the music.
    a. meter                              c. tempo
    b. syncopation                      d. dynamics
Ans. c
p. 29

98. The Italian term _____ is a tempo marking to indicate a moderately slow or walking pace.
    a. andante          b. allegro          c. adagio          d. largo
Ans. a
p. 29

99. The Italian term _____ is a tempo marking to indicate a lively pace.
    a. andante                            c. adagio
    b. allegro                        d. vivace
Ans. d
p. 29

100. A gradual slowing-down of tempo is indicated by the term
    a. accelerando                        c. ritardando
    b. andante                        d. crescendo
Ans. c
p. 30

101. A _____ is an apparatus that produces ticking sounds or flashes of light at any desired musical speed.
    a. clock                              c. metronome
    b. beat                              d. stopwatch
Ans. c
p. 30

102. A staff is a
    a. set of five horizontal lines
    b. black or white oval used in notation
    c. piece of wood used by a conductor
    d. symbol indicating silence rather than sound
Ans. a
p. 31

103. A _____ is placed at the beginning of a staff to show the exact pitch of each line and space.
    a. note          b. clef          c. ledger line          d. sharp sign
Ans. b
p. 31

104. In musical notation, pitches are written on a set of five horizzontal lines called a
    a. clef                              c. staff
    b. bar                              d. stem
Ans. c
p. 31

105. The treble clef is used for
    a. relatively low pitches, such as those played by a pianist's left hand
    b. relatively high pitches, such as those played by the pianist's right hand
    c. drums and non-pitched percusssion instruments
    d. middle range pitches, such as those played by the violas

Ans. b
p. 31

106. In musical notation, silence is indicated by
    a. notes                      c. rests
    b. clefs                     d. beams

Ans. c
p. 33

107. By adding a dot to the right of a note we
    a. increase its duration by half      c. add a dynamic accent
    b. decrease its duration by half     d. double the note's value

Ans. a
p. 33

108. In the full score of an orchestral composition, the families of instruments
are arranged from top to bottom in the order of
    a. strings, woodwinds, brass, percussion     c. brass, woodwinds, percussion, strings
    b. woodwinds, brass, percussion, strings     d. percussion, woodwinds, brass, strings

Ans. b
p. 34

109. In a musical time signature, the upper number tells
    a. what kind of note gets a beat
    b. how many beats fall in a measure
    c. how many notes there are in a measure
    d. how many measures there are in a composition

Ans. b
p. 35

110. Melody may be defined as
    a. an emotional focal point in a tune
    b. a resting place at the end of a phrase
    c. a series of single notes that add up to a recognizable whole
    d. the organization of beats into regular groupings

Ans. c
p. 35

111. A series of single tones that add up to a recognizable whole is called a
    a. cadence                c. melody
    b. rhythm               d. sequence

Ans. c
p. 35
SG

112. A melody is said to move by steps if it moves by
    a. repeating the same notes       c. large intervals
    b. having rests between the notes    d. adjacent scale tones

Ans. d
p. 35
SG

113. The emotional focal point of a melody is called the
    a. sequence              c. cadence
    b. theme                d. climax

Ans. d
p. 35
SG

114. A part of a melody is called a
    a. cadence                c. phrase
    b. sequence            d. step

Ans. c
p. 36
SG

115. *Staccato* refers to playing or singing a melody      Ans. a
    a. in a short detached manner      c. at a higher or lower pitch      p. 36
    b. in a smooth, connected manner      d. in small steps

116. A short, detached style of playing a melody is known as      Ans. b
    a. legato      c. glissando      p. 36
    b. staccato      d. vibrato      SG

117. A smooth, connected style of playing a melody is known as      Ans. a
    a. legato      c. glissando      p. 36
    b. staccato      d. vibrato

118. *Legato* refers to playing or singing a melody      Ans. b
    a. in a short, detached manner      c. at a higher or lower pitch      p. 36
    b. in a smooth, connected style      d. by small steps      SG

119. A melodic phrase ending that sets up expectations for continuation is known as      Ans. a
    a. an incomplete cadence      c. a sentence      p. 36
    b. a complete cadence      d. a theme      SG

120. *Sequence* may be defined as      Ans. d
    a. a resting place at the end of a phrase      p. 36
    b. the emotional focal point of a melody
    c. a part of a melody
    d. the repetition of a melodic pattern at a higher or lower pitch

121. The repetition of a melodic pattern at a higher or lower pitch is called a      Ans. b
    a. climax      c. cadence      p. 36
    b. sequence      d. phrase      SG

122. A cadence is      Ans. b
    a. the emotional focal point of a melody      p. 36
    b. a resting place at the end of a phrase
    c. a melody that serves as the starting point for a more extended piece of music
    d. the repetition of a melodic pattern at a higher or lower pitch

123. A resting place at the end of a phrase is called a      Ans. d
    a. climax      c. stop      p. 36
    b. melody      d. cadence      SG

124. A melodic phrase ending that sets up expectations for continuation is known as      Ans. a
    a. an incomplete cadence      c. a sentence      p. 36
    b. a complete cadence      d. a theme      SG

125. A melody that serves as the starting point for a more extended piece of music      Ans. a
    is called a      p. 37
    a. theme      b. tune      c. climax      d. cadence      SG

126. A theme is                                                        Ans. c
   a. the emotional focal point of a melody                            p. 37
   b. a resting place at the end of a phrase
   c. a melody that serves as the starting point for a more extended piece of music
   d. the repetition of a melodic pattern at a higher or lower pitch

127. _____ in music adds support, depth, and richness to a melody.   Ans. d
   a. rhythm                          c. meter                         p. 38
   b. tempo                           d. harmony                       SG

128. The musical element that refers to the way chords are             Ans. a
   constructed and how they follow each other is                       p. 38
   a. harmony                         c. melody
   b. tempo                           d. meter

129. *Harmony* refers to                                               Ans. a
   a. the way chords are constructed and how they follow each other    p. 38
   b. living in peace with other people                                SG
   c. a pattern of beats per measure
   d. a chord built upon the first step of the scale

130. A combination of three or more tones sounded at the same time is called   Ans. c
   a. harmony                         c. a chord                       p. 38
   b. consonance                      d. dissonance                    SG

131. A chord is                                                        Ans. b
   a. a pattern of accents used in music                               p. 38
   b. a combination of three or more tones sounded at once
   c. a series of individual tones heard one after another
   d. a resting point at the end of a phrase

132. A progression is                                                  Ans. a
   a. a series of chords                                               p. 38
   b. a combination of three or more tones sounded at once
   c. a broken chord
   d. music of a higher level than what came before

133. A series of chords is called a(n)                                 Ans. b
   a. triad                           c. arpeggio                      p. 38
   b. progression                     d. consonance                    SG

134. A consonance is a combination of tones that                       Ans. b
   a. is considered unstable and tense   c. are sounded one after the other   p. 39
   b. is considered stable and restful   d. form a melody

135. A combination of tones that is considered stable and restful is called a   Ans. a
   a. consonance                      c. progression                   p. 39
   b. dissonance                      d. chord                         SG

136. A combination of tones that is considered unstable and tense is called a
   a. consonance
   b. progression
   c. dissonance
   d. chord

Ans. c
p. 39
SG

137. A dissonance is a combination of tones that
   a. is considered unstable and tense
   b. is considered stable and restful
   c. are sounded one after the other
   d. form a melody

Ans. a
p. 39

138. The triad built on the first step of the scale is called
   a. the tonic chord
   b. the dominant chord
   c. a progression
   d. the resolution

Ans. a
p. 39

139. Traditionally, a composition would almost always end on a
   a. progression
   b. dissonant chord
   c. dominant chord
   d. tonic chord

Ans. d
p. 39
SG

140. The dominant chord is the triad built on the _____ step of the scale.
   a. first
   b. second
   c. fourth
   d. fifth

Ans. d
p. 39

141. The triad built on the fifth step of the scale is called the
   a. tonic chord
   b. dominant chord
   c. progression
   d. resolution

Ans. b
p. 39
SG

142. When a dissonance moves to a consonance, it is called a
   a. triad
   b. chord
   c. resolution
   d. broken chord

Ans. c
p. 39

143. *Resolution* refers to a(n)
   a. dissonant chord moving to a consonant chord
   b. consonant chord moving to a dissonant chord
   c. composer resolving to write a composition
   d. arpeggio

Ans. a
p. 39
SG

144. Dynamic tension that demands onward motion in music is usually the result of
   a. the performer's technical ability
   b. the impulse of dissonance to be resolved
   c. the audience's response
   d. a high volume level

Ans. b
p. 39

145. The simplest, most basic chord used in western music is the
   a. consonance
   b. dissonance
   c. dyad
   d. triad

Ans. d
p. 39

146. When the individual tones of a chord are sounded one after another instead of simultaneously, it is called a broken chord or
   a. cadence
   b. arpeggio
   c. allegro
   d. progression

Ans. b
p. 40
SG

147. *Key* refers to
    a. the major scale
    b. a central tone, scale, and chord
    c. any twelve random pitches
    d. a musical symbol placed at the beginning of the staff

Ans. b
p. 40
SG

148. The keynote, or tonic, of a melody is the _____ of the melody.
    a. central tone
    b. opening note
    c. climax
    d. key signature

Ans. a
p. 40

149. The central tone around which a musical composition is organized is called the
    a. scale
    b. dominant
    c. tonic
    d. modulation

Ans. c
p. 40
SG

150. The sense of relatedness to a central tone is known as
    a. modulation
    b. tonality
    c. transposition
    d. atonal

Ans. b
p. 40

151. *Tonality* is another term for
    a. key
    b. scale
    c. chromaticism
    d. modulation

Ans. a
p. 40

152. In traditional western music, the _____ is the smallest interval between successive tones of a scale.
    a. quarter step
    b. whole step
    c. half step
    d. octave

Ans. c
p. 41
SG

153. Sharp or flat signs immediately following the clef sign at the beginning of the staff of a musical composition are called the
    a. time signature
    b. music signature
    c. key signature
    d. meter

Ans. c
p. 43

154. The word *chromatic* comes from the Greek word *chroma*, color, and is used in music to refer to the
    a. twelve tones of the octave
    b. eight tones of the octave
    c. color of the instrumentation
    d. use of colorful descriptions of the music

Ans. a
p. 43

155. *Modulation* refers to
    a. the central tone of a musical composition
    b. the use of all keys in one octave
    c. the sharp or flat signs immediately following the clef sign at the beginning of the staff of a musical composition
    d. a shift from one key to another within the same composition

Ans. d
p. 43

156. A shift from one key to another within the same composition is called
    a. key
    b. resolution
    c. scale
    d. modulation

Ans. d
p. 43
SG

157. *Musical texture* refers to
    a. how many different layers of sound are heard at the same time
    b. what kind of layers of sound are heard (melody or harmony)
    c. how layers of sound are related to each other
    d. all of the above

Ans. d
p. 44
SG

158. Monophonic texture consists of
    a. a single melodic line without accompaniment
    b. one main melody accompanied by chords
    c. two or more melodies of relatively equal interest performed simultaneously
    d. all of the above

Ans. a
p. 44

159. If a flute player were to play a solo without any other accompaniment,
the texture would be
    a. contrapuntal               c. monophonic
    b. homophonic              d. polyphonic

Ans. c
p. 44

160. The texture of a single melodic line without accompaniment is
    a. contrapuntal               c. monophonic
    b. homophonic              d. polyphonic

Ans. c
p. 44
SG

161. Performance of a single melodic line by more than one instrument or voice
is described as playing or singing in
    a. unison                    c. harmony
    b. counterpoint             d. imitation

Ans. a
p. 44
SG

162. When two or more melodic lines of equal interest are performed simultaneously,
the texture is
    a. monophonic              c. polyphonic
    b. homophonic              d. heterophonic

Ans. c
p. 45
SG

163. Polyphonic texture consists of
    a. a single melodic line without accompaniment
    b. one main melody accompanied by chords
    c. two or more melodies of relatively equal interest performed simultaneously
    d. two or more different versions of the same basic melody performed simultaneously

Ans. c
p. 45

164. The technique of combining several melodic lines into
a meaningful whole is called
    a. texture                    c. unison
    b. imitation                d. counterpoint

Ans. d
p. 45
SG

165. When a melodic idea is presented by one voice or instrument and then restated
immediately by another voice or instrument, the technique is called
    a. counterpoint             c. copying
    b. imitation               d. all of the above

Ans. b
p. 45
SG

166. *Contrapuntal texture* is sometimes used in place of the term          Ans. c
  a. monophonic texture                    c. polyphonic texture            p. 45
  b. homophonic texture                    d. unisonal performance          SG

167. A *round* is an example of                                            Ans. c
  a. homophonic texture                    c. strict imitation             p. 45
  b. monophonic texture                    d. sloppy singing               SG

168. A song in which several people sing the same melody but each singer    Ans. c
  starts at a different time is an example of                               p. 45
  a. homophonic texture                    c. strict imitation
  b. monophonic texture                    d. sloppy singing

169. When harmonized by chords, *Row, Row, Row Your Boat* is an example of   Ans. b
  a. monophonic texture                    c. polyphonic texture           p. 45
  b. homophonic texture                    d. a round

170. Homophonic texture consists of                                         Ans. b
  a. a single melodic line without accompaniment                           p. 46
  b. one main melody accompanied by chords
  c. two or more melodies of relatively equal interest performed simultaneously
  d. two or more different versions of the same basic melody performed simultaneously

171. When there is one main melody accompanied by chords, the texture is    Ans. b
  a. polyphonic                            c. monophonic                   p. 46
  b. homophonic                            d. imitative                    SG

172. *Form* in music is                                                     Ans. c
  a. a statement followed by a contrasting statement                       p. 48
  b. the technique of combining several melodic lines into a meaningful whole
  c. the organization of musical ideas in time
  d. constant repetition of a musical idea

173. The organization of musical ideas in time is called                    Ans. a
  a. form                                  c. ternary                      p. 48
  b. repetition                            d. variation                    SG

174. Repetition is a technique widely used in music because it              Ans. d
  a. creates a sense of unity                                              p. 49
  b. helps engrave a melody in the memory                                  SG
  c. provides a feeling of balance and symmetry
  d. all of the above

175. Retaining some features of a musical idea while changing others is called   Ans. d
  a. form                                  c. repetition                   p. 49
  b. contrast                              d. variation                    SG

176. Forward motion, conflict, and change of mood all come from                Ans. a
    a. contrast                              c. homogeneity               p. 49
    b. repetition                          d. dynamics

177. When some features of a musical idea are changed, but others are retained,        Ans. d
    the technique is referred to as        p. 49
    a. form                                 c. repetition
    b. contrast                         d. variation

178. A musical statement followed by a contrasting statement and then a        Ans. a
    return of the original statement would be called        p. 49
    a. ternary form                     c. free form
    b. binary form                    d. double form

179. Three-part form can be represented as        Ans. d
    a. A B A                            c. statement, contrast, return    p. 49
    b. A B A'                         d. all of the above                  SG

180. The form consisting of a musical statement followed by a counterstatement        Ans. b
    would be called        p. 51
    a. ternary                           c. free                       SG
    b. binary                           d. all of the above

181. In music, _____ refers to a characteristic way of using        Ans. c
    melody, rhythm, tone color, dynamics, harmony, texture, and form.        p. 53
    a. fashion                            c. style
    b. technique                       d. convention

182. Which of the following would be a good example of a change in musical style?        Ans. b
    a. The treble clef is used for relatively high pitch ranges, but the bass clef is used        p. 53
        for lower ranges.        SG
    b. The major and minor scales were the basic scales of western music from the 1600s
        to the 1900s, but in the twentieth century many composers abandoned tonality.
    c. The men in the New York Philharmonic wear white tie and tails during the winter
        season, but for  the summer concerts they wear black tie and white dinner jackets.
    d. each of the above.

183. Changes in musical style from one historical period to the next are usually        Ans. a
    a. continuous        p. 53
    b. recognizable only by scholars and professional musicians        SG
    c. very abrupt
    d. for the worse

184. The Renaissance, as a stylistic period in western music,  encompassed the years        Ans. a
    a. 1450-1600                       c. 1750-1820              p. 53
    b. 1600-1750                       d. 1820-1900

185. The baroque period in western music is usually given as
    a. 450-1450                                c. 1600-1750
    b. 1450-1600                             d. 1750-1820

Ans. c
p. 53

186. We know little about the music of very ancient civilizations because
    a. there probably was almost none
    b. it was too primitive to interest later generations
    c. it is too difficult to be played today
    d. hardly any notated music has survived from these cultures

Ans. d
p. 53
SG

# II. THE MIDDLE AGES AND RENAISSANCE

1. The phrase *Middle Ages* refers to the period of European history spanning
   a. 450-1000
   b. 1000-1150
   c. 1150-1450
   d. 450-1450

   Ans. d
   p. 56

2. The romanesque period in Europe encompassed the years
   a. 450-1000
   b. 1000-1150
   c. 1150-1450
   d. 1450-1600

   Ans. b
   p. 56

3. The gothic period in Europe encompassed the years
   a. 450-1000
   b. 1000-1150
   c. 1150-1450
   d. 1450-1600

   Ans. c
   p. 56

4. The "dark ages" in Europe
   a. began about 450 with the disintegration of the Roman Empire
   b. was a period of peace and tranquility
   c. was a period of cultural growth
   d. all of the above

   Ans. a
   p. 56

5. In the Middle Ages, most important musicians were
   a. priests
   b. traveling entertainers
   c. peasants
   d. women

   Ans. a
   p. 56

6. A virtual monopoly on learning during the Middle Ages was held by
   a. knights in castles
   b. professors in universities
   c. monks in monasteries
   d. wandering minstrels or *jongleurs*

   Ans. c
   p. 56

7. An important woman composer of the Middle Ages was
   a. Alicia de la Rocha
   b. Amy Beach
   c. Hildegard of Bingen
   d. Mary Lowell

   Ans. c
   p. 56

8. Most medieval music was
   a. instrumental
   b. vocal
   c. for the piano
   d. for the organ

   Ans. b
   p. 56

9. During the Middle Ages, women
   a. were not permitted to sing in church
   b. sang at all church services
   c. could sing only in monasteries
   d. were not permitted to participate in church services

   Ans. a
   p. 56

10. The view of the later medieval church on music during religious services was that it should be
    a. performed by as many musical instruments as possible
    b. used only as a discreet accompaniment
    c. banned entirely
    d. used only with wind instruments

    Ans. b
    p. 56

11. In the Middle Ages the organ                                                    Ans. d
    a. had not as yet been invented                                                 p. 56
    b. was considered the "king of instruments"
    c. could be carried around the neck
    d. was a prominent church instrument

12. Church authorities in the Middle Ages _____ their religious services.     Ans. c
    a. encouraged the use of music as a highlight of                                p. 56
    b. forbade the use of music in
    c. wanted music only as a discreet accompaniment to
    d. preferred instrumental music in

13. The church modes were                                                           Ans. c
    a. forms of religious ritual                                                    p. 56
    b. only used in the music of the Catholic church
    c. the basic scales of western music during the Middle Ages
    d. chalices to hold holy relics

14. The church modes are                                                            Ans. c
    a. different from the major and minor scales in that they consist of only       p. 56
       six different tones                                                          SG
    b. different from the major and minor scales in that they consist of only five
       different tones
    c. like the major and minor scales in that they consist of seven tones and
       an eighth tone that duplicates the first an octave higher
    d. completely different from any other form of scale

15. Gregorian chant                                                                 Ans. d
    a. is set to sacred Latin texts                                                 p. 57
    b. is sung without accompaniment                                                SG
    c. was the official music of the Roman Catholic church for more than 1,000 years
    d. all of the above

16. Gregorian chant                                                                 Ans. a
    a. is monophonic in texture          c. is homophonic in texture                p. 57
    b. is polyphonic in texture          d. has no texture                         SG

17. Gregorian chant consists of                                                     Ans. b
    a. one instrument playing alone      c. several voices singing in harmony       p. 57
    b. melody sung without accompaniment d. several instruments playing together

18. Which of the following is *not* true of Gregorian chant?                        Ans. d
    a. It conveys a calm, otherworldly quality.                                     p. 57
    b. Its exact rhythm is uncertain.
    c. The melodies tend to move stepwise within a narrow range of pitches.
    d. It is usually polyphonic in texture.

19. Gregorian chant melodies tend to move
    a. by leaps over a wide range of pitches
    b. stepwise within a narrow range of pitches
    c. infrequently, remaining on a single tone for long stretches
    d. only by perfect intervals

Ans. b
p. 58

20. Gregorian chant is named after Pope Gregory I, who
    a. composed all the chants presently in use
    b. had his name put on the first printed edition
    c. was credited by medieval legend with having created it, even though it evolved over many centuries
    d. wrote the texts for the chants

Ans. c
p. 58
SG

21. Pope Gregory the Great
    a. composed all of the Gregorian chants
    b. published all of the Gregorian chants
    c. reorganized the liturgy of the Catholic church during his reign from 590 to 604
    d. all of the above

Ans. c
p. 58

22. *Alleluia*
    a. may be translated as "praise ye the Lord"
    b. is a Latinized form of the Hebrew word *hallelujah*
    c. is often used in Gregorian chants
    d. all of the above

Ans. d
p. 58

23. The earliest surviving chant manuscripts date from about the _____ century.
    a. sixth          b. nint h          c. thirteenth          d. fourteenth

Ans. b
p. 58

24. The form of the chant *Alleluia: Vidimus stellam* is
    a. theme and variations          c. through-composed
    b. ABA          d. ABACABA

Ans. b
p. 59

25. The first large body of secular songs that survives in decipherable notation was composed
    a. during the twelfth and thirteenth centuries  c. from 590 to 604
    b. during the ninth century          d. during the fifteenth century

Ans. a
p. 60

26. The first large body of secular songs that survives in decipherable notation was composed
    a. during the ninth century by monks for church services
    b. during the twelfth and thirteenth centuries by French nobles called *troubadours* and *trouvères*
    c. during the fifteenth century by wandering minstrels called *jongleurs*
    d. around 1250 by the royal family, like *Danse royale (Royal Dance)*

Ans. b
p. 60
SG

27. Trouvère songs of the Middle Ages dealt with all of the following subjects *except*
    a. love          c. the Crusades
    b. dancing          d. religion

Ans. d
p. 60

28. The first large body of secular songs that survives
    in decipherable notation was composed by
    a. priests and monks
    b. French nobles called *troubadours* and *trouvère*
    c. wandering minstrels or *jongleurs*
    d. professional dancers and singers

    Ans. b
    p. 60

29. The French secular songs of the Middle Ages usually dealt with
    a. the Crusades
    b. spinning

    c. love
    d. all of the above

    Ans. d
    p. 60
    SG

30. A famous French woman troubadour was
    a. Hildegard of Bingen
    b. Frauenlob

    c. Péronne d'Armentières
    d. Beatriz de Dia

    Ans. d
    p. 60

31. The notation of the secular songs of the Middle Ages does not indicate
    a. rhythm
    b. pitch

    c. duration
    d. any of the above

    Ans. a
    p. 60
    SG

32. Surviving manuscripts of troubadour and trouvère melodies show no indication of
    a. rhythm          b. pitch          c. duration          d. tempo

    Ans. a
    p. 60

33. An *estampie* is a medieval
    a. dance
    b. method of soil cultivation

    c. type of jewelry
    d. version of apple pie

    Ans. a
    p. 61

34. The medieval *jongleurs*, important sources of information in a time when there
    were no newspapers, were
    a. ranked on a high social level
    b. on the lowest social level
    c. equal in rank to the troubadours and trouvères
    d. welcomed by the nobility as distinguished guests

    Ans. b
    p. 61

35. The wandering minstrels, or *jongleurs*, of the Middle Ages
    a. performed music and acrobatic tricks in castles, taverns, and town squares
    b. lived on the lowest level of society
    c. played instrumental dances on harps, fiddles, and lutes
    d. all of the above

    Ans. d
    p. 61
    SG

36. Which of the following statements is *not* true of the medieval *estampie*?
    a. It is one of the earliest surviving pieces of instrumental music.
    b. It was intended for religious services.
    c. It is monophonic in texture.
    d. The manuscript does not indicate which instrument should play the melody.

    Ans. b
    p. 61

37. In the recording of the medieval *estampie*, the melody is played on a rebec, a
    a. medieval drum
    b. bowed string instrument

    c. tubular wind instrument
    d. plucked string instrument

    Ans. b
    p. 61
    SG

38. The first step in a revolution that eventually transformed            Ans. a
    western music began sometime between 700 and 900 with the             p. 62
    a. addition of a second melodic line to Gregorian chant
    b. addition of an organ accompaniment
    c. transcription of the music for several different instruments
    d. addition of chords to the melody line

39. The first steps toward the development of polyphony were taken sometime   Ans. c
    between 700 and 900, when                                             p. 62
    a. musicians composed new music to accompany dancing                 SG
    b. the French nobles began to sing hunting songs together
    c. monks in monastery choirs began to add a second melodic line to Gregorian chant
    d. all of the above

40. The center of polyphonic music in Europe after 1150 was              Ans. a
    a. Paris                          c. Reims                            p. 62
    b. Rome                           d. London                           SG

41. _____ is a term applied to medieval music that consists of   Ans. b
    Gregorian chant and one or more additional melodic lines.            p. 62
    a. alleluia        b. organum        c. jongleurs        d. ostinato

42. Medieval music that consists of Gregorian chant and one or           Ans. b
    more additional melodic lines is called                             p. 62
    a. a fugue         b. organum        c. a madrigal       d. an oratorio

43. Medieval music that consists of Gregorian chant and one or more additional   Ans. b
    melodic lines is called                                             p. 62
    a. *ars nova*      b. organum        c. cantus firmus    d. *alleluia*  SG

44. The melody added to the Gregorian chant to form organum around 1100  Ans. b
    was usually _____ the original chant.                      p. 62
    a. much slower than              c. note against note of
    b. much faster than              d. a duplication at a lower pitch of

45. Leonin and Perotin are notable because they                          Ans. d
    a. are the first important composers known by name                   p. 62
    b. indicated definite time values and a clearly defined meter        SG
    c. were the leaders of the school of Notre Dame
    d. all of the above

46. The earliest known composers to write music with measured rhythm were   Ans. c
    a. Pope Gregory and Chastelain de Couci     c. Leonin and Perotin       p. 62
    b. Machaut and Josquin                       d. all of the above

47. An outstanding composer of the Notre Dame school was                 Ans. a
    a. Perotin                        c. Hildegard of Bingen              p. 62
    b. Guillaume de Machaut           d. Pope Gregory I                   SG

48. Secular music in the fourteenth century
    a. became more important than sacred music
    b. was not based on Gregorian chant
    c. included drinking songs and pieces in which bird calls, barks of dogs,
       and hunters' shouts are imitated
    d. all of the above

Ans. d
p. 62
SG

49. The term *ars nova* refers to
    a. French and Italian music of the fourteenth century
    b. German music of the sixteenth century
    c. the new art of baroque painters
    d. paintings from the new world

Ans. a
p. 63

50. One of the major characteristics of *ars nova* music is its use of
    a. syncopation                    c. Gregorian chant
    b. organum                        d. monophonic texture

Ans. a
p. 63

51. A new system of music notation which allowed composers to
    specify almost any rhythmical pattern had evolved by the
    a. late twelfth century           c. early fourteenth century
    b. early thirteenth century       d. late fourteenth century

Ans. c
p. 63

52. The *ars nova* differed from older music in that
    a. the music emphasized homophonic texture  c. there was no syncopation
    b. rhythm could be notated more precisely    d. the subjects were all secular

Ans. b
p. 63
SG

53. Machaut's compositions consist mainly of
    a. music for church services
    b. Gregorian chants
    c. dance music
    d. love songs with instrumental accompaniment

Ans. d
p. 63

54. The foremost composer of fourteenth-century France was
    a. Guillaume de Machaut           c. Charles V
    b. Hildegard of Bingen            d. Perotin

Ans. a
p. 63
SG

55. An outstanding composer of the *ars nova* was
    a. Perotin                        c. Leonin
    b. Guillaume de Machaut           d. Pope Gregory I

Ans. b
p. 63
SG

56. Guillaume de Machaut was a _____ as well musician.
    a. court official                 c. priest
    b. poet                           d. all of the above

Ans. d
p. 63

57. Which of the following is *not* a part of the mass ordinary?
    a. Ave Maria                      c. Kyrie
    b. Gloria                         d. Credo

Ans. a
p. 63
SG

58. The *Notre Dame* Mass by Guillaume de Machaut was
    a. written for three voices without instrumental accompaniment
    b. written for the Cathedral of Notre Dame in Paris
    c. the first polyphonic treatment of the mass ordinary by a known composer
    d. all of the above

Ans. c
p. 63
SG

59. The Renaissance may be described as an age of
    a. curiosity and individualism       c. the "rebirth" of human creativity
    b. exploration and adventure         d. all of the above

Ans. d
p. 64

60. The intellectual movement called *humanism*
    a. condemned any remnant of pagan antiquity
    b. focused on human life and its accomplishments
    c. treated the madonna as a childlike earthly creature
    d. focused on the afterlife in heaven and hell

Ans. b
p. 66
SG

61. The dominant intellectual movement of the Renaissance was called
    a. feudalism                         c. classicism
    b. humanism                          d. paganism

Ans. b
p. 66
SG

62. A movement called _____ was the dominant intellectual movement
    of the Renaissance.
    a. humanism                          c. paganism
    b. feudalism                         d. classicism

Ans. a
p. 66

63. Which of the following statements is *not* true of the intellectual movement
    of the Renaissance known as humanism?
    a. The madonna was treated as a beautiful young woman.
    b. The humanists were basically atheistic in their beliefs.
    c. The humanists were captivated by the pagan cultures of ancient Greece and Rome.
    d. The humanists focused on human life and its accomplishments.

Ans. b
p. 66

64. Which of the following statements is *not* true of the Renaissance?
    a. Education was considered a status symbol by aristocrats and the upper
       middle class.
    b. The Catholic church was even more powerful in the Renaissance than during
       the Middle Ages.
    c. Every educated person was expected to be trained in music.
    d. Musical activity gradually shifted from the church to the court.

Ans. b
p. 66

65. Which of the following statements is *not* true of Renaissance music?
    a. The texture of Renaissance music is chiefly polyphonic.
    b. Instrumental music became more important than vocal music during
       the Renaissance.
    c. The Renaissance period is sometimes called "the golden age" of *a cappella*
       choral music because the music did not need instrumental accompaniment.
    d. Renaissance composers often used *word painting,* a musical representation
       of specific poetic images.

Ans. b
p. 67

66. The Renaissance in music occurred between                          Ans. c
   a. 1000 and 1150            c. 1450 and 1600         p. 67
   b. 1150 and 1450            d. 1600 and 1750

67. Renaissance music sounds fuller than medieval music because        Ans. d
   a. composers considered the harmonic effect of chords rather than     p. 67
      superimposing one melody above another
   b. the bass register is used for the first time
   c. the typical choral piece has four, five, or six voice parts of nearly equal melodic interest
   d. all of the above

68. The texture of Renaissance music is chiefly                        Ans. c
   a. monophonic            c. polyphonic         p. 67
   b. homophonic            d. heterophonic       SG

69. Many prominent Renaissance composers, who held important posts all over   Ans. b
the continent, came from an area of Europe  known at that time as      p. 68
   a. Great Britain            c. Spain
   b. Flanders              d. Scandinavia

70. *A cappella* refers to                                             Ans. a
   a. unaccompanied choral music                                       p. 68
   b. men taking their hats off in church                              SG
   c. singing in a hushed manner because one is in church
   d. any form of music appropriate for church use

71. Renaissance melodies are usually easy to sing because              Ans. d
   a. the level of musicianship in the Renaissance was not very high, and so     p. 68
      easy music was composed                                        SG
   b. the music was mostly homophonic, so that one could sing it with a group
   c. there was a sharply defined beat, which kept the performers together
   d. the melody usually moves along a scale with few large leaps

72. The two main forms of sacred Renaissance music are the mass and the   Ans. b
   a. Kyrie       b. motet       c. madrigal       d. cantata         p. 68

73. Which of the following is *not* a part of the Renaissance mass?    Ans. d
   a. Agnus Dei       b. Gloria       c. Sanctus       d. Alleluia        p. 68

74. The Renaissance motet is a                                         Ans. d
   a. polyphonic choral composition made up of five sections          p. 68
   b. piece for several solo voices set to a short poem, usually about love
   c. dancelike song for several solo voices
   d. polyphonic choral work set to a sacred Latin text other than the ordinary of the mass

75. Josquin Desprez spent much of his life in                         Ans. a
   a. Italy             c. Germany           p. 68
   b. Spain            d. the Netherlands   SG

76. Josquin Desprez was a contemporary of
   a. Christopher Columbus
   b. Perotin
   c. Palestrina
   d. Henry VIII of England

Ans. a
p. 68

77. Which of the following statements is *not* true?
   a. Josquin's compositions strongly influenced other composers, and were enthusiastically praised by music lovers.
   b. Josquin spent most of his life in the province of Hainaut, today a part of Belgium.
   c. Josquin's compositions include masses, motets, and secular vocal pieces.
   d. Josquin's *Ave Maria . . . Virgo serena* uses polyphonic imitation, a technique typical of the period.

Ans. b
p. 69

78. Palestrina's career centered in
   a. the Netherlands
   b. Florence
   c. Naples
   d. Rome

Ans. d
p. 70
SG

79. Giovanni Pierluigi da Palestrina's
   a. career centered in Florence
   b. training, like Josquin's, was in Flanders
   c. music includes 104 masses and some 450 other sacred works
   d. all of the above

Ans. c
p. 70

80. Palestrina's *Pope Marcellus* Mass sounds fuller than Josquin's *Ave Maria* because
   a. Palestrina was a better composer
   b. it is set for six voices instead of four
   c. the recording engineer adjusted the levels differently
   d. all of the above

Ans. b
p. 71
SG

81. The Renaissance madrigal began around 1520 in
   a. England
   b. France
   c. Italy
   d. Flanders

Ans. c
p. 72
SG

82. The Renaissance madrigal is a
   a. polyphonic choral composition made up of five sections
   b. piece for several solo voices set to a short poem, usually about love
   c. dancelike song for several solo voices
   d. polyphonic choral work set to a sacred Latin text

Ans. b
p. 72

83. A madrigal, like a motet, is a vocal composition that combines homophonic and polyphonic textures; but it differs from the motet in that it
   a. uses a vernacular rather than Latin text
   b. more often uses word painting and unusual harmonies
   c. both a and b
   d. neither a nor b

Ans. c
p. 72
SG

84. The madrigal anthology *The Triumphes of Oriana* was written in honor of
   a. Queen Anne
   b. King Henry VIII
   c. the goddess Diana
   d. Queen Elizabeth I

Ans. d
p. 72
SG

85. The development of the English madrigal can be traced to 1588 and considered    Ans. d
    a result of    p. 72
    a. the Spanish armada    SG
    b. a decree by Queen Elizabeth
    c. the writings of Shakespeare
    d. the publication in London of a volume of translated Italian madrigals

86. Thomas Weelkes's *As Vesta Was Descending* is notable for its    Ans. a
    a. word painting                    c. instrumental accompaniment    p. 72
    b. completely homophonic texture    d. monophonic texture    SG

87. Which of the following statements regarding the Renaissance is *not* true?    Ans. d
    a. Secular vocal music was written for groups of solo voices and for solo voice    p. 73
        with instrumental accompaniment.
    b. Secular music contained more rapid changes of mood than sacred music.
    c. A wealth of dance music published during the sixteenth century has survived.
    d. Much of the instrumental music composed during the Renaissance was intended
        for church use.

88. Much of the instrumental music composed during the Renaissance    Ans. c
    was intended for    p. 73
    a. the concert hall          c. dancing    SG
    b. religious worship         d. the piano

89. Andrea Gabrieli, an important Renaissance composer, was organist at    Ans. c
    St. Mark's Cathedral in    p. 73
    a. Rome          c. Venice
    b. Florence      d. Vienna

90. The ricercar is a    Ans. c
    a. dancelike song for several solo voices    p. 74
    b. polyphonic choral work set to a vernacular text
    c. polyphonic instrumental composition employing imitation
    d. homophonic instrumental composition

91. A polyphonic instrumental composition employing imitation is the    Ans. c
    a. madrigal          c. ricercar    p. 74
    b. ballett           d. motet    SG

# III. THE BAROQUE PERIOD

1. The word *baroque* has at various times meant all of the following except
   a. elaborately ornamented
   b. flamboyant
   c. bizarre
   d. naturalistic

   Ans. d
   p. 78

2. Modern historians use the term baroque to indicate
   a. a particular style in the arts
   b. a period of decline in the arts
   c. a class of musical instruments that no longer function
   d. a scientific movement popular in the seventeenth century

   Ans. a
   p. 78

3. All of the following were baroque painters except
   a. Gian Lorenzo Bernini
   b. Isaac Newton
   c. Peter Paul Rubens
   d. Rembrandt van Rijn

   Ans. b
   p. 78

4. Baroque painters exploited their materials to expand the potential of _____ to create totally structured worlds.
   a. color
   b. ornament and detail
   c. depth
   d. all of the above

   Ans. d
   p. 78

5. Baroque style flourished in music during the period
   a. 1000-1250
   b. 1250-1450
   c. 1450-1600
   d. 1600-1750

   Ans. d
   p. 78

6. The baroque, as a stylistic period in western art music, encompassed the years
   a. 1450-1600
   b. 1600-1750
   c. 1750-1820
   d. 1820-1900

   Ans. b
   p. 78

7. The two giants of baroque composition were George Frideric Handel and
   a. Johann Christian Bach
   b. Johann Sebastian Bach
   c. Giovanni Gabrieli
   d. Galileo Galilei

   Ans. b
   p. 78

8. All of the following were major baroque composers except
   a. Wolfgang A. Mozart
   b. Claudio Monteverdi
   c. Antonio Vivaldi
   d. Arcangelo Corelli

   Ans. a
   p. 78

9. Which of the following statements is *not* true?
   a. Baroque art is a complex mixture of rationalism, sensuality, materialism, and spirituality.
   b. The late baroque period was one of the most revolutionary periods in music history.
   c. Early baroque composers favored homophonic texture over the polyphonic texture typical of Renaissance music.
   d. Regardless of form, baroque music features contrasts between bodies of sound.

   Ans. b
   p. 80

10. One of the most revolutionary periods in music history was the
    a. Renaissance
    b. early baroque
    c. middle baroque
    d. late baroque

    Ans. b
    p. 80
    SG

11. The early baroque was characterized by
    a. elaborate counterpoint
    b. homophonic texture
    c. development of the standardized orchestra
    d. diffusion of the style into every corner of Europe

Ans. b
p. 80
SG

12. Monteverdi, an early baroque composer, strove to create music that was
    a. difficult to perform          c. extremely complex
    b. passionate and dramatic       d. placid and smooth

Ans. b
p. 80

13. The early and late baroque periods differed in that composers in the early baroque
    a. favored polyphonic texture    c. used extremely complex harmonies
    b. favored homophonic texture    d. favored purely instrumental music

Ans. b
p. 80

14. The middle baroque was characterized by
    a. elaborate counterpoint
    b. homophonic texture
    c. the development of the standardized orchestra
    d. a diffusion of the style into every corner of Europe

Ans. d
p. 80
SG

15. By about _____, major or minor scales were the tonal
    basis of most compositions.
    a. 1500          b. 1600          c. 1680          d. 1750

Ans. c
p. 80

16. *Affections* in baroque usage refers to
    a. the nobility's manner of deportment    c. terraced dynamics
    b. the doctrine of universal brotherhood  d. emotional states or moods of music

Ans. d
p. 80
SG

17. A baroque musical composition usually expresses _____ within the
    same movement.
    a. one basic mood                c. constantly changing moods
    b. a wide variety of moods

Ans. a
p. 80

18. The baroque principle of ____ may be temporarily suspended in vocal music when
    drastic changes of emotion in a text inspires corresponding changes in the music.
    a. basso continuo     b. unity of mood     c. terraced dynamics     d. all of the above

Ans. b
p. 80

19. Instrumental music became as important as vocal music for
    the first time in the _____ period.
    a. Renaissance        b. early baroque     c. middle baroque     d. late baroque

Ans. d
p. 80

20. The compelling drive and energy in baroque music are usually provided by
    a. a sexy text                   c. repeated rhythmic patterns
    b. complex harmonic progressions d. the high dynamic level

Ans. c
p. 80

21. Baroque melodies often are
    a. elaborate and ornamental      c. impossible to play
    b. easy to sing and remember     d. short and simple

Ans. a
p. 81

22. Baroque melodies give the impression of                                      Ans. d
    a. balance and symmetry              c. tonal vagueness                       p. 81
    b. being carelessly composed         d. dynamic expansion

23. Melodic sequence refers to                                                   Ans. c
    a. a composition by Vivaldi                                                  p. 81
    b. a preferred method of tuning an instrument
    c. the successive repetition of a musical idea at higher or lower pitch levels
    d. the pedagogical steps in learning to play an instrument

24. A characteristic often found in baroque melodies is                          Ans. d
    a. one long continuous phrase with long sustained notes                      p. 81
    b. one short phrase followed by continuous repetition of the same phrase
    c. a symmetrical frame with two long phrases of equal length
    d. a short opening phrase followed by a longer phrase with an unbroken flow
       of rapid notes

25. Terraced dynamics refers to                                                  Ans. c
    a. a gradual change from soft to loud                                        p. 81
    b. a gradual change from loud to soft
    c. the sudden alternation from one dynamic level to another
    d. dynamics that are not written in the music but added by the performer

26. In the baroque era, dynamics consisted mainly of sudden alterations          Ans. b
    between loud and soft called                                                 p. 81
    a. cantus firmus        b. terraced dynamics   c. basso continuo    d. basso ostinato

27. The main keyboard instruments of the baroque period were the                 Ans. b
    organ and the                                                               p. 81
    a. clavichord           b. harpsichord         c. piano             d. accordion

28. A popular keyboard instrument in which sound was produced                     Ans. a
    by means of brass blades striking the strings was the                        p. 81
    a. clavichord           b. harpsichord         c. basso continuo    d. organ     SG

29. The most characteristic feature of baroque music is its use of               Ans. c
    a. gradual dynamic changes           c. basso continuo                       p. 82
    b. monophonic texture                d. simple singable melodies

30. A bass part together with numbers (figures) that specify the chords          Ans. a
    to be played above it, characteristic of the baroque, is called              p. 82
    a. basso continuo                    c. basso profundo
    b. harpsichord                       d. counterpoint

31. The orchestra evolved during the baroque period into a performing group      Ans. a
    based on instruments of the _____ family.                             p. 83
    a. violin               b. woodwind            c. brass             d. percussion

32. A section that sounds fairly complete and independent but              Ans. a
    is part of a larger composition is called a                            p. 84
    a. movement          b. phrase              c. song              d. sentence

33. The word *movement* in music normally refers to                       Ans. b
    a. music for the ballet                                                p. 84
    b. a piece that sounds fairly complete and independent but is part of a larger composition
    c. the rising and falling of the melodic contour
    d. the rhythm of a piece

34. A common variation form in the baroque is based upon the              Ans. a
    use of a ground bass, or                                               p. 84
    a. basso ostinato                          c. basso continuo
    b. basso profundo                          d. thoroughbass

35. _____ is a musical idea repeated over and over in the bass while   Ans. a
    melodies above it constantly change.                                  p. 84
    a. basso ostinato     b. basso profundo    c. basso continuo    d. thoroughbass

36. A concerto grosso most often has _____ movement(s).            Ans. c
    a. one               b. two                c. three             d. four     p. 85

37. The large group of players in a concerto grosso is known as the       Ans. d
    a. concertino        b. orchestra          c. soloists          d. tutti    p. 85

38. Which of the following statements is *not* true?                      Ans. c
    a. A concerto grosso normally involves two to four soloists, and       p. 85
       anywhere from eight to twenty or more musicians for the tutti.
    b. A concerto grosso presents a contrast of texture between the tutti and the soloists,
       who assert their individuality and appeal for attention through brilliant and
       fanciful melodic lines.
    c. A concerto grosso normally involves a large group of soloists accompanied by
       an equal number of supporting players.
    d. The first and last movements of concerti grossi are often in ritornello form,
       a form that features the alternation between tutti and solo sections.

39. The concerto grosso most often has three movements whose tempo markings are   Ans. a
    a. fast, slow, fast                        c. slow, fast, slow              p. 85
    b. fast, fast, slow                        d. slow, slow, fast

40. The first and last movements of the concerto grosso are often in _____ form.   Ans. b
    a. sonata                                  c. theme and variations          p. 85
    b. ritornello                              d. ternary

41. The solo instruments in Bach's *Brandenburg* Concerto No. 5           Ans. c
    are the _____, violin, and harpsichord.                           p. 86
    a. trumpet           b. cello              c. flute             d. oboe

42. Bach's *Brandenburg* Concerto No. 5 is unusual in that
    a. it consists of a single movement
    b. it consists of four movements
    c. it gives a solo role to the harpsichord
    d. the first movement is not in typical ritornello form

Ans. c
p. 86

43. A musical ornament consisting of the rapid alternation
    of two tones that are a whole or half step apart is a
    a. trill          b. shake          c. blurb          d. wobble

Ans. a
p. 86

44. A polyphonic composition based on one main theme, a cornerstone
    of baroque music, is the
    a. subject          b. concerto          c. episode          d. fugue

Ans. d
p. 88

45. The main theme of a fugue is called the
    a. answer          b. subject          c. countersubject          d. episode

Ans. b
p. 88

46. When the subject of a fugue is presented in the dominant scale, it is called the
    a. answer          b. countersubject          c. episode          d. stretto

Ans. a
p. 89

47. In many fugues, the subject in one voice is constantly
    accompanied in another voice by a different melodic idea called a(n)
    a. answer          b. countersubject          c. episode          d. stretto

Ans. b
p. 89

48. Transitional sections of a fugue that offer either new material
    or fragments of the subject or countersubject are called
    a. answers          b. episodes          c. preludes          d. strettos

Ans. b
p. 89

49. _____ is a musical procedure in which a fugue subject
    is imitated before it is completed.
    a. augmentation                    c. retrograde
    b. diminution                      d. stretto

Ans. d
p. 90

50. A _____ is a single tone, usually in the bass, that is held while the
    other voices produce a series of changing harmonies against it.
    a. pedal point                     c. basso continuo
    b. pitch                           d. basso ostinato

Ans. a
p. 90

51. Turning the subject of a fugue upside down, or reversing
    the direction of each interval, is called
    a. inversion                       c. retrograde
    b. stretto                         d. countersubject

Ans. a
p. 90

52. Presenting the subject of a fugue going from right to left, or beginning
    with the last and proceeding backward to the first note, is called
    a. inversion                       c. augmentation
    b. stretto                         d. retrograde

Ans. d
p. 90

53. Presenting the subject of a fugue in lengthened time values  is called
    a. inversion
    b. augmentation
    c. retrograde
    d. diminution

    Ans. b
    p. 90

54. Presenting the subject of a fugue in shortened time values is called
    a. inversion
    b. augmentation
    c. retrograde
    d. diminution

    Ans. d
    p. 90

55. Very often an independent fugue is introduced by a short piece called a(n)
    a. overture      b. prelude      c. concerto      d. pedal point

    Ans. b
    p. 90

56. An _____ is a play, set to music, sung to orchestral accompaniment, with scenery, costumes, and action.
    a. overture      b. opera      c. aria      d. ensemble

    Ans. b
    p. 93

57. The text, or book, of a musical dramatic work is called the
    a. text      b. libretto      c. story      d. score

    Ans. b
    p. 93

58. Which of the following statements is *not* true?
    a. The terms ensemble and chorus are synonymous.
    b. Voice categories in opera are divided more finely than in other musical genres.
    c. Operas may contain spoken dialogue, but most are entirely sung.
    d. Opera soloists must create a wide variety of characters, and so need acting skills as well as vocal artistry.

    Ans. a
    p. 93

59. A song for solo voice with orchestral accompaniment is called
    a. aria      b. duet      c. ensemble      d. solo

    Ans. a
    p. 93

60. _____ refers to a vocal line that imitates the rhythms and pitch fluctuations of speech.
    a. aria      b. duet      c. recitative      d. ensemble

    Ans. c
    p. 94

61. An _____ is an orchestral composition performed before the curtain rises on a dramatic work.
    a. overture      b. aria      c. opera      d. opening

    Ans. a
    p. 94

62. Members of the Camerata wanted to create a new vocal style based on the
    a. music of the ancient Greek tragedies
    b. glories of their aristocratic patrons
    c. organum of the Middle Ages
    d. polyphonic madrigal

    Ans. a
    p. 94
    SG

63. The members of the Florentine Camerata wanted the vocal line of their music to follow
    a. standard rules of musical theory
    b. the rhythms and pitch fluctuations of speech
    c. the lines of contrapuntal writing
    d. set metrical and melodic patterns

    Ans. b
    p. 94

64. Which of the following statements is *not* true?                                             Ans. b
    a. Most early baroque operas were based on Greek mythology and ancient history.             p. 94
    b. The members of the Florentine Camerata based their theories on actual dramatic
       music that had come down to them from the Greeks.
    c. The members of the Florentine Camerata wanted to create a new vocal style
       modeled on the music of ancient Greek tragedy.
    d. Polyphony was rejected by the members of the Florentine Camerata because
       different words sounding simultaneously would obscure the text.

65. The earliest opera that has been preserved is Jacopo Peri's                                  Ans. a
    a. *Euridice*          b. *Orfeo*          c. *Nerone*          d. *Arsace*                   p. 94

66. Most early baroque operas were based on Greek mythology and                                  Ans. d
    a. contemporary political events                                                             p. 95
    b. contemporary lyric poetry                                                                 SG
    c. contemporary exploration of the new world
    d. ancient history

67. The stage machinery of baroque opera                                                         Ans. b
    a. was very primitive                    c. was nonexistent                                  p. 95
    b. bordered on the colossal              d. replaced set designs

68. The first opera house in Europe to offer entry to anyone                                     Ans. d
    with the price of admission opened in 1637 in                                                p. 95
    a. Hamburg           b. London           c. Rome           d. Venice

69. A _____ is a singer with a low range who usually takes comic roles.                        Ans. b
    a. tenor              b. basso buffo      c. basso profundo    d. buffoon                     p. 93

70. A _____ is a singer with a very low range and powerful voice, who usually                  Ans. c
    takes roles calling for great dignity.                                                       p. 93
    a. tenor              b. basso buffo      c. basso profundo    d. buffoon

71. A(n) ____ is a musical number for two solo voices with orchestral accompaniment.             Ans. c
    a. aria               b. ensemble         c. duet              d. chorus                      p. 94

72. A(n) _____ is an operatic number involving three or more lead singers.                     Ans. b
    a. aria               b. ensemble         c. duet              d. chorus                      p. 94

73. The _____ is the person who beats time, indicates expression, cues in                      Ans. d
    musicians, and controls the balance among instruments and voices.                            p. 94
    a. prima donna        b. prompter         c. concertmaster     d. conductor

74. A virtuoso is a performer who has                                                            Ans. c
    a. a great natural talent                                                                    p. 95
    b. learned to sing or play an instrument                                                     SG
    c. developed an extraordinary technical mastery
    d. an uncle in the business

75. Castrati
    a. received the highest fees of any musicians
    b. combined the lung power of a man with the vocal range of a woman
    c. were male singers who had been castrated before puberty
    d. all of the above

Ans. d
p. 95

76. Speechlike melody accompanied only by a basso continuo is called
    a. basso ostinato                    c. secco recitative
    b. accompanied recitative            d. congregational singing

Ans. c
p. 95

77. A typical baroque operatic form was the da capo aria in
    ABA form in which the singer
    a. would make a literal repetition of the opening A section after the B section
    b. was expected to embellish the returning melody with ornamental tones
    c. would insert recitatives between the sections for added variety
    d. improvise new words for the returning A section

Ans. b
p. 95

78. Embellishments are
    a. ornamental tones not printed in the music that seventeenth- and
       eighteenth-century performers were expected to add to the melody
    b. music created at the same time it is performed
    c. notes printed in the music that embellish the melody
    d. obsolete in contemporary performances

Ans. a
p. 95

79. Monteverdi spent the greater part of his career in the most
    important church post in Italy, that of
    a. Notre Dame, Paris                 c. St. Mark's, Venice
    b. The Duomo, Florence               d. the Vatican, Rome

Ans. c
p. 95

80. To achieve intensity of expression, Monteverdi used _____ with
    unprecedented freedom and daring.
    a. consonance      b. dissonance      c. basso continuo      d. texts

Ans. b
p. 96
SG

81. Orpheus goes to Hades in the hope of bringing _____ back to life.
    a. Apollo                             c. Mantua
    b. Eurydice                           d. Monteverdi

Ans. b
p. 96
SG

82. Orpheus goes to Hades in the hope of bringing _____ back to life.
    a. Eurydice        b. Phyllis         c. Persephone        d. Oriana

Ans. a
p. 96

83. Which of the following statements is *not* true?
    a. Monteverdi's *Orfeo*, written in 1607, is considered to be
       the earliest operatic masterpiece.
    b. All twelve of Monteverdi's operas are regularly performed in Europe and America.
    c. Monteverdi creates variety in *Orfeo* by using many kinds of music, combining recitatives,
       arias, duets, choruses, and instrumental interludes into one dramatic whole.
    d. Monteverdi's works form a musical bridge between the sixteenth and seventeenth
       centuries and greatly influenced composers of the time.

Ans. b
p. 96

84. The sonata in the baroque period was a composition in several movements for   Ans. d
   a. a solo instrument          c. two to four instruments   p. 97
   b. three solo instruments     d. one to eight instruments   SG

85. Baroque trio sonatas usually involve _____ performers.   Ans. c
   a. two                        c. four   p. 97
   b. three                      d. five   SG

86. Corelli's Trio Sonata in E Minor, Op. 3, no. 7, is scored for   Ans. c
   a. two violins                c. two violins and basso continuo   p. 98
   b. solo violin and orchestra  d. piano, violin and cello   SG

87. Corelli's Trio Sonata in E Minor, Op. 3, no. 7, consists   Ans. b
   of four short movements, all in the same   p. 98
   a. meter          b. key          c. tempo          d. mood

88. Characteristic of baroque trio sonatas, the second movement of Corelli's Trio   Ans. c
   Sonata in E Minor, Op. 3, no. 7, is   p. 98
   a. slow and dignified   b. songlike          c. fuguelike          d. a dance   SG

89. Vivaldi spent most of his life working at an institution   Ans. b
   for orphaned and illegitimate girls in   p. 98
   a. Rome          b. Venice          c. Florence          d. Cremona

90. Vivaldi is closely identified with the musical life of   Ans. b
   a. Rome                        c. Florence   p. 98
   b. Venice                      d. Cremona   SG

91. Vivaldi was famous and influential as a virtuoso   Ans. d
   a. harpsichordist             c. lutenist   p. 98
   b. opera singer               d. violinist   SG

92. Vivaldi wrote approximately _____ concerti grossi and solo concertos.   Ans. d
   a. 10          b. 30          c. 95          d. 450   p. 99

93. A Vivaldi concerto usually has _____ movements.   Ans. b
   a. two                        c. four   p. 99
   b. three                      d. a variable number of   SG

94. Vivaldi wrote concertos   Ans. c
   a. only for string instruments     c. for a great variety of instruments   p. 99
   b. only for violins with continuo  d. only for keyboard instruments   SG

95. The abbreviation *op.* stands for *opus,* Latin for   Ans. c
   a. a cartoon character        c. work   p. 99
   b. Spring                     d. opulent   SG

96. The longest period of Bach's professional life was spent
    as director of music at St. Thomas's Church in
    a. Rome            b. Leipzig            c. Cöthen            d. Eisenach

Ans. b
p. 101

97. While at Leipzig, Bach
    a. taught organ and composition, gave recitals, and was
       often asked to judge the construction of organs
    b. was responsible for the musical education of some fifty-five students in
       the St. Thomas school
    c. rehearsed, conducted, and usually composed an extended work for chorus, soloists
       and orchestra for each Sunday and holiday of the church year
    d. all of the above

Ans. d
p. 101

98. Which of the following statements is *not* true?
    a. Bach's church music uses operatic forms such as the aria and recitative.
    b. Bach was recognized as the most eminent composer of his day.
    c. Bach created masterpieces in every baroque form except opera.
    d. Bach's music is unique for its combination of rich harmony and polyphonic texture.

Ans. b
p. 101

99. Of Bach's twenty children, _____ went on to become well-known composers.
    a. two                                   c. four
    b. three                                 d. five

Ans. c
p. 101
SG

100. Bach was recognized as the most eminent _____ of his day.
    a. organist                              c. violinist
    b. composer                              d. cellist

Ans. a
p. 101
SG

101. Improvisation is
    a. a technique used only in jazz and nonwestern music
    b. music created at the same time as it is performed
    c. the addition of ornaments not indicated in the printed music
    d. all of the above

Ans. b
p. 101

102. Bach created masterpieces in every baroque form except the
    a. opera                                 c. fugue
    b. concerto                              d. sonata

Ans. a
p. 102
SG

103. Bach's personal music style was drawn from
    a. Italian concertos                     c. German church music
    b. French dance pieces                   d. all of the above

Ans. d
p. 102
SG

104. Bach achieves unity of mood in his compositions by using
    a. homophonic texture                    c. an insistent rhythmic drive
    b. musical symbolism                     d. simple melodic ideas

Ans. c
p. 102
SG

105. A collection of compositions that displays all the
resources of fugue writing is Bach's
   a. *Art of the Fugue*                  c. *St. Matthew Passion*
   b. *Well-Tempered Clavier*             d. *Wachet Auf*

Ans. a
p. 102

106. A collection of twice twenty-four preludes and fugues, one in each major
and minor key, basic to the repertoire of keyboard players today, is Bach's
   a. *Art of the Fugue*                  c. *St. Matthew Passion*
   b. *Well-Tempered Clavier*             d. *Brandenburg* Concertos

Ans. b
p. 102

107. Sets of dance-inspired instrumental movements are called
   a. sonatas          b. concertos          c. suites          d. cantatas

Ans. c
p. 103

108. Which of the following statements is *not* true?
   a. Baroque suites often begin with a French overture.
   b. The baroque suite is a musical form exclusive to the orchestra.
   c. A baroque suite is made up of different movements that are all written
      in the same key but differ in tempo, meter, and character.
   d. The various dances of the baroque suite are usually in AABB form.

Ans. b
p. 103

109. Which of the following is *not* a part of the baroque suite?
   a. allemande                           c. sarabande
   b. waltz                               d. gigue

Ans. b
p. 103
SG

110. Although all the movements of a baroque suite are written in the same key,
they differ in
   a. meter                               c. tempo
   b. national origin                     d. all of the above

Ans. d
p. 103
SG

111. The various dances of the baroque suite are usually
   a. polyphonic in texture               c. in AABB form
   b. in theme and variation form         d. in ABA form

Ans. c
p. 103
SG

112. Baroque suites frequently begin with a
   a. French overture      b. bourrée          c. allemande          d. gigue

Ans. a
p. 103

113. The French overture has
   a. two sections: slow-fast             c. three sections: fast-slow-fast
   b. two sections: fast-slow             d. one continuous section

Ans. a
p. 103
SG

114. In Bach's day, the Lutheran church service lasted about _____ hour(s).
   a. one                                 c. three
   b. two                                 d. four

Ans. d
p. 104
SG

115. The _____ is a Lutheran congregational hymn tune.
   a. cantata                             c. chorale prelude
   b. chorale                             d. recitative

Ans. b
p. 105
SG

116. A _____ is a hymn tune for congregational use.
   a. chorale　　　　　　b. song　　　　　c. chorale prelude　　　d. cantata

Ans. a
p. 105

117. The _____ is an instrumental composition based on a chorale.
   a. cantata　　　　　　　　　　　　　c. chorale prelude
   b. solo concerto　　　　　　　　　　d. French overture

Ans. c
p. 105
SG

118. A _____ is a short instrumental composition based on a
   hymn tune that reminds the congregation of the hymn's melody.
   a. chorale prelude　　　b. fugue　　　　c. cantata　　　　　d. chorale

Ans. a
p. 105

119. A sung piece, or choral work with or without vocal soloists, usually
   with orchestral accompaniment, is the
   a. cantata　　　　　　　　　　　　　c. concerto grosso
   b. chorale prelude　　　　　　　　　d. sonata

Ans. a
p. 105
SG

120. The _____ is a choral work, or sung piece, with or without vocal
   soloists, usually with orchestral accompaniment.
   a. chorale　　　　　　　　　　　　　c. chorale prelude
   b. sonata　　　　　　　　　　　　　　d. cantata

Ans. d
p. 105

121. In their use of aria, duet, and recitative, Bach's cantatas closely resembled
   the _____ of the time.
   a. suites　　　　　　b. operas　　　　c. concertos　　　　d. sonatas

Ans. b
p. 105
SG

122. Which of the following statements is *not* true?
   a. Oratorios first appeared in England.
   b. Oratorio differs from opera in that it has no acting, scenery, or costumes.
   c. An oratorio is a large-scale composition for chorus, vocal soloists, and orchestra,
      usually set to a narrative text.
   d. The first oratorios were based on stories from the Bible.

Ans. a
p. 109

123. A large-scale composition for chorus, vocal soloists, and orchestra,
   usually set to a narrative biblical text, is called
   a. chorale　　　　　　b. aria　　　　　c. recitative　　　　d. oratorio

Ans. d
p. 109

124. Oratorio differs from opera in that it has no
   a. orchestral accompaniment　　　　c. choral parts
   b. acting, scenery, or costumes　　　d. vocal soloists

Ans. b
p. 109
SG

125. The first oratorios were based on
   a. Greek mythology　　　　　　　　　c. Greek and Roman literature
   b. contemporary literature　　　　　d. stories from the Bible

Ans. d
p. 109
SG

126. The _____ in an oratorio is especially important and
   serves either to comment on or to participate in the drama.
   a. narrator　　　　　　　　　　　　　c. orchestra
   b. chorus　　　　　　　　　　　　　　d. vocal soloist

Ans. b
p. 109

127. An element of the oratorio that is especially important and serves    Ans. b
     to comment on or participate in the drama is the                      p. 109
     a. narrator          b. chorus          c. vocal soloist          d. orchestra    SG

128. Pieces of an oratorio are usually connected together by means of      Ans. a
     a. a narrator's recitatives          c. duets                          p. 109
     b. choruses                          d. arias

129. In oratorio, the story is carried forward by the                      Ans. c
     a. arias                             c. narrator's recitatives         p. 109
     b. chorus                            d. duets                          SG

130. Oratorios first appeared in                                           Ans. c
     a. Germany                           c. Italy                          p. 110
     b. England                           d. France                         SG

131. Handel's *Messiah* is an example of                                   Ans. a
     a. an oratorio                       c. musical theater                p. 110
     b. an opera                          d. a song                         SG

132. George Frideric Handel was born in 1685, the same year as             Ans. a
     a. Johann Sebastian Bach             c. Claudio Monteverdi             p. 110
     b. Arcangelo Corelli                 d. Antonio Vivaldi                SG

133. Handel spent the major portion of his life in                         Ans. b
     a. Germany                           c. Italy                          p. 110
     b. England                           d. Ireland                        SG

134. In addition to being a composer and opera impresario, Handel was a virtuoso    Ans. b
     a. violinist                         c. cellist                        p. 110
     b. organist                          d. trumpeter                      SG

135. Although Handel wrote a great deal of instrumental music, the core     Ans. a
     of his huge output consists of English oratorios and Italian           p. 111
     a. operas          b. songs          c. chorales          d. madrigals  SG

136. Handel's oratorios are usually based on                               Ans. a
     a. the Old Testament                 c. the New Testament              p. 111
     b. Greek mythology                   d. Roman history                  SG

137. Which of the following statements is *not* true?                      Ans. b
     a. The focus of the Handelian oratorio is usually the chorus.         p. 111
     b. Most of Handel's oratorios are without plot or characters since
        they were primarily intended for church use.
     c. *Messiah*, set to a text compiled by Charles Jennings from the Old and New
        Testaments, is meditative rather than as dramatic as Handel's other oratorios.
     d. Handel's oratorios are usually based on the Old Testament.

138. Which of the following oratorios is *not* by Handel?                 Ans. b
   a. *Messiah*                         c. *Israel in Egypt*              p. 111
   b. *Elijah*                          d. *Joshua*                       SG

139. The focus of a Handel oratorio is usually the                       Ans. b
   a. soprano soloist                   c. orchestra                     p. 111
   b. chorus                            d. conductor                     SG

# IV. THE CLASSICAL PERIOD

1. Classicism, as a stylistic period in western art music, roughly
   encompassed the years
   a. 1450-1600          b. 1600-1750          c. 1750-1820          d. 1820-1900

   Ans. c
   p. 118

2. The preclassical period roughly encompassed the years
   a. 1600-1750          b. 1730-1770          c. 1770-1820          d. 1820-1900

   Ans. b
   p. 118

3. The fully developed classical style in music flourished during the period
   a. 1600-1750          b. 1730-1770          c. 1770-1820          d. 1820-1900

   Ans. c
   p. 118

4. Which of the follwing statements is *not* true of the classical period?
   a. Philosophers and writers in the classical period believed that custom and tradition,
      rather than reason, were the best guides to human conduct.
   b. During the early  eighteenth century, the heavy, monumental baroque style gave
      way to the more intimate rococo style, with its light colors, curved lines, and
      graceful ornaments.
   c. By the late eighteenth century, the rococo style had been superseded by the neoclassical
      style, which attempted to recapture the "noble simplicity and calm grandeur"
      of ancient Greek and Roman art.
   d. Philosophers and writers in the classical period saw their time as a great turning point in
      history and called it the "age of enlightenment."

   Ans. a
   p. 118

5. Carl Philipp Emanuel Bach and _____ were two of the more important
   preclassical composers.
   a. Jean Honoré Fragonard                  c. Johann Sebastian Bach
   b. Johann Christian Bach                  d. Joseph Haydn

   Ans. b
   p. 118

6. Which of the following composers is *not* considered a
   master of the classical period?
   a. Johann Christian Bach                  c. Wolfgang A. Mozart
   b. Ludwig van Beethoven                   d. Joseph Haydn

   Ans. a
   p. 121

7. Joseph Haydn was content to spend most of his life
   a. as an independently wealthy composer   c. serving a wealthy aristocratic family
   b. as a professional free-lance musician  d. as a church musician and organist

   Ans. c
   p. 121

8. Composers in the classical period took middle-class tastes into account by
   a. flavoring their serious compositions with folk and popular music
   b. writing comic operas that sometimes ridiculed the aristocracy
   c. writing dance music for public balls
   d. all of the above

   Ans. d
   p. 121

9. Which of the following characteristics is *not* typical of
   the music of the classical period?
   a. Classical melodies are tuneful and easy to remember.
   b. Classical compositions fluctuate in mood.
   c. A classical composition has a wealth of rhythmic patterns.
   d. Classical music is basically polyphonic.

   Ans. d
   p. 122

10. Which of the following statements is *not* true?                                    Ans. c
    a. In the classical period, composers were influenced by folk and popular music.    p. 122
    b. While a late baroque musical composition may convey a single emotion,
       a classical composition will fluctuate in mood.
    c. Composers in the classical period tended to continue to use terraced dynamics
       in their compositions.
    d. The basso continuo was gradually abandoned during the classical period.

11. Which of the following statements is *not* true of the music of the classical period?   Ans. c
    a. Classical composers stressed balance and clarity of structure.                   p. 123
    b. The standard orchestra comprised of four sections evolved during the classical period.
    c. The basso continuo was the nucleus of the instrumental ensemble.
    d. Classical melodies are among the most tuneful and easy to remember.

12. The typical orchestra of the classical period consisted of                          Ans. b
    a. a loose ensemble of available instruments                                        p. 123
    b. strings, pairs of woodwinds, horns, trumpets, and timpani
    c. strings with harpsichord continuo
    d. woodwinds, trombones, drums, and strings

13. Which of the following instruments were not normally                                Ans. b
    included in the classical orchestra?                                                p. 123
    a. french horns          b. trombones          c. timpani          d. trumpets

14. A symphony is a                                                                     Ans. a
    a. sonata for orchestra              c. work for chorus and orchestra               p. 124
    b. work for solo instrument          d. work for piano solo

15. Which of the following is *not* part of a sonata form movement?                     Ans. b
    a. recapitulation        c. exposition                                              p. 125
    b. rondo                 d. development

16. Sonata form consists of three main sections, exposition, development, and           Ans. b
    a. introduction                      c. motives                                     p. 125
    b. recapitulation                    d. transition

17. Sonata form is used frequently as the form for the _____ movement of a           Ans. a
    multimovement work.                                                                 p. 125
    a. first                             c. final fast                                  SG
    b. slow                              d. all of the above

18. In the exposition of a sonata-form movement                                         Ans. c
    a. the closing theme is in the tonic key                                            p. 125
    b. a new theme is always presented in the bridge                                    SG
    c. the second theme is in a new key
    d. a new meter enters with the second theme

19. In the recapitulation of a sonata-form movement                                     Ans. a
    a. the closing section is in the tonic key      c. the second theme is in a new key p. 125
    b. a new theme is presented in the bridge       d. there is no second theme         SG

20. At the end of a classical exposition there usually is a                                    Ans. c
    a. new tempo indication              c. repeat sign                                          p. 126
    b. new time signature                d. coda sign                                            SG

21. Which of the following statements is *not* true?                                           Ans. b
    a. The term *sonata form* refers to the form of a single movement, and it should           p. 126
       not be confused with the term *sonata*, which is used for a whole composition
       made up of several movements.
    b. The second theme returns in the recapitulation of a sonata form movement in
       an exact repetition of its statement in the exposition.
    c. The coda of a sonata form movement rounds off the movement by repeating themes
       or developing them further.
    d. A fast movement in sonata form is sometimes preceded by a slow introduction
       that creates a strong feeling of expectancy.

22. A transitional passage that leads to a contrasting section is called a                     Ans. c
    a. coda              b. theme              c. bridge           d. motive                    p. 126

23. A modulation from the home key to a new key in the                                         Ans. c
    exposition of a sonata form movement takes place in the                                    p. 126
    a. coda              b. theme              c. bridge           d. motive

24. The three main sections of a sonata-form movement are often followed                       Ans. a
    by a concluding section known as the                                                       p. 126
    a. coda              b. theme              c. bridge           d. motive

25. A feeling of harmonic tension and forward motion is                                        Ans. a
    created in the exposition of a sonata form movement by                                     p. 126
    a. the conflict of tonalities between the first and second themes
    b. the introduction of a new theme in the bridge
    c. retaining the same tonality for both themes
    d. changing the meter of the second theme

26. Short musical ideas or fragments of themes that are                                        Ans. d
    developed within a composition are called                                                  p. 126
    a. codas             b. rides              c. melodies         d. motives

27. Sonata form should be viewed as                                                            Ans. c
    a. a rigid mold into which musical ideas are poured                                        p. 127
    b. another term for the symphony                                                           SG
    c. a set of principles that serve to shape and unify contrasts of theme and key
    d. a composition containing several movements

28. The standard catalog of the compositions of Mozart was made by                            Ans. a
    a. Ludwig von Köchel              c. Lorenzo da Ponte                                       p. 127
    b. Franz X. Süssmayr              d. Friedrich Kuhlau

29. Each successive variation in a theme with variations                                       Ans. a
    a. retains some elements of the theme       c. is usually in the same key                  p. 131
    b. is usually in a new key                  d. presents a new melodic idea                 SG

30. Which of the following statements is *not* true?                                          Ans. c
   a. Each variation in a theme and variations form movement is unique and may                p. 131
      differ in mood from the theme.
   b. The form called theme and variations is widely used in the classical period, either as an
      independent piece or as one movement of a symphony, sonata, or string quartet.
   c. The first movement of Haydn's *Surprise* symphony is in theme and variations form.
   d. In a theme and variations movement, a basic musical idea is repeated over and over
      and is changed each time.

31. Theme-and-variations form may be schematically outlined as                                Ans. b
   a. AABB                                         c. ABA                                      p. 131
   b. AA'A"A'"A""                                  d. ABACADA                                  SG

32. Which of the following elements is usually *not* changed in                               Ans. c
   varying the theme in theme and variations form?                                            p. 131
   a. melody            b. harmony            c. length            d. rhythm

33. The ___ movement of Haydn's *Surprise* Symphony is in theme-and-variations form.          Ans. b
   a. first                                        c. third                                    p. 131
   b. second                                       d. fourth                                   SG

34. The minuet and trio movement of a classical symphony,                                     Ans. a
   string quartet, or other work, is in _____ form.                                       p. 134
   a. ABA                                          c. AA'A"A'"A""
   b. AABB                                         d. ABACABA

35. The movement of a sonata-type composition often patterned after a dance is the            Ans. c
   a. first              b. second            c. third            d. fourth                    p. 134

36. The minuet is generally the _____ movement of a classical symphony.                   Ans. c
   a. first                                        c. third                                    p. 134
   b. second                                       d. fourth                                   SG

37. The form known as minuet and trio is employed as the _____ movement of               Ans. c
   classical symphonies, string quartets, and other works.                                    p. 134
   a. first              b. second            c. third            d. fourth

38. The minuet first appeared around 1650 as a(n)                                             Ans. c
   a. instrumental composition for concert performance                                        p. 134
   b. prayer in Germany at the end of the Thirty Years War                                    SG
   c. dance at the court of Louis XIV of France
   d. country dance in England

39. The character of the minuet is best described as                                          Ans. d
   a. brisk and lively                             c. heavy and ponderous                      p. 134
   b. quiet and relaxed                            d. stately and dignified                    SG

40. The minuet as a whole may be outlined as                                                  Ans. a
   a. ABA                                          c. ABC                                      p. 134
   b. AABB                                         d. AABBCC                                   SG

41. Which of the following statements is *not* true?  Ans. b
    a. The minuet movement of a symphony or string quartet is  p. 134
       written for listening, not dancing.
    b. The character of the minuet is best described as brisk and lively.
    c. In many of Beethoven's compositions, the third movement is not a minuet but
       a related form in triple meter called a scherzo.
    d. The scherzo differs from the minuet in that it moves more quickly, generating
       energy, rhythmic drive, and rough humor.

42. Which of the following is *not* true of the minuet?  Ans. c
    a. triple meter                    c. quick, lively tempo  p. 134
    b. moderate tempo                  d. ABA form

43. In many of Beethoven's works, there is a _____ movement instead of the minuet.  Ans. b
    a. presto                          c. fugato  p. 134
    b. scherzo                         d. ritornello  SG

44. The scherzo differs from the minuet in that it  Ans. a
    a. moves more quickly              c. has a different  meter  p. 134
    b. has a different form            d. all of the above  SG

45. A _____ is a musical composition that is usually light  Ans. c
    in mood, and meant for evening entertainment.  p. 135
    a. minuet and trio     b. aubade        c. serenade          d. rondo

46. The double bass in the classical orchestra, as in  Ans. c
    Mozart's *Eine Kleine Nachtmusik*, usually  p. 135
    a. has a separate and distinct bass part     c. doubles the cello part an octave lower .
    b. doubles the cello part in the same register     d. plays only accents on stressed beats

47. The rondo may be schematically outlined as  Ans. a
    a. ABACABA           b. AABB            c. ABBABC        d. ABA  p. 136

48. A common rondo pattern is  Ans. a
    a. ABACA                           c. ABBABC  p. 136
    b. ABACBA                          d. ABCBA  SG

49. Another common rondo pattern is  Ans. b
    a. ABCBCD                          c. ABCBAC  p. 136
    b. ABACABA                         d. ABACDC  SG

50. The return of the main theme in rondo form is all the more welcome  Ans. b
    because it is usually  p. 136
    a. in a contrasting key            c. slow and dignified
    b. in the tonic key                d. in varied form

51. The sonata-rondo  Ans. d
    a. may be outlined as ABA-development section-ABA  p. 136
    b. combines rondo form with elements of sonata form
    c. usually has a lively, pleasing, and simple to remember theme
    d. all of the above

52. The main theme of the rondo
    a. returns only once in the movement
    b. is usually slow and dignified
    c. seldom ends the movement
    d. is usually in the tonic key

Ans. d
p. 136
SG

53. Because of its liveliness, regularity, and buoyancy, the
    rondo most often serves as a
    a. slow movement
    b. first movement
    c. set of variations
    d. finale

Ans. d
p. 136

54. Because of its character, the rondo most often serves as a
    a. slow movement
    b. first movement
    c. set of variations
    d. finale

Ans. d
p. 136
SG

55. Which of the following statements is *not* true?
    a. A rondo movement features a tuneful main theme which returns several times
       in alternation with other themes.
    b. The rondo as a musical form was not used in musical compositions after
       the classical period.
    c. A common rondo pattern is ABACABA.
    d. Rondo form is often combined with elements of sonata form to produce
       the sonata-rondo.

Ans. b
p. 136

56. The rondo was used
    a. only in the classical symphony and quartet
    b. only as an independent composition
    c. as late as the twentieth century
    d. exclusively in the classical period

Ans. c
p. 136
SG

57. *Symphony* may be defined as a(n)
    a. musical composition for orchestra, usually in four movements
    b. sonata for orchestra
    c. extended, ambitious composition exploiting the expanded range of tone color
       and dynamics of the classical orchestra
    d. all of the above

Ans. d
p. 138
SG

58. The usual order of movements in a classical symphony is
    a. fast, dance-related, slow, fast
    b. fast, slow, dance-related, fast
    c. fast, slow, fast, slow
    d. slow, fast, slow, fast

Ans. b
p. 138
SG

59. The first movement of a classical symphony is almost always fast, and in _____ form.
    a. sonata
    b. rondo
    c. minuet
    d. ABA

Ans. a
p. 138
SG

60. Which of the following is *not* true of the symphony?
    a. A musical composition for orchestra, usually in four  movements.
    b. A sonata for orchestra.
    c. An extended, ambitious composition exploiting the expanded range of the color
       and dynamics of the classical orchestra.
    d. A musical composition for solo instrument and orchestra.

Ans. d
p. 138

61. ABA form is typical of the minuet or scherzo movement and is also common in the
    a. finale
    b. first movement
    c. slow movement
    d. all of the above

Ans. c
p. 138
SG

62. Which of the following statements is *not* true?   Ans. c
    a. In most classical symphonies, each movement is a self-contained composition   p. 138
       with its own set of themes.
    b. Beethoven's concluding movement of a symphony tends to be more triumphant
       and heroic in character and sometimes is meant as the climax of the whole symphony.
    c. The opening movement of a classical symphony is almost always slow and in
       ABA form.
    d. A classical symphony usually consists of four movements that evoke a wide range
       of emotions through contrasts of tempo and mood.

63. The lyrical slow movement of a symphony is most often the   Ans. b
    a. first               b. second               c. third               d. fourth   p. 138

64. Unlike the other movements in the symphony, the _____ movement   Ans. b
    is generally *not* in the tonic key.   p. 138
    a. first               b. second               c. third               d. fourth

65. The slow movement of a classical symphony   Ans. b
    a. is usually in theme and variations form   p. 138
    b. is generally not in the tonic key
    c. tends to be more heroic and triumphant in character
    d. all of the above

66. The last movement of a classical symphony   Ans. d
    a. is most often in sonata or sonata-rondo form   p. 138
    b. is usually fast, lively, and brilliant, but somewhat lighter in mood than
       the opening movement
    c. is always in the tonic key of the symphony
    d. all of the above

67. Unity is achieved in the classical symphony partly by the use of the same   Ans. a
    a. key in three of its four movements      c. key in all four movements   p. 139
    b. theme in each of its four movements     d. rhythm in all four movements

68. A symphony is unified partly by the use of the same   Ans. a
    a. key in three of its movements      c. tempo throughout   p. 139
    b. theme for each of its movements    d. all of the above   SG

69. A concerto is a large-scale work in several movements for   Ans. b
    a. an instrumental soloist            c. any combination of instruments   p. 139
    b. an instrumental soloist and orchestra   d. symphonic orchestra

70. Which of the following statements is *not* true?   Ans. c
    a. A classical concerto combines the virtuosity and interpretive abilities of a soloist   p. 139
       with the wide range of tone color and dynamics of the orchestra.
    b. Cadenzas in a classical concerto were indicated in the score by a fermata, and the
       soloist was expected to improvise, there being no music in the score at that point.
    c. A typical sequence of movements in a classical concerto is fast, slow, dance-related, fast.
    d. The first movement of a classical concerto is in sonata form, but has two expositions,
       one for the orchestra and one for the soloist.

71. A classical concerto is a three-movement work for

    a. instrumental soloist and orchestra    c. instrumental soloist and piano

    b. symphonic orchestra    d. vocal soloist and orchestra

Ans. a
p. 139
SG

72. Mozart and Beethoven wrote a number of concertos for their favorite solo instrument, the

    a. cello    b. violin    c. flute    d. piano

Ans. d
p. 139

73. The favored solo instrument in the classical concerto was the

    a. violin    c. piano

    b. cello    d. clarinet

Ans. c
p. 139
SG

74. A typical sequence of movements in a classical concerto is

    a. fast, slow, fast    c. fast, dance-related, fast

    b. slow, fast, slow    d. fast, slow, dance-related, fast

Ans. a
p. 139

75. The classical concerto differs from the symphony in that it does not have a _____ movement.

    a. sonata form    b. slow    c. minuet or scherzo    d. rondo finale

Ans. c
p. 139

76. The symphonic movement usually lacking in the concerto is the

    a. sonata-form movement    c. minuet or scherzo

    b. slow movement    d. rondo finale

Ans. c
p. 139
SG

77. A brilliant solo section in a concerto designed to display the performer's virtuosity is called

    a. a cadenza    b. a fermata    c. a pause    d. da capo

Ans. a
p. 139

78. An unaccompanied showpiece for the concerto's soloist is known as a

    a. fermata    c. concerto's solo

    b. cadenza    d. pause

Ans. b
p. 139
SG

79. In the first movement and sometimes in the last movement of a classical concerto there is a special unaccompanied showpiece for the soloist, the

    a. coda    b. fermata    c. cadenza    d. finale

Ans. c
p. 139

80. A pause in the score of a concerto is indicated by a

    a. signal from the soloist    c. signal from the conductor

    b. signal from the concertmaster    d. fermata

Ans. d
p. 139
SG

81. The first movement of a classical concerto

    a. is in the same form as a classical symphony    c. is usually a long cadenza

    b. has two expositions    d. does not have a development section

Ans. b
p. 140
SG

82. Classical chamber music is designed

    a. to display the virtuosity of the players

    b. for the intimate setting of a small room

    c. exclusively for performance by paid professional musicians

    d. to be conducted by experienced orchestral directors

Ans. b
p. 140
SG

83. A major factor that distinguishes chamber music from the symphony or concerto is that chamber music
   Ans. d
   p. 140
   SG
   a. does not use sonata form
   b. is performed in concert in concert halls
   c. does not have difficult parts
   d. is performed by one player per part

84. The most important form of classical chamber music is the
   Ans. c
   p. 140
   SG
   a. piano trio
   b. string quintet
   c. string quartet
   d. violin and piano sonata

85. The string quartet
   Ans. d
   p. 140
   a. usually consists of four movements
   b. is the most important form in classical chamber music
   c. is written for two violins, viola, and cello
   d. all of the above

86. The classical string quartet is a musical composition for
   Ans. b
   p. 140
   SG
   a. violin, viola, cello, and bass
   b. two violins, viola, and cello
   c. violin, guitar, viola, and cello
   d. all of the above

87. Which of the following statements is *not* true?
   Ans. b
   p. 141
   a. Classical chamber music does not need a conductor.
   b. The piano trio is a musical composition for three pianos.
   c. Chamber music is subtle and intimate, intended to please the performer as much as the listener.
   d. The most important form in classical chamber music is the string quartet.

88. The usual order of movements in a classical string quartet is
   Ans. a
   p. 141
   SG
   a. fast, slow, minuet or scherzo, fast
   b. fast, slow, fast, slow
   c. slow, fast, slow, fast
   d. fast, slow, fast

89. The piano trio is a musical composition for
   Ans. c
   p. 141
   SG
   a. three pianos
   b. violin and piano
   c. violin, cello, and piano
   d. all of the above

90. Haydn was fortunate in having a long and fruitful, as well as financially stable relationship with the noble Hungarian family of
   Ans. a
   p. 141
   a. Esterházy          b. Stefanházy          c. Liszt          d. Kadar

91. Which of the following was not one of Haydn's duties while in the service of the Esterházys?
   Ans. d
   p. 141
   a. composing all the music requested by his patron
   b. conducting the orchestra of about 25 players
   c. coaching the singers for operatic performances
   d. teaching music to the choir boys

92. Haydn's duties while in the service of the Esterházys included
   Ans. d
   p. 141
   SG
   a. composing all the music requested by his patron
   b. conducting the orchestra of about 25 players
   c. coaching the singers for operatic performances
   d. all of the above

93. Haydn's contract of employment shows that he was considered                 Ans. a
    a. a skilled servant                c. a visiting guest composer      p. 141
    b. a free-lance musician           d. an equal by his employer        SG

94. The twelve symphonies written for the concert manager J. P. Salomon for    Ans. d
performance at his public concerts are also known as the _____ symphonies   p. 141
for the city in which they were first performed.
    a. Paris           b. Esterháza        c. Vienna          d. London

95. Which of the following statements is *not* true?                    Ans. c
    a. Haydn's position at Esterháza was that of a highly skilled servant.      p. 142
    b. Haydn was good-humored and unselfish, and cared about the personal interests
        of his musicians.
    c. Haydn composed two oratorios, *The Creation* and *Judas Maccabaeus*.
    d. Haydn was a master at developing themes, able to build whole movements
        out of single main themes.

96. Haydn was a prolific composer, as demonstrated in part             Ans. d
by his 68 string quartets and 104                           p. 142
    a. operas           b. serenades        c. songs          d. symphonies

97. Haydn's two popular oratorios are entitled *The Seasons* and          Ans. a
    a. *The Creation*     b. *The Magic Flute*    c. *Judas Maccabaeus*    d. *Elijah*     p. 142

98. Along with his symphonies, Haydn's ___ are considered his most important works.   Ans. b
    a. operas                        c. baryton trios              p. 142
    b. string quartets                d. serenades                 SG

99. Mozart was born in                                            Ans. a
    a. Salzburg, Austria                c. Bonn, Germany           p. 144
    b. Eisenach, Germany              d. Rohrau, Austria           SG

100. Which of the following statements is *not* true?                   Ans. c
    a. Mozart wrote masterpieces in all the musical forms of his time.       p. 144
    b. Between the ages of six and fifteen, Mozart was continually on tour in England
        and Europe.
    c. In his later years, Mozart was financially well off, widely acclaimed, and sought after
        by an adoring public.
    d. Mozart's trips to Italy enabled him to study and master the current operatic style.

101. Between the ages of six and fifteen, Mozart                     Ans. c
    a. received an excellent formal education in Salzburg            p. 144
    b. went to Vienna to study with Haydn                   SG
    c. was continually on tour in England and Europe
    d. played in the archbishop's orchestra in Salzburg

102. Mozart's trips to Italy                                        Ans. a
    a. enabled him to study and master the Italian operatic style        p. 144
    b. were quite rare                                  SG
    c. were the scenes of his greatest triumphs
    d. enabled him to secure several permanent posts

103. By the age of six, Mozart could    Ans. d
  a. play the harpsichord and violin    c. read music perfectly at sight    p. 144
  b. improvise fugues and write minuets    d. all of the above    SG

104. Which of the following is *not* one of Mozart's three masterpieces of Italian opera?    Ans. c
  a. *Così fan tutte*    c. *Orfeo*    p. 145
  b. *The Marriage of Figaro*    d. *Don Giovanni*    SG

105. Mozart's finest German opera was    Ans. a
  a. *The Magic Flute*    c. *Don Giovanni*    p. 145
  b. *The Marriage of Figaro*    d. *Fidelio*    SG

106. Mozart composed his Requiem    Ans. c
  a. for his own funeral    c. on commission from a stranger    p. 145
  b. as an exercise for his composition teacher    d. to help his pupil Süssmayr

107. Mozart's Requiem was    Ans. d
  a. composed by a nobleman using Mozart's name    p. 145
  b. a high point in his career    SG
  c. an early work
  d. finished by one of his pupils

108. Don Giovanni, in Mozart's opera of that name, is    Ans. b
  a. a despotic Italian nobleman    c. Sir John Falstaff    p. 146
  b. the legendary Spanish lover    d. the servant to Leporello    SG

109. Mozart's Symphony No. 40    Ans. c
  a. is in G major    c. is one of his last three symphonies    p. 152
  b. has only three movements    d. all of the above    SG

110. Which of the following is *not* true of the late eighteenth-century fortepiano?    Ans. b
  a. Its tone was softer and lasted a shorter time than the modern piano.    p. 155
  b. It weighed the same as the modern piano.    SG
  c. It had thinner strings held by a frame of wood, rather than metal.
  d. Its pitch range was smaller than the modern piano.

111. Which of the following statements is *not* true?    Ans. c
  a. The finale of Beethoven's Ninth Symphony is based on Schiller's poem about    p. 159
      human brotherhood, *Ode to Joy*.
  b. Beethoven opened new realms of musical expression that profoundly influenced
      composers throughout the nineteenth century.
  c. Like Haydn and many other composers of the classical period, Beethoven was
      most successful financially when in the service of the aristocracy.
  d. In the finale of his Ninth Symphony, Beethoven took the unprecedented step
      of using a chorus and four solo vocalists.

112. Beethoven    Ans. d
  a. was a brilliant pianist    p. 159
  b. was self-educated and had read widely, but was weak in elementary arithmetic
  c. began to feel the first symptoms of deafness in his twenty-ninth year
  d. all of the above

113. The Third Symphony of Beethoven was originally composed to commemorate            Ans. b
    the deeds of _____ as the embodiment of heroism and democratic ideals.          p. 159
    a. George Washington                    c. the Marquis de Lafayette
    b. Napoleon Bonaparte                   d. the Duke of Wellington

114. We have a record of Beethoven's struggle with his musical material                Ans. b
    because of his habit of                                                            p. 160
    a. carrying a pocket tape recorder      c. telling his troubles to his friends
    b. carrying musical sketchbooks         d. keeping a diary

115. Beethoven's late works, composed after he was totally deaf, include               Ans. d
    a. piano sonatas                        c. the Ninth Symphony                       p. 160
    b. string quartets                      d. all of the above                        SG

116. Beethoven's greatest liturgical music is to be found in his                       Ans. b
    a. Mass in B Minor                      c. *Fidelio*                                p. 160
    b. *Missa Solemnis*                     d. Eighth Symphony                          SG

117. The musical heir of Haydn and Mozart, Beethoven bridged the                       Ans. c
    the _____ and _____ periods.                                               p. 160
    a. Renaissance, baroque                 c. classical, romantic
    b. baroque, classical                   d. romantic, impressionist

118. A piano sonata is a musical composition in two or more movements for             Ans. a
    a. piano                                c. piano and orchestra                      p. 160
    b. piano, violin, and cello             d. flute and piano

119. The choral finale of Beethoven's Ninth Symphony is based on                       Ans. c
    a. Dante's *Inferno*                    c. Schiller's *Ode to Joy*                  p. 161
    b. Shakespeare's *Midsummer Night's Dream*   d. Shelley's *Ode to the West Wind*   SG

120. Beethoven's Ninth Symphony is unusual in that it is scored                        Ans. b
    for _____ as well as orchestra.                                            p. 161
    a. a chorus                             c. a piano soloist
    b. four vocal soloists and a chorus     d. a violin soloist

121. Beethoven's sixteen _____ are generally considered among the greatest        Ans. b
    music ever composed.                                                               p. 161
    a. piano concertos   b. string quartets   c. piano sonatas   d. symphonies         SG

122. Beethoven greatly expanded the _____ section of the sonata-form          Ans. c
    movement and made it more dramatic.                                                p. 161
    a. introduction   b. exposition   c. development   d. recapitulation               SG

123. Beethoven's only opera is entitled                                                Ans. d
    a. *The Magic Flute*   b. *Madame Butterfly*   c. *Don Giovanni*   d. *Fidelio*     p. 161

# V. THE ROMANTIC PERIOD

*A* 1. Romantic style flourished in music during the period      Ans. c
       p. 176
     a. 1600-1750        b. 1750-1820        c. 1820-1900        d. 1900-1950

*B* 2. Romanticism, as a stylistic period in western art music,      Ans. d
     encompassed the years      p. 176
     a. 1450-1600        b. 1600-1750        c. 1750-1820        d. 1820-1900

*A* 3. Which of the following is *not* characteristic of romanticism?      Ans. b
     a. A fascination with fantasy.      p. 176
     b. An emphasis on balance and clarity of structures.
     c. An enthusiasm for the culture of the Middle Ages.
     d. An interest in exoticism and the past.

*B* 4. Which of the following is *not* a characteristic aspect of      Ans. a
     romanticism in literature and painting?      p. 176
     a. emotional restraint        c. exoticism
     b. emotional subjectivity        d. fantasy

*A* 5. Which of the following is *not* characteristic of romanticism?      Ans. b
     a. nationalism        c. individualism      p. 176
     b. emotional restraint        d. supernaturalism

*B* 6. Of all the inspirations for romantic art, none was more important than      Ans. c
     a. the aristocracy        c. nature      p. 176
     b. ancient Greek art and culture        d. the church

*A* 7. Which of the following composers is *not* associated with the romantic period?      Ans. b
     a. Giuseppe Verdi        c. Robert Schumann      p. 178
     b. Wolfgang Amadeus Mozart        d. Frédéric Chopin

*B* 8. The composer whose career was a model for many romantic composers was      Ans. a
     a. Ludwig van Beethoven        c. Johann Sebastian Bach      p. 178
     b. Joseph Haydn.        d. Antonio Vivaldi

9. Which of the following statements is *not* true?      Ans. d
     a. Romantic composers wrote primarily for a middle-class audience whose      p. 179
       size and prosperity had increased because of the industrial revolution.
     b. Romantic musicians often composed to fulfill an inner need rather than
       to execute a commission or meet the demands of an aristocratic or church patron.
     c. Music conservatories were founded in Europe and the United States
       during the romantic period.
     d. Romantic composers rejected the basic forms of the classical period and
       preferred to develop new forms of their own.

10. The rise of the urban middle class led to the
    a. piano becoming a fixture in every middle-class home
    b. formation of many orchestras and opera groups
    c. development of regular subscription concerts
    d. all of the above

Ans. d
p. 179

11. A very important musical part of every middle-class home
    during the romantic period was the
    a. resident composer/performer          c. violin
    b. piano                                d. flute

Ans. b
p. 179

12. All of the following romantic composers were also virtuoso
    instrumentalists giving solo recitals except
    a. Clara Wieck Schumann                 c. Niccolò Paganini
    b. Hector Berlioz                       d. Franz Liszt

Ans. b
p. 179

13. A romantic composer who earned his living as a touring virtuoso was
    a. Franz Liszt.                         c. Ludwig van Beethoven
    b. Hector Berlioz                       d. Frédéric Chopin

Ans. a
p. 179

14. The deliberate intent to draw creative inspiration from the composer's own
    homeland is known as
    a. exoticism       b. individualism       c. nationalism       d. *verismo*

Ans. c
p. 180

15. Composers expressed musical nationalism in their music by
    a. using the rhythms of the dances of their homelands
    b. using their national legends as subject matter
    c. basing their music on the folk songs of their country
    d. all of the above

Ans. d
p. 180

16. Drawing creative inspiration from cultures of lands foreign
    to the composer is known as
    a. exoticism       b. nationalism       c. program music       d. *verismo*

Ans. a
p. 181

17. Fascination with national identity also led composers to draw on
    colorful materials from foreign lands, a trend known as musical
    a. nationalism                          c. collectivism
    b. exoticism                            d. individualism

Ans. b
p. 181

18. Program music is
    a. music that depicts aspects of nature
    b. vocal music that tells a story
    c. instrumental music associated with a story, poem, idea, or scene
    d. all of the above

Ans. c
p. 181

19. Instrumental music that is associated with a story, poem, idea, or scene
    is called _____ music.
    a. absolute       b. program       c. exotic       d. natural

Ans. b
p. 181

20. Which of the following statements is *not* true?
    a. Romantic music puts unprecedented emphasis on self-expression
       and individuality of style.
    b. Fascination with the melodies, rhythms, and colorful materials from
       distant lands is a romantic trend known as musical nationalism.
    c. Romantic composers relied upon a more prominent use of chromatic
       harmony, or the use of chords containing tones not found in the
       prevailing major or minor scale.
    d. A romantic composition tends to have a wide variety of keys and rapid modulations.

Ans. b
p. 181

21. An orchestra toward the end of the romantic period might include close
    to _____ musicians.
    a. 24             b. 40            c. 60            d. 100

Ans. d
p. 181

22. The orchestra in the romantic period
    a. was basically the same as in the classical period
    b. ranged from twenty to sixty players
    c. was larger and more varied in tone color than the classical orchestra
    d. had a limited dynamic range due to the primitive nature of the brass instruments

Ans. c
p. 181

23. The 1844 *Treatise on Modern Instrumentation and Orchestration* that signaled
the recognition of orchestration as an art in itself was written by
    a. Franz Liszt                  c. Hector Berlioz
    b. Robert Schumann         d. Bedřich Smetana

Ans. c
p. 182

24. Which of the following statements is *not* true of the piano in
the early romantic period?
    a. A cast-iron frame was introduced to hold the strings under greater tension.
    b. The use of the damper pedal allowed a sonorous blend of tones from
       all registers of the piano.
    c. The piano's range remained basically the same as in the classical period.
    d. The piano's hammers were covered with felt.

Ans. c
p. 182

25. A slight holding back or pressing forward of tempo in
music is known as
    a. ritardando                 c. accelerando
    b. rubato                    d. fermata

Ans. b
p. 183

26. A slight slowing down or speeding up of the tempo, characteristically
employed in the performance of much romantic music, is
    a. ostinato                 c. syncopation
    b. chromatic               d. rubato

Ans. d
p. 183

27. Altering the character of a melody by changes in dynamics, orchestration,
or rhythm is a romantic technique known as
    a. thematic transformation       c. rubato
    b. melodic evolution           d. development

Ans. a
p. 184

A 28. An art song is a musical composition for                                   Ans. a
   a. solo voice and piano          c. multiple voices                           p. 184
   b. solo voice and orchestra      d. all of the above

B 29. The word _____ is commonly used for a romantic art song                Ans. a
   with a German text.                                                           p. 184
   a. *lied*                        c. *chanson*
   b. *durchkomponiert*             d. *ballade*

30. The German composers of art songs favored, among others, the lyric poetry   Ans. a
   of Johann Wolfgang von Goethe and                                             p. 184
   a. Heinrich Heine                c. William Wordsworth
   b. Victor Hugo                   d. Walt Whitman

31. Which of the following statements is *not* true of the romantic art song?    Ans. a
   a. The art song is restricted to strophic or through-composed form.           p. 185
   b. A song cycle is a set of romantic art songs that may be unified by a story
      line that runs through the poems, or by musical ideas linking the songs.
   c. Through-composed, a translation of the German term *durchkomponiert*,
      is a song form that allows music to reflect a poem's changing moods.
   d. The accompaniment of a romantic art song is an integral part of the
      composer's conception, and it serves as an interpretive partner to the voice.

32. The mood of an art song is often set by a brief piano introduction and       Ans. b
   summed up at the end by a piano section called a                              p. 185
   a. conclusion        b. postlude        c. song cycle        d. finale

A 33. When the same music is repeated for each stanza of a poem                   Ans. b
   the form is known as                                                          p. 185
   a. song form                     c. through-composed
   b. strophic                      d. repetitious

B 34. When a composer writes new music for each stanza of a poem                  Ans. c
   the form is known as                                                          p. 185
   a. song form                     c. through-composed
   b. strophic                      d. unending

A 35. Schubert's primary source of income came from his                          Ans. d
   a. position as music director to a noble court                                p. 186
   b. touring as a virtuoso performer
   c. performing as church organist
   d. musical compositions

B 36. Schubert
   a. was widely acknowledged as a composer in his lifetime                      Ans. d
   b. was very self-critical, which accounts for his meager output               p. 186
   c. produced his greatest works after the age of forty                         SG
   d. was the first great master of the romantic art song

37. Which of the following statements is *not* true?                           Ans. b
    a. Franz Schubert led a bohemian existence, living with friends because     p. 186
       he had no money to rent a room of his own.
    b. Schubert labored at great length over each of his compositions,
       which accounts for his small output.
    c. At the time of his death, Schubert's reputation was mainly that
       of a fine song composer.
    d. In addition to symphonies, operas, string quartets and other chamber works,
       Schubert composed over six hundred songs.

*A* 38. Schubert's songs number more than                                       Ans. d
    a. 50                              c. 250                                    p. 186
    b. 100                             d. 600                                    SG

39. Schubert wrote compositions in every musical genre except                   Ans. b
    a. string quartets    b. piano concertos    c. symphonies    d. operas      p. 186

*B* 40. Schubert was eighteen years old when he composed the                    Ans. d
    song *Erlkönig*, set to a poem by                                           p. 187
    a. Schubert himself                c. Victor Hugo
    b. Heinrich Heine                  d. Johann Wolfgang von Goethe

*A* 41. *The Erlking* is a poem by                                              Ans. c
    a. Heinrich Heine                  c. Johann Wolfgang von Goethe            p. 187
    b. Schubert himself                d. Robert Schumann                       SG

*B* 42. The form of *The Erlking* is                                           Ans. c
    a. strophic                        c. through-composed                      p. 187
    b. modified strophic               d. none of the above                     SG

*A* 43. Schubert's song *Erlkönig* is an example of _____ form.            Ans. d
    a. modified strophic               c. AABA                                  p. 187
    b. strophic                        d. through-composed

*B* 44. The Erlking, in Schubert's song of that name, is a romantic personification of   Ans. b
    a. ghosts                          c. nature                                p. 187
    b. death                           d. a galloping horse                     SG

*A* 45. The piano's relentless rhythm in *Erlkönig* (*The Erlking*) unifies     Ans. a
    the episodes of the song and suggests the                                   p. 188
    a. galloping horse                 c. calmness of the father                SG
    b. joy of the child                d. approach of death

46. Robert Schumann's works are                                                 Ans. d
    a. intensely autobiographical                                               p. 190
    b. usually linked with descriptive titles, texts, or programs               SG
    c. essentially lyrical in nature
    d. all of the above

47. Which of the following is *not* typical of Robert Schumann's works?      Ans. d
    a. intensely autobiographical      p. 190
    b. usually have descriptive titles, texts, or programs
    c. essentially lyrical in nature
    d. all written for the piano

48. As a writer and critic, Robert Schumann      Ans. d
    a. founded and edited the *New Journal of Music*      p. 191
    b. discovered and made famous some of the leading composers of his day      SG
    c. wrote appreciative reviews of young "radical" composers like Chopin and Berlioz
    d. all of the above

49. Clara Wieck was      Ans. d
    a. the daughter of Schumann's piano teacher      p. 191
    b. a virtuoso pianist      SG
    c. Schumann's wife
    d. all of the above

50. During the first ten years of his creative life, Schumann published only      Ans. b
    a. songs                          c. symphonies      p. 192
    b. piano pieces                   d. musical criticism      SG

51. Which of the following statements regarding Robert Schumann is *not* true?      Ans. a
    a. Schumann's short piano pieces often express a wide variety of moods.      p. 192
    b. Schumann's symphonies are romantic in their emphasis on lyrical second
       themes, use of thematic transformation, and connections between movements.
    c. During the first ten years of his creative life, Schumann published only piano pieces.
    d. Schumann's genius is most characteristically expressed in his songs and short piano
       pieces, both of which he usually organized into sets or cycles.

52. *Im wunderschönen Monat Mai (In the Lovely Month of May)* is part      Ans. c
    of Robert Schumann's      p. 192
    a. *Fantasiestücke (Fantasy Pieces)*      c. *Dichterliebe (Poet's Love)*      SG
    b. *Kinderscenen (Scenes of Childhood)*      d. *Carnaval (Carnival)*

53. Clara Wieck Schumann was      Ans. d
    a. a composer                     c. the mother of a large family      p. 193
    b. a concert pianist              d. all of the above      SG

54. Clara Wieck was      Ans. d
    a. one of the leading concert pianists of the nineteenth century      p. 193
    b. a child prodigy
    c. the wife of composer Robert Schumann
    d. all of the above

55. Clara Schumann frequently performed the works of her husband and her
close friend
    a. Hector Berlioz               c. Johann Sebastian Bach
    b. Richard Wagner           d. Johannes Brahms

Ans. d
p. 193
SG

56. Johannes Brahms
    a. was an admirer of Robert Schumann, but never met him
    b. was a violinist who performed Clara Schumann's compositions
    c. was a close friend of Clara and Robert Schumann
    d. married Clara Schumann after her husband died

Ans. c
p. 193

57. Clara Schumann
    a. composed many works for orchestra
    b. stopped composing at the age of thirty-six when her husband died
    c. gave up concertizing when she got married
    d. continued to compose music throughout her life

Ans. b
p. 194
SG

58. As a composer, Clara Schumann
    a. wrote only short lyrical piano pieces
    b. wrote only operas
    c. never performed her own music
    d. wrote songs, piano pieces, a piano concerto, and a trio for piano, violin, and cello

Ans. d
p. 194
SG

59. A leading pianist of the nineteenth century, Clara Schumann
    a. never composed any music
    b. did some composing, but considered herself primarily a performer
    c. composed many works throughout her long life
    d. performed only the music of her husband Robert

Ans. b
p. 194

60. *Romanze (romance)* in the nineteenth century was often used for a(n)
    a. steamy, sexy novel
    b. short, lyrical piece for piano or solo instrument with piano accompaniment
    c. autobiographical song cycle
    d. descriptive programmatic symphony

Ans. b
p. 194
SG

*A* 61. In the 1830s, Paris was    *Most of Chopin's musical career*
    a. a center of romanticism    *was associated with.*
    b. the artistic capital of Europe    *London, Paris, Vienna,*
    c. the home of Victor Hugo, Balzac, and Heine    *warsaw.*
    d. all of the above

Ans. d
p. 197
SG

62. Chopin was
    a. an extroverted virtuoso        c. sloppy and careless in dress
    b. robust and flamboyant        d. shy and reserved

Ans. d
p. 197
SG

63. Chopin expressed his love of Poland by composing polonaises and
    a. polkas                 c. waltzes
    b. folk songs           d. mazurkas

Ans. d
p. 197

64. While in Paris, Chopin
    a) married the famous writer Aurore Dudevant
    b. earned a good living by teaching piano to the daughters of the rich
    c. gave a great number of successful public concerts
    d. all of the above

Ans. b
p. 197

65. Most of Chopin's pieces
    a. are exquisite miniatures
    b. are for a wide range of media
    c. have a limited variety of moods
    d. have literary programs or titles

Ans. a
p. 197
SG

66. A slow, lyrical, intimate composition for piano,
    associated with evening and night time, is the
    a. étude          b. mazurka          c. waltz          d. nocturne

Ans. d
p. 197

67. A study piece, designed to help a performer master
    specific technical difficulties, is known as
    a. nocturne          b. étude          c. polonaise          d. lied

Ans. b
p. 200

68. Chopin's *Revolutionary* Étude develops the pianist's left hand because
    a. the left hand must play rapid passages throughout
    b. it is played only by the left hand
    c. it takes nearly an hour to perform
    d. the left hand plays the main melody

Ans. a
p. 200
SG

69. Which of the following statements is *not* true?
    a. In the 1830s Paris was a center of romanticism and the
       artistic capital of Europe.
    b. Chopin was a shy, reserved man who disliked crowds and preferred to play
       in salons rather than in public concert halls.
    c. Many of Chopin's most poetic effects come from the sensitive exploitation
       of the piano's pedals.
    d. Chopin's piano études, compositions designed to help a performer master specific
       technical difficulties, are primarily technical exercises without much musical value.

Ans. d
p. 200

70. The _____ is a dance in triple meter that originated as a stately
    procession for the Polish nobility.
    a. polka                    c. waltz
    b. mazurka                  d. polonaise

Ans. d
p. 200

71. As a youth, Liszt was influenced by the performances of
    a. Richard Wagner           c. Robert Schumann
    b. Hector Berlioz           d. Niccolò Paganini

Ans. d
p. 201
SG

72. When he was nineteen, Liszt was overwhelmed by the virtuosity of
    a. Ludwig van Beethoven     c. Robert Schumann
    b. Niccolò Paganini         d. Joseph Haydn

Ans. b
p. 201

73. During his teens and twenties, Liszt lived in
   a. Rome                                          c. Paris
   b. Weimar                                        d. Budapest

Ans. c
p. 201
SG

74. Until the age of thirty-six, Liszt toured Europe as a virtuoso
   a. pianist                                       c. cellist
   b. conductor                                     d. all of the above

Ans. a
p. 201
SG

75. During the 1840s, Liszt toured Europe as a virtuoso
   a. violinist          b. cellist          c. conductor          d. pianist

Ans. d
p. 201

76. Liszt abandoned his career as a traveling virtuoso to become court conductor
   at _____, where he championed works by contemporary composers.
   a. Rome          b. Weimar          c. Paris          d. Budapest

Ans. b
p. 201
SG

77. Liszt became court conductor and a champion of modern music in the city of
   a. Paris          b. Weimar          c. London          d. Prague

Ans. b
p. 201

78. The writer whose literary works greatly inspired Franz Liszt was
   a. William Shakespeare                            c. Robert Schumann
   b. Johann Wolfgang von Goethe                     d. Marie d'Agoult

Ans. b
p. 202

79. Among Liszt's favorite inspirations were the literary works of
   a. Johann Wolfgang von Goethe                     c. Heinrich Heine
   b. Carolyne Sayn-Wittgenstein                     d. Richard Wagner

Ans. a
p. 202
SG

80. Liszt typified the romantic movement because he
   a. had a charismatic personality                 c. was an innovative composer
   b. was a stupendous performer                     d. all of the above

Ans. d
p. 202
SG

81. Liszt created the _____, a one-movement orchestral composition
   based to some extent on a literary or pictorial idea.
   a. concert overture                              c. piano concerto
   b. symphonic poem                                d. sonata

Ans. b
p. 202
SG

82. The symphonic poem, or tone poem, a one-movement orchestral composition
   based to some extent on literary or pictorial ideas, was created by
   a. Robert Schumann                               c. Franz Liszt
   b. Richard Strauss                               d. Franz Schubert

Ans. c
p. 202

83. In many of his works, Liszt unified contrasting moods by a process known as
   a. motivic repetition                            c. sequential restatement
   b. thematic transformation                       d. cohesive unification

Ans. b
p. 202
SG

84. Liszt's piano works are characterized by
   a. an unprecedented range of dynamics            c. arpeggios
   b. rapid octaves and daring leaps                d. all of the above

Ans. d
p. 202
SG

85. By the age of thirteen, Mendelssohn had written _____ of astounding quality.    Ans. d
    a. vocal works.                          c. symphonies and concertos    p. 205
    b. sonatas                               d. all of the above

86. Mendelssohn is known as the man who rekindled an interest in the music of    Ans. b
    a. Giovanni Pierluigi da Palestrina      c. George Frideric Handel    p. 206
    b. Johann Sebastian Bach                 d. Franz Schubert            SG

87. Mendelssohn earned an international reputation, and rekindled    Ans. b
    an interest in the earlier composer's music, by conducting    p. 206
    the first performance since the composer's death of
    a. Josquin's *Ave Maria*                 c. Handel's *Messiah*
    b. Bach's *St. Matthew Passion*          d. Schubert's Mass in C

88. The high point of Mendelssohn's career was the triumphant premiere    Ans. d
    of his oratorio _____ in England.    p. 206
    a. *Elijah*                              c. A *Midsummer Night's Dream*    SG
    b. *Hebrides*                            d. *Fingal's Cave*

89. Mendelssohn's career reached its high point at the    Ans. a
    triumphant premiere of his oratorio *Elijah* in    p. 206
    a. Birmingham, England                   c. Leipzig, Germany
    b. Paris, France                         d. Berlin, Germnay

90. Mendelssohn wrote in all musical forms except    Ans. b
    a. symphonies                            c. string quartets    p. 206
    b. operas                                d. oratorios

91. The three movements of Mendelssohn's Violin Concerto    Ans. d
    a. are unified by the process of thematic transformation    p. 206
    b. are all in the same key    SG
    c. all have separate cadenzas
    d. are played without pause

92. Mendelssohn's Violin Concerto in E Minor opens with a(n)    Ans. b
    a. orchestral exposition typical in concertos    p. 207
    b. soloist, who presents the main theme    SG
    c. slow introduction by the orchestra
    d. single bassoon tone

93. The opening of Mendelssohn's Violin Concerto in E minor    Ans. b
    is unusual in that    p. 207
    a. there is a trumpet fanfare introduction
    b. the main theme is presented by the soloist
    c. there is a slow introduction by the orchestra
    d. the orchestra presents the main theme without the soloist

94. In the first movement of the Violin Concerto, the cadenza
    a. is left to the performer to improvise
    b. appears at the end of the recapitulation, as is common in classical concertos
    c. is frequently omitted in performance
    d. appears at the end of the development section as a transition to the recapitulation

Ans. d
p. 208
SG

*B* 95. Instrumental music associated with a story, poem, idea,
    or scene, popular during the romantic period, is called
    a. absolute music                    c. program music
    b. opera                             d. symphony

Ans. c
p. 208

*A* 96. Instrumental music endowed with literary or pictorial associations
    is called _____ music.
    a. absolute          b. synthetic          c. program          d. rap

Ans. c
p. 208

97. The work referred to by Beethoven as an "expression of feeling rather than
    painting" was his
    a. Symphony No. 5                    c. *Eroica* Symphony
    b. *Fidelio* Overture                d. Symphony No. 6

Ans. d
p. 208
SG

98. Which of the following statements is *not* true?
    a. Musicians and audiences in the romantic period liked to read stories.
       into all music, whether intended by the composer or not.
    b. The romantic concert overture was modeled after the opera overture, but
       the concert overture is not intended to usher in a stage work, being instead
       an independent composition.
    c. The symphonic poem, or tone poem, is a one-movement composition
       in sonata-allegro form.
    d. While music alone makes no definite reference to ideas, emotions, or objects,
       it can create moods, emotions, and atmosphere.

Ans. c
p. 208

*B* 99. Nonprogram music is also known as _____ music.
    a. pure                              c. concert
    b. absolute                          d. symphonic

Ans. b
p. 208
SG

*A* 100. Instrumental music written for its own sake, and for
    which the composer did not intend a program, is called
    a. absolute music                    c. opera
    b. program music                     d. music for its own sake

Ans. a
p. 208

101. Absolute music is also known as
    a. program music                     c. concert music
    b. nonprogram music                  d. chamber music

Ans. b
p. 208

*B* 102. A _____ is an instrumental composition in several
    movements based to some extent on a literary or pictorial idea.
    a. nocturne                          c. polonaise
    b. program symphony                  d. concert overture

Ans. b
p. 209

*A*

103. A _____ is a one-movement orchestral composition based to some      Ans. c
extent on a literary or pictorial idea.                                            p. 209
  a. mazurka                                 c. symphonic poem      SG
  b. program symphony                     d. nocturne

*B*

104. The composer who developed the symphonic poem was                             Ans. a
  a. Franz Liszt                                   c. Franz Schubert      p. 209
  b. Ludwig van Beethoven                 d. Richard Strauss      SG

105. The symphonic poem, or tone poem, a one-movement orchestral composition        Ans. c
based to some extent on literary or pictorial ideas, was developed by               p. 209
  a. Robert Schumann                        c. Franz Liszt
  b. Richard Strauss                         d. Hector Berlioz

*A*

106. Music intended to be performed before and during a play to set the mood         Ans. b
for scenes or highlight dramatic action is known as                                 p. 209
  a. music drama     b. incidental music     c. absolute music     d. play music

107. Today's movie scores may be regarded as examples of                            Ans. b
  a. pure music                                  c. folk music      p. 209
  b. incidental music                     d. absolute music      SG

*B*

108. The musical scores composed for moving pictures may be                         Ans. a
regarded as examples of _____ music.                                      p. 209
  a. incidental       b. occasional       c. absolute         d. rock

109. In 1830 the Paris Conservatory awarded Berlioz                                 Ans. d
  a. a graduate fellowship                 c. a position on the faculty      p. 210
  b. a scholarship                         d. the Prix de Rome      SG

110. The writer whose works had the greatest impact on the young Berlioz was        Ans. b
  a. Victor Hugo                                c. Honoré de Balzac      p. 210
  b. William Shakespeare                   d. Heinrich Heine

111. The *Fantastic Symphony* reflects Berlioz's                                     Ans. c
  a. intense nationalism                                                     p. 210
  b. experiences in Rome                                                      SG
  c. love for the actress Harriet Smithson
  d. interrest in composing for small, intimate ensembles

112. In order to support his family, Berlioz turned to                              Ans. b
  a. medicine                                   c. teaching      p. 210
  b. musical journalism                     d. arranging concerts      SG

113. Unable to gain sufficient financial support from his                           Ans. a
compositions, Berlioz turned to                                                     p. 210
  a. musical journalism    b. medicine            c. music copying       d. acting

114. Parisians were startled by Berlioz's *Fantastic Symphony* because of its
    a. sensationally autobiographical program
    b. amazingly novel orchestration
    c. vivid description of the weird and diabolical
    d. all of the above

Ans. d
p. 210
SG

115. Which of the following statements is *not* true?
    a. Berlioz was an extraordinarily imaginative and innovative orchestrator.
    b. All of Berlioz's major works are dramatic in nature and relate either to
       a literary program or to a text.
    c. In 1830 Berlioz won the Paris Conservatory's Prix de Rome which granted
       him two years' subsidized study in Rome.
    d. Berlioz's reputation outside France was even lower than it was in his homeland.

Ans. d
p. 211

116. Outside France, Berlioz enjoyed a great career as a(n)
    a. conductor                    c. singer
    b. concert pianist             d. impresario

Ans. a
p. 211
SG

117. As one of the first great _____, Berlioz influenced a whole
generation of musicians.
    a. orchestral conductors         c. impresarios
    b. composition teachers          d. guitarists

Ans. a
p. 211

118. Berlioz was extraordinarily imaginative in treating
the orchestra, creating _____ never before heard.
    a. tone colors                 c. harmonies
    b. rhythms                   d. forms

Ans. a
p. 211

119. Which of the following was *not* composed by Berlioz?
    a. *Romeo and Juliet*            c. *The Sorcerer's Apprentice*
    b. *The Damnation of Faust*       d. Requiem

Ans. c
p. 211
SG

120. Which of the following statements is *not* true of Berlioz's *Fantastic Symphony*?
    a. The fourth movement depicts a dream of a witches' sabbath.
    b. Berlioz incorporates the medieval chant *Dies irae*, traditionally sung in
       the mass for the dead, in the last movement.
    c. The second movement is a waltz, the most popular dance of the Romantic period.
    d. The *idée fixe* appears in all five movements and unifies the contrasting episodes
       of the symphony.

Ans. a
p. 212

121. The contrasting episodes of Berlioz's *Fantastic Symphony*
are unified by the recurrence of a theme known as the
    a. subject                  c. leitmotif
    b. Smithson theme          d. *idée fixe*

Ans. d
p. 212

122. Berlioz's *Fantastic Symphony* is unified by the recurrence of a theme
known as the
    a. germ motive      b. *thème varié*      c. basic motive      d. *idée fixe*

Ans. d
p. 212
SG

123. The second movement of Berlioz's *Fantastic Symphony* is a _____,    Ans. a
the most popular dance of the romantic era.    p. 212
    a. waltz              b. minuet              c. country dance       d. gavotte    SG

124. The fourth movement of the *Fantastic Symphony* depicts a    Ans. a
    a. march to the scaffold         c. dream of a witches' sabbath    p. 212
    b. ball                          d. scene in the country    SG

125. The liturgical melody quoted in the last movement of the *Fantastic*    Ans. d
*Symphony* is the    p. 214
    a. *Ave Maria*        b. alleluia        c. benedictus       d. *Dies irae*    SG

126. The strongest impact of musical nationalism was felt in    Ans. d
    a. Russia                        c. Bohemia    p. 217
    b. the Scandinavian countries    d. all of the above

127. Which of the following countries did *not* produce    Ans. b
important composers whose music had a national flavor?    p. 217
    a. Norway             b. Portugal        c. Russia           d. Bohemia

128. Antonin Dvořák's Symphony no. 9    Ans. d
    a. is his most famus work    p. 217
    b. is subtitled *From the New World*
    c. glorifies both the Czech and the American folk spirit
    d. all of the above

129. The opera that laid the groundwork for a Russian national style, *A Life*    Ans. d
*for the Tsar*, was composed by    p. 217
    a. Modest Mussorgsky             c. Nikolai Rimsky-Korsakov    SG
    b. César Cui                     d. Mikhail Glinka

130. The most original, and probably the greatest of the Russian five, was    Ans. b
    a. César Cui                     c. Alexander Borodin    p. 218
    b. Modest Mussorgsky             d. Mily Balakirev    SG

131. Bedřich Smetana    Ans. a
    a. was the founder of Czech national music    p. 218
    b. was a leading composer of symphonies
    c. served as a member of the Austrian provincial government
    d. all of the above

132. The founder of Czech national music was    Ans. c
    a. César Cui                     c. Bedřich Smetana    p. 218
    b. Antonin Dvořák                d. Boris Godunov    SG

133. Smetana grew up when Bohemia was under _____ domination.    Ans. b
    a. German                        c. Polish    p. 218
    b. Austrian                      d. Russian    SG

B. 34. The composer Bedřich Smetana was associated
with ____ nationalism
a. Russian   b. Norwegian   c. Bohemian
   d. Hungarian

134. Smetana's most popular opera is                                    Ans. a
   a. *The Bartered Bride*              c. *Boris Godunov*              p. 218
   b. *My Country*                      d. *The Moldau*                 SG

composition heard in class is

A  135. Bedřich Smetana's most famous opera is  (c) a program symphony  Ans. d
   a. *The Moldau* (a) d. concert overture  c. *Russalka*              p. 218
   b. *Eugene Onegin* (b) a symphonic     d. *The Bartered Bride*
                    poem                  (d) incidental music

B  136. Even though Smetana was deaf at the time, he composed a musical work   Ans. a
   depicting Bohemia's main river as it flows through the countryside. The name   p. 218
   of the river, and the musical composition, is the                            SG
   a. Moldau        b. Seine           c. Danube           d. Thames

137. Which of the following statements is *not* true?                   Ans. b
   a. Bedřich Smetana was active in Prague as a composer, pianist, conductor,   p. 218
      teacher, and tireless propagandist for Czech musical nationalism.
   b. Smetana passed the last few years of his life teaching and conducting in Prague.
   c. *The Moldau* is one of the six symphonic poems in Smetana's cycle *Má Vlast (My
      Country)*, a romantic representation of nature and a display of Czech nationalism.
   d. A peasant wedding is suggested in Smetana's *The Moldau* by a rustic polka.

A  138. Peter Ilyich Tchaikovsky                                        Ans. d
   a. was a child prodigy, learning music at an early age              p. 220
   b. preferred his government position to music
   c. studied music theory and violin as a teenager
   d. began to study music theory at the age of twenty-one

139. Which of the following statements is *not* true?                   Ans. b
   a. Tchaikovsky's progress in music was so rapid that after graduating from the   p. 220
      St. Petersburg Conservatory he became professor of harmony at the new
      Moscow Conservatory.
   b. Tchaikovsky was a happily-married family man with a cheerful self-confident
      outlook.
   c. Tchaikovsky, while not a member of the "Russian five," considered himself
      as *Russian* in the fullest sense of the word.
   d. Tchaikovsky, with elements of French, Italian, and German music as well as
      Russian folk songs, fused national and international elements to produce
      intensely subjective and passionate music.

140. Nadezhda von Meck was                                              Ans. b
   a. one of Tchaikovsky's lovers                                       p. 220
   b. a wealthy benefactress who provided Tchaikovsky with an annuity   SG
   c. Tchaikovsky's wife
   d. the inspiration for his *Romeo and Juliet*

141. Tchaikovsky's Sixth Symphony                                       Ans. d
   a. is in the usual four-movement form    c. has five movements       p. 221
   b. was left unfinished by the composer   d. ends with a slow, despairing finale   SG

142. Which of the following was *not* composed by Tchaikovsky?
    a. *Romeo and Juliet*               c. *Swan Lake*
    b. *Boris Godunov*                  d. Symphony no. 6 *(Pathétique)*

Ans. b
p. 221

143. Which of the following was *not* composed by Tchaikovsky?
    a. *The Sleeping Beauty*            c. *Marche slave*
    b. *Russian Easter* Overture        d. *Overture 1812*

Ans. b
p. 221
SG

144. Which of the following is *not* a ballet by Tchaikovsky?
    a. *Swan Lake*                      c. *The Nutcracker*
    b. *The Sleeping Beauty*            d. *Coppelia*

Ans. d
p. 221

145. Tchaikovsky's *Romeo and Juliet* is a(n)
    a. opera                           c. symphonic poem
    b. program symphony                d. concert overture

Ans. d
p. 222
SG

146. Tchaikovsky's Overture-Fantasy *Romeo and Juliet* is
    a. an overture to an opera         c. a symphonic poem
    b. an overture to a ballet         d. a concert overture

Ans. d
p. 222

147. At its premiere in 1870, Tchaikovsky's *Romeo and Juliet* Overture was
    a. a tremendous success
    b. a dismal failure
    c. performed by a large orchestra, with chorus and cannon
    d. enthusiastically applauded by the tsar

Ans. b
p. 222
SG

148. Tchaikovsky's *Romeo and Juliet* is
    a. a ballet based on Shakespeare's play *Romeo and Juliet*
    b. a medley of popular melodies taken from his opera of that name
    c. an early programmatic symphony inspired by the characters in Shakespeare's play
    d. a concert overture consisting of a slow introduction and a fast movement
       in sonata form

Ans. d
p. 222

149. The course of Brahms's artistic and personal life was shaped by
    the influence of the composer
    a. Antonin Dvořák                  c. Franz Liszt
    b. Robert Schumann and his wife Clara   d. Richard Wagner

Ans. b
p. 224
SG

150. The fourth movement of Brahms's Fourth Symphony is a _____, a
    baroque variation form.
    a. passamezzo                      c. passacaglia
    b. passionato                      d. passaggio

Ans. c
p. 224
SG

151. In Vienna, Brahms
    a. conducted a Viennese musical society
    b. edited baroque and classical compositions
    c. collected music manuscripts
    d. all of the above

Ans. d
p. 225

152. Which of the following statements is *not* true?                 Ans. a
  a. One of Brahms's musical trademarks is his exotic orchestration.    p. 225
  b. When he was thirteen, Brahms studied piano, music theory, and composition during the day, and played dance music for prostitutes and their clients in waterfront bars at night.
  c. Brahms was a romantic who breathed new life into classical forms.
  d. As conductor of a Viennese musical society, Brahms introduced many forgotten works of Bach, Handel, and Mozart.

153. In comparison to some earlier composers, Brahms's musical output may be   Ans. c
  considered small. This is explained in part by the fact that Brahms      p. 225
  a. was too busy conducting and performing to find time to compose
  b. was insecure and lazy, unable to concentrate on composing
  c. was extremely critical of his own work
  d. died before he had a chance to realize himself fully

154. Brahms wrote masterpieces in many musical forms, but never any      Ans. b
  a. art songs                  c. choral works            p. 225
  b. operas                    d. chamber music

155. Brahms's works, though very personal in style, are rooted in the music of  Ans. d
  a. Joseph Haydn              c. Ludwig van Beethoven    p. 225
  b. Wolfgang Amadeus Mozart     d. all of the above         SG

156. Brahms's musical trademarks included                 Ans. b
  a. bombastic flamboyance        c. the use of da capo arias    p. 225
  b. the use of two notes against three   d. all of the above         SG

157. The original source for the theme of the fourth movement of Brahms's   Ans. b
  Fourth Symphony was a                          p. 226
  a. piece for wind instruments     c. song by Brahms         SG
  b. cantata by Bach              d. piano piece by Schumann

158. Verdi studied music in _____, the city where Italy's most important  Ans. d
  opera house, La Scala, is located.                      p. 230
  a. Rome        b. Florence       c. Venice       d. Milan     SG

159. Verdi's first great success, an opera with strong political overtones, was  Ans. c
  a. *Oberto*                  c. *Nabucco*            p. 230
  b. *Aïda*                   d. *La Traviata*       SG

160. Which of the following operatic masterpieces was *not* composed by Verdi?  Ans. b
  a. *La Traviata*            c. *Il Trovatore*         p. 230
  b. *Cavalleria rusticana*   d. *Otello*

161. Which of the following operas is *not* by Verdi?              Ans. b
  a. *La Traviata*            c. *Il Trovatore*         p. 230
  b. *Cavalleria rusticana*   d. *Otello*               SG

162. Critics were often scandalized by the subject matter of Verdi's operas because they     Ans. d
    a. symbolized a free and unified Italy     p. 230
    b. commemorated the Suez canal, which was not even in Europe     SG
    c. were based on Shakespearean plays
    d. seemed to condone rape, suicide, and free love

163. Verdi's great comic masterpiece, written when he was seventy-nine, is     Ans. c
    a. *Il Trovatore*                    c. *Falstaff*     p. 230
    b. *Otello*                      d. *Aïda*     SG

164. Remarkably, at the age of seventy-nine, Verdi completed his     Ans. d
comic masterpiece     p. 230
    a. *Oberto*        b. *La Traviata*        c. *Nabucco*        d. *Falstaff*

165. Which of the following statements is *not* true?     Ans. c
    a. Giuseppe Verdi, the most popular of all opera composers, was born     p. 230
        to a poor family in a tiny Italian village.
    b. The soul of a Verdi opera is its expressive vocal melody.
    c. Verdi composed primarily for the Italian musical elite, those who
        would best appreciate his talents.
    d. In the course of his long life, Verdi's style became less conventional, more subtle
        and flexible, with more imaginative orchestrations and richer accompaniments.

166. Verdi mainly composed his operas     Ans. d
    a. for the Italian musical elite          c. to promote Italian unification     p. 230
    b. to glorify the singers               d. to entertain a mass public     SG

167. The soul of a Verdi opera is     Ans. b
    a. extensive thematic development        c. the situation comedy     p. 231
    b. expressive vocal melody            d. atmospheric orchestral parts     SG

168. Verdi's later operas differ from his earlier ones in that they have     Ans. d
    a. less difference between aria and recitative     p. 231
    b. greater musical continuity     SG
    c. more imaginative orchestrations
    d. all of the above

169. Rigoletto, the title role in Verdi's opera, is all of the following except     Ans. d
    a. a hunchback                  c. the father of Gilda     p. 231
    b. a court jester to the Duke of Mantua    d. the romantic lover

170. Rigoletto, the title character in Verdi's opera, is     Ans. d
    a. a hunchback                  c. the father of Gilda     p. 231
    b. court jester to the duke of Mantua     d. all of the above     SG

171. The famous aria *La donna è mobile* is taken from Verdi's opera     Ans. a
    a. *Rigoletto*                  c. *Falstaff*     p. 231
    b. *Aïda*                   d. *Il Trovatore*     SG

172. Puccini's first successful opera was
    a. *Madame Butterfly*               c. *Manon Lescaut*
    b. *La Bohème*                 d. *Turandot*

    Ans. c
    p. 232
    SG

173. Which of the following operas was *not* composed by Puccini?
    a. *Tosca*                    c. *Turandot*
    b. *Madame Butterfly*          d. *I Pagliacci*

    Ans. d
    p. 232
    SG

174. Which of the following operas was *not* composed by Puccini?
    a. *Aïda*                    c. *Turandot*
    b. *Manon Lescaut*           d. *La Bohème*

    Ans. a
    p. 232

175. Puccini's operas have lasting appeal because
    a. he had a marvelous sense of theater
    b. his melodies have short, memorable phrases and are intensely emotional
    c. he minimized the difference between aria and recitative, thus creating
       a continuous flow of music
    d. all of the above

    Ans. d
    p. 232
    SG

176. Puccini, in his operas,
    a. achieved unity and continuity by using the same material in different acts
    b. used the orchestra to reinforce the vocal melody and to suggest mood
    c. composed melodies that have short memorable phrases and are intensely emotional
    d. all of the above

    Ans. d
    p. 232

177. An artistic trend of the 1890s, in which operas dealt with ordinary people
and true-to-life situations, was known as
    a. *opera seria*              c. exoticism
    b. *Cavalleria rusticana*      d. *verismo*

    Ans. d
    p. 232
    SG

178. The movement in opera known as *verismo* is best exemplified by
    a. Claudio Monteverdi       c. Giacomo Puccini
    b. Wolfgang Amadeus Mozart    d. Richard Wagner

    Ans. c
    p. 232

179. Which of the following operas is considered an example of *verismo*?
    a. *Turandot*              c. *Nabucco*
    b. *Tosca*                 d. *Die Walküre*

    Ans. b
    p. 232
    SG

180. Some of Puccini's operas feature exoticism, as in his use of melodic and
rhythmic elements derived from Japanese and Chinese music in his operas
    a. *Turandot* and *Manon Lescaut*    c. *Madame Butterfly* and *Turandot*
    b. *La Bohème* and *Madame Butterfly*    d. *Tosca* and *Turandot*

    Ans. c
    p. 232

181. Puccini used melodic and rhythmic elements derived from Asian music
in his operas
    a. *Turandot* and *Manon Lescaut*    c. *Tosca* and *Turandot*
    b. *Madame Butterfly* and *Turandot*    d. *La Bohème* and *Madame Butterfly*

    Ans. b
    p. 232
    SG

182. Which of the following statements is *not* true?
    a. Puccini achieved unity and continuity in his operas by using the same material in different acts.
    b. After 1896, Puccini was wealthy and world-famous from the enormous success of *La Bohème*, which portrays a "bohemian" life similar to his own as an impoverished music student.
    c. Puccini composed long highly ornamented melodies that are difficult to remember and perform well.
    d. As Verdi did in his late works, Puccini minimized the difference between aria and recitative, thus creating a continuous flow of music.

Ans. c
p. 232

183. *La Bohème* takes place in
    a. Seville
    b. Milan
    c. Rome
    d. Paris

Ans. d
p. 233
SG

184. In *La Bohème*, Rodolfo is a young
    a. painter
    b. poet
    c. philosopher
    d. musician

Ans. b
p. 233
SG

185. Mimi and Rodolfo meet for the first time in *La Bohème* because she has come to his door to ask for a
    a. light for her candle
    b. drink of wine
    c. dinner date
    d. cup of sugar

Ans. a
p. 233
SG

186. In *La Bohème*, who sings the aria *Che gelida manina (What a cold little hand)*?
    a. Mimi
    b. Schaunard
    c. Rodolfo
    d. Marcello

Ans. c
p. 238
SG

187. Wagner's preeminence was such that an opera house of his own design was built in _____, solely for performances of his music dramas.
    a. Paris, France
    b. Geneva, Switzerland
    c. Leipzig, Germany
    d. Bayreuth, Bavaria

Ans. d
p. 240

188. Wagner had an opera house built to his own specifications in
    a. Munich
    b. Weimar
    c. Dresden
    d. Bayreuth

Ans. d
p. 240
SG

189. Which of the following statements is *not* true?
    a. As a young man, Wagner spent many years studying music theory and developing a virtuosic piano technique.
    b. During the last decades of the nineteenth century, Wagner's operas and artistic philosophy influenced not only musicians, but poets, painters, and playwrights as well.
    c. Wagner revolutionized opera by shifting the focus from the voice to the orchestra and treating the orchestra symphonically.
    d. Wagner used leitmotifs, or short musical ideas associated with a person, object, or thought, to unify his greatly extended music dramas.

Ans. a
p. 240

190. The composer who had an overwhelming influence on the young Wagner was
    a. Johann Sebastian Bach         c. Johannes Brahms
    b. Ludwig van Beethoven       d. Hector Berlioz

Ans. b
p. 240
SG

191. When he was fifteen, Wagner was overwhelmed by the power
of the music of
    a. Franz Liszt               c. Robert Schumann
    b. Ludwig van Beethoven       d. Giuseppe Verdi

Ans. b
p. 240

192. Wagner was appointed conductor of the Dresden opera
mainly because of the success of his first opera
    a. *The Ring of the Nibelung*     c. *Parsifal*
    b. *Götterdämmerung*         d. *Rienzi*

Ans. d
p. 241

193. Wagner's first successful opera was
    a. *Tannhäuser*           c. *The Twilight of the Gods*
    b. *Rienzi*              d. *Die Walküre*

Ans. b
p. 241
SG

194. Which of the following operas was *not* composed by Wagner?
    a. *Tannhäuser*           c. *Fidelio*
    b. *Tristan and Isolde*        d. *Parsifal*

Ans. c
p. 241
SG

195. The librettos to *The Ring of the Nibelung* were written by
    a. Arrigo Boito           c. King Ludwig of Bavaria
    b. Wagner himself        d. Hans von Bülow

Ans. b
p. 241
SG

196. Wagner's last opera was
    a. *Götterdämmerung (The Twilight of the Gods)*   c. *Rienzi*
    b. *Tannhäuser*           d. *Parsifal*

Ans. d
p. 241
SG

197. Wagner called his works *music dramas* rather than operas because
    a. there is a continuous musical flow within each act
    b. there are no breaks where applause can interrupt
    c. the vocal line is inspired by the rhythms and pitches of the German text
    d. all of the above

Ans. d
p. 242
SG

198. A short musical idea associated with a person, object, or thought, used by
Wagner in his operas, is called
    a. leitmotif            c. unending melody
    b. lied               d. speech-song

Ans. a
p. 242
SG

199. Wagner spins an orchestral web out of recurrent musical themes called
    a. *Sprechstimme*        c. speech-songs
    b. leitmotifs           d. melodies

Ans. b
p. 242

200. Valhalla, in Wagner's *Ring* cycle, is
    a. a city in New York State     c. the home of Siegfried
    b. the castle of the gods      d. the magic ring

Ans. b
p. 242
SG

201. Siegmund, in Wagner's opera *Die Walküre*, is                                Ans. d
  a. Sieglinde's brother, then wife        c. Siegfried's father                 p. 243
  b. Wotan's son by a mortal woman         d. all of the above                   SG

202. Which of the following statements concerning Wagner's *Ring* cycle is *not* true?   Ans. d
  a. Valhalla is the castle of the gods.                                         p. 243
  b. Siegmund is Sieglinde's brother and husband.
  c. Wotan, the king of the gods, stole the ring from the dwarf Alberich.
  d. Sieglinde is a Valkyrie, one of the daughters of Wotan.

# VI. THE TWENTIETH CENTURY

1. In music, the early twentieth century was a time of
   a. revolt and change
   b. the continuation of old forms
   c. stagnation
   d. disinterest

   Ans. a
   p. 250

2. Which of the following statements is *not* true?
   a. The years following 1900 saw more fundamental changes in the language of music than any time since the beginning of the baroque era.
   b. Twentieth-century music follows the same general principles of musical structure as earlier periods.
   c. Twentieth-century music relies less on preestablished relationships and expectations.
   d. After 1900 each musical composition is more likely to have a unique system of pitch relationships, rather than be organized around a central tone.

   Ans. b
   p. 250

3. The most famous riot in music history occurred in Paris in 1913 at the first performance of
   a. Arnold Schoenberg's *Gurrelieder*
   b. Igor Stravinsky's *The Rite of Spring*
   c. Richard Wagner's *Siegfried*
   d. Igor Stravinsky's *Les Noces*

   Ans. b
   p. 250

4. All of the following composers worked in the early years of the twentieth century *except*
   a. Claude Debussy
   b. Arnold Schoenberg
   c. Igor Stravinsky
   d. Hector Berlioz

   Ans. d
   p. 252

5. Composers in the twentieth century drew inspiration from
   a. folk and popular music from all cultures
   b. the music of Asia and Africa
   c. European art music from the Middle Ages through the nineteenth century
   d. all of the above

   Ans. d
   p. 252
   SG

6. Twentieth-century composers incorporated elements of folk and popular music within their personal styles because
   a. it made their music more commercially viable
   b. they were attracted to the unconventional rhythms, sounds, and melodic patterns
   c. it simplified technical problems of musical composition
   d. all of the above

   Ans. b
   p. 252

7. A great twentieth-century composer who was also a leading scholar of the folk music of his native land was
   a. Claude Debussy
   b. Samuel Barber
   c. Béla Bartók
   d. Igor Stravinsky

   Ans. c
   p. 252

8. Which of the following was *not* stimulated by the folklore of his native land?
   a. Igor Stravinsky
   b. Anton Webern
   c. Béla Bartók
   d. Charles Ives

   Ans. b
   p. 252
   SG

9. Which of the following statements is *not* true?                                    Ans. c
   a. Modern composers drew inspiration from a wider historical range of music.        p. 252
   b. The range of musical styles during the first half of the twentieth century was vast.
   c. Composers in the early twentieth century drew inspiration only from serious
      art music and their own intellect, ignoring popular and folk music.
   d. Western composers were more receptive and sympathetic to Asian and African cultures.

10. All of the following twentieth-century composers were                             Ans. c
    stimulated by the folklore of their native country *except*                       p. 252
    a. Charles Ives                           c. Arnold Schoenberg
    b. Igor Stravinsky                        d. Béla Bartók

11. American jazz, with its syncopated rhythms and                                    Ans. d
    improvisational quality, had an influence on                                       p. 252
    a. the French composer Claude Debussy
    b. the Russian composer Igor Stravinsky
    c. the American composers Aaron Copland and George Gershwin
    d. all of the above

12. Which of the following statements is *not* true?                                   Ans. b
    a. New technological advances, such as phonograph records, tape recordings,        p. 253
       radio, and television, have brought music to a larger audience than ever before,
       besides vastly increasing the amount and scope of music available.
    b. Audiences in the first half of the twentieth century, as in Mozart's time, demanded
       and got the latest music, and concert programs consisted mainly of recent works.
    c. Wagner was a potent influence on modern composers who used him as a point of
       departure or reacted violently against his style.
    d. Twentieth-century composers use baroque dances and forms like the passacaglia
       and concerto grosso.

13. In twentieth-century music                                                        Ans. d
    a. string players are sometimes called upon to use the wood instead of the         p. 254
       hair on their bows                                                              SG
    b. percussion instruments have become very prominent and numerous
    c. dissonance has been emancipated
    d. all of the above

14. The glissando, a technique widely used in the twentieth century, is               Ans. b
    a. the combination of two traditional chords sounding together                     p. 254
    b. a rapid slide up or down a scale
    c. a motive or phrase that is repeated persistently at the same pitch throughout a section
    d. a chord made up of tones only a half step or a whole step apart

15. In modern music                                                                   Ans. d
    a. instruments are played at the very top or bottom of their ranges                p. 254
    b. uncommon playing techniques have become normal
    c. noiselike and percussive sounds are often used
    d. all of the above

16. Among the unusual playing techniques that are widely used during the twentieth     Ans. b
century is the _____, a rapid slide up or down a scale.                            p. 254
   a. buzz                 b. glissando              c. slip              d. ostinato    SG

17. A piano is often used in twentieth-century orchestral music to                     Ans. d
   a. "sing" a beautiful melody                                                          p. 254
   b. play important cadenzas in slow movements
   c. provide a nucleus for the orchestra similar to the baroque basso continuo
   d. add a percussive edge

18. Which of the following statements is *not* true?                                   Ans. c
   a. The "emancipation of the dissonance" does not prevent composers from              p. 255
      differentiating between chords of greater or lesser tension.
   b. By the early twentieth century, the traditional distinction between consonance
      and dissonance was abandoned in much music.
   c. The general principle that determines whether a chord is stable or not remains the
      same in the twentieth century as it did in the nineteenth.
   d. Up to about 1900, all chords except the three-tone triad were considered dissonant.

19. Which of the following is *not* an alternative to the traditional organization      Ans. b
   of pitch used by twentieth-century composers?                                        p. 256
   a. bitonality                           c. atonality
   b. tone clusters                        d. polytanlity

20. The combination of two traditional chords sounding together is known as            Ans. d
   a. polytonality                         c. a tone cluster                            p. 256
   b. bitonality                           d. a polychord                                SG

21. A fourth chord is                                                                   Ans. c
   a. a combination of four tones                                                       p. 256
   b. the chord built on the fourth step of the scale
   c. a chord in which the tones are a fourth apart, instead of a third
   d. all of the above

22. A chord made of tones only a half step or a whole step apart is known as           Ans. d
   a. polytonality                         c. bitonality                                p. 256
   b. a polychord                          d. a tone cluster                             SG

23. Striking a group of adjacent keys on a piano with the                              Ans. a
   fist or forearm will result in                                                       p. 256
   a. a tone cluster                       c. a polychord
   b. a broken piano keyboard              d. polytonality

24. The technique of using two or more tonal centers at the same time is called        Ans. b
   a. expanded tonality                    c. atonality                                 p. 257
   b. polytonality                         d. twelve-tone

25. The use of two or more keys at one time is known as
   a. polytonality
   b. a tone cluster
   c. atonality
   d. the twelve-tone system

Ans. a
p. 257
SG

26. To create fresh sounds, twentieth-century composers used
   a. scales borrowed from nonwestern cultures
   b. scales they themselves invented
   c. ancient church modes
   d. all of the above

Ans. d
p. 257
SG

27. The absence of key or tonality in a musical composition is known as
   a. polytonality
   b. ostinato
   c. a tone cluster
   d. atonality

Ans. d
p. 257
SG

28. The complete rejection of a tonal center, or treating each of the twelve tones equally, is called
   a. expanded tonality
   b. polytonality
   c. atonality
   d. modality

Ans. c
p. 257

29. The purposeful avoidance of any tonal relationship is called
   a. modality   b. transposition   c. atonality   d. tonality

Ans. c
p. 257

30. Using all twelve tones without regard to their traditional relationship to major or minor scales, avoiding traditional chord progressions, is known as
   a. polytonality   b. bitonality   c. freetonality   d. atonality

Ans. d
p. 257

31. The first significant atonal pieces were composed around 1908 by
   a. Igor Stravinsky
   b. Claude Debussy
   c. Arnold Schoenberg
   d. Aaron Copland

Ans. c
p. 257

32. Which of the following statements is *not* true?
   a. In the twentieth century, new rhythmic procedures are drawn from many sources, including folk music from all over the world, jazz, and European art music from the Middle Ages through the nineteenth century.
   b. The rhythmic resources of twentieth-century music have been expanded through the use of unconventional meters.
   c. Twentieth-century composers depended on predictable rhythmic patterns.
   d. Twentieth-century music often uses two or more contrasting and independent rhythms at the same time.

Ans. c
p. 258

33. The use of two or more contrasting and independent rhythms at the same time is known as
   a. polyrhythm   b. jazz   c. polytonality   d. ostinato

Ans. a
p. 259

34. *Ostinato* refers to a
   a. rapid slide through different pitches
   b. chord made of tones only a half step or whole step apart
   c. combination of two traditional chords sounding together
   d. motive or phrase that is repeated persistently at the same pitch throughout a section

Ans. d
p. 259

35. A motive or phrase that is repeated persistently at the same pitch throughout a section is called
   a. polytonality         b. glissando          c. ostinato          d. atonality

Ans. c
p. 259
SG

36. Impressionism as a movement originated in
   a. France                               c. Germany
   b. Italy                                d. England

Ans. a
p. 260
SG

37. Impressionist painting and symbolist poetry as artistic movements originated in
   a. Bohemia         b. Austria          c. France          d. Spain

Ans. b
p. 260

38. The most important impressionist composer was
   a. Richard Wagner                       c. Arnold Schoenberg
   b. Béla Bartók                          d. Claude Debussy

Ans. d
p. 260

39. The term *impressionist* derived from a critic's derogatory reaction to *Impression: Sunrise*, a painting by
   a. Claude Debussy                       c. Claude Monet
   b. Camille Pissarro                     d. Auguste Renoir

Ans. c
p. 261

40. The term *impressionist* derived from a French critic's derogative reaction to Claude Monet's painting
   a. *Impression: Sunrise*                c. *Rouen Cathedral*
   b. *Vetheuil in Summer*                 d. *La Grenouillère*

Ans. a
p. 261

41. When viewed closely, impressionist paintings are made up of
   a. fine lines                           c. tiny black dots
   b. large bands of color                 d. tiny colored patches

Ans. d
p. 261
SG

42. Impressionist painters were primarily concerned with the effect of light, color, and
   a. rhythm          b. atmosphere          c. detail          d. clarity

Ans. b
p. 261

43. The impressionist painters were particularly obsessed with portraying
   a. water                                c. scenes of ancient glories
   b. religious scenes                     d. battle scenes

Ans. a
p. 261
SG

44. Which of the following is *not* considered a symbolist poet?
   a. Stéphane Mallarmé                     c. Victor Hugo
   b. Paul Verlaine                        d. Arthur Rimbaud

Ans. c
p. 261
SG

45. Which of the following statements is *not* true?
   a. Both impressionist painting and symbolist poetry were catalysts for many developments during the twentieth century.
   b. Symbolist writers emphasized the purely musical, or sonorous, effects of words.
   c. When viewed closely, impressionist paintings are made up of tiny colored patches.
   d. The impressionist painters were particularly obsessed with portraying scenes of ancient French glories.

Ans. d
p. 261

46. Many of Debussy's songs are set to poems by the symbolist poet                Ans. b
    a. Stéphane Mallarmé                    c. Jean Paul Sartre                    p. 261
    b. Paul Verlaine                        d. Arthur Rimbaud

47. Debussy's most famous orchestral work was inspired by a poem by              Ans. a
    a. Stéphane Mallarmé                    c. Jean-Paul Sartre                    p. 261
    b. Paul Verlaine                        d. Arthur Rimbaud                      SG

48. As a result of his summer sojourns away from France during his teens, Debussy   Ans. d
    developed a lifelong interest in the music of                                 p. 261
    a. Italy                               c. England                             SG
    b. Hungary                             d. Russia

49. Having the opportunity of working away from France as a pianist while still in his   Ans. b
    teens, Debussy developed a lifelong interest in the music of                  p. 261
    a. Germany          b. Russia          c. Norway          d. Sweden

50. At the Paris International Exhibition of 1889 Debussy was strongly influenced by   Ans. d
    a. the advantages of modern technology    c. the Eiffel Tower                 p. 261
    b. performances of the music of Bach      d. performances of Asian music      SG

51. Which of the following statements is *not* true?                              Ans. a
    a. Debussy was greatly inspired by his three years of study in Italy, made possible   p. 261
       by his winning the Prix de Rome in 1884.
    b. Debussy was both attracted to and repelled by the music of Richard Wagner.
    c. Debussy's treatment of harmony was revolutionary in that he tends to use a chord
       more for its special color and sensuous quality than for its function in a standard
       harmonic progression.
    d. Literary and pictorial ideas often inspired Debussy, and most of his compositions
       have descriptive titles.

52. A dramatic turning point in Debussy's career came in 1902 when                Ans. a
    a. his opera *Pelléas et Mélisande* was premiered                             p. 262
    b. he undertook a series of concert tours
    c. he went to Italy to study
    d. he went to Bayreuth to hear Wagner's music

53. Which of the following characteristics is *not* usually associated with impressionism?   Ans. b
    a. fleeting mood                       c. misty atmosphere                    p. 262
    b. clearly delineated forms            d. symbolism

54. A five-tone scale, such as that produced by the five black keys of the piano in   Ans. a
    succession, is called a _____ scale.                               p. 263
    a. pentatonic          b. hexatonic          c. whole-tone          d. pentagon

55. A scale made up of six different notes each a whole step                      Ans. c
    away from the next is called a _____ scale.                                p. 263
    a. pentatonic          b. octatonic          c. whole-tone          d. Gypsy

56. There are _____ different tones in the whole-tone scale.

    a. five                     b. six                     c. eight                     d. ten

Ans. b
p. 263

57. Debussy's music tends to

    a. sound free and spontaneous, almost improvised

    b. have a strong sense of tonality

    c. have a strong rhythmic pulse

    d. use the orchestra for massive effects

Ans. a
p. 263
SG

58. Impressionism in music is characterized by

    a. the recurrence of strong accents on the downbeat

    b. a stress on tone color, atmosphere, and fluidity

    c. an adherence to traditional harmonic chord progressions

    d. all of the above

Ans. b
p. 263

59. Which of the following techniques did Debussy *not* use to weaken the grip of major-minor tonality?

    a. pentatonic scale       b. twelve-tone scale       c. whole-tone scale       d. modality

Ans. c
p. 263

60. In order to "drown the sense of tonality," Debussy

    a. turned to the medieval church modes

    b. borrowed pentatonic scales from Javanese music

    c. developed the whole-tone scale

    d. all of the above

Ans. d
p. 263
SG

61. Debussy's opera *Pelléas et Mélisande* is an almost word-for-word setting of the symbolist play by

    a. Paul Verlaine                     c. Maurice Maeterlinck

    b. Arthur Rimbaud                 d. Stéphane Mallarmé

Ans. c
p. 264
SG

62. In which of the following areas did Debussy *not* create masterpieces?

    a. symphonies                     c. chamber music

    b. art songs                       d. piano music

Ans. a
p. 264
SG

63. The poem that inspired the *Prelude to "The Afternoon of a Faun"* was written by

    a. Paul Verlaine                     c. Maurice Maeterlinck

    b. Arthur Rimbaud                 d. Stéphane Mallarmé

Ans. d
p. 264
SG

64. The faun evoked in Debussy's famous composition is a

    a. baby deer                       c. beautiful young maiden

    b. creature who is half man, half goat     d. sensitive musician

Ans. b
p. 264
SG

65. The neoclassical movement in music roughly encompassed the years

    a. 1890-1915             b. 1900-1920           c. 1920-1950          d. 1945-1970

Ans. c
p. 266

66. Neoclassical composers favored

    a. unusual and exotic scales             c. programmatic music

    b. clear polyphonic textures          d. homophonic textures

Ans. b
p. 266

67. Favoring clear polyphonic textures, neoclassical composers wrote
 a. fugues
 b. baroque dance suites
 c. concerti grossi
 d. all of the above

Ans. d
p. 266
SG

68. Neoclassical compositions are characterized by
 a. forms and stylistic features of earlier periods
 b. whole-tone scales
 c. harsh dissonances
 d. the use of the twelve-tone system

Ans. a
p. 266
SG

69. Which of the following is *not* characteristic of neoclassicism?
 a. emotional restraint
 b. clarity
 c. misty atmosphere
 d. balance

Ans. c
p. 266
SG

70. Neoclassical composers modeled many of their works after the compositions of
 a. Richard Wagner
 b. Guillaume de Machaut
 c. Johann Sebastian Bach
 d. Franz Liszt

Ans. c
p. 266

71. Neoclassicism was a reaction against
 a. romanticism and impressionism
 b. humanism
 c. classicism
 d. traditional forms

Ans. a
p. 266
SG

72. Which of the following statements concerning neoclassicism is *not* true?
 a. Neoclassical composers reacted against twentieth-century harmonies and rhythms, and preferred to revive old forms and styles exactly as they were.
 b. Neoclassical compositions use the musical forms and stylistic features of earlier periods, particularly of the eighteenth century.
 c. Since many neoclassical compositions were modeled after Bach's music, the term *neobaroque* might have been more appropriate.
 d. Neoclassicism was an important trend in other art forms such as painting and poetry.

Ans. a
p. 267

73. Neoclassical composers favored
 a. tonality
 b. atonality
 c. program music
 d. large orchestras

Ans. a
p. 267
SG

74. A painter who went through a neoclassical phase, and who designed sets for Stravinsky's first neoclassical work, was
 a. Claude Monet
 b. Pablo Picasso
 c. Auguste Renoir
 d. Wassily Kandinsky

Ans. b
p. 267
SG

75. The painter who designed the sets for Stravinsky's *Pulcinella*, and who went through a phase that showed the influence of ancient Greek art, was
 a. Pablo Picasso
 b. Henri Matisse
 c. Wassily Kandinsky
 d. Ernst Kirchner

Ans. a
p. 267

76. Stravinsky's composition teacher was
 a. Sergei Diaghilev
 b. Modest Mussorgsky
 c. Nikolai Rimsky-Korsakov
 d. Claude Debussy

Ans. c
p. 267
SG

77. Stravinsky's life took a sudden turn in 1909, when he met the director of the Russian Ballet,
    a. Michel Fokine
    b. Sergei Diaghilev
    c. Vaclav Nijinsky
    d. George Balanchine

    Ans. b
    p. 267

78. Sergei Diaghilev was a famous
    a. writer    b. composer    c. ballet impresario    d. pianist

    Ans. c
    p. 267

79. Sergei Diaghilev was the director of the
    a. Moscow Conservatory
    b. Leningrad Philharmonic
    c. Russian Ballet
    d. Orchestre de Paris

    Ans. c
    p. 267
    SG

80. The immense success of Stravinsky's 1910 ballet _____ established him as a leading young composer.
    a. *The Firebird*    b. *The Rite of Spring*    c. *Petrushka*    d. *Pulcinella*

    Ans. a
    p. 267

81. The famous riot in 1913 was caused by the first performance of Stravinsky's ballet
    a. *Pulcinella*
    b. *The Fairy's Kiss*
    c. *Agon*
    d. *The Rite of Spring*

    Ans. d
    p. 267
    SG

82. The legendary riot that erupted in the audience in Paris in 1913 occurred at the first performance of Stravinsky's ballet
    a. *Pulcinella*    b. *The Firebird*    c. *The Rite of Spring*    d. *Petrushka*

    Ans. c
    p. 267

83. Stravinsky's enormous influence on twentieth-century music is due to his innovations in
    a. rhythm
    b. harmony
    c. tone color
    d. all of the above

    Ans. d
    p. 268
    SG

84. Which of the following ballets is *not* from Stravinsky's Russian period?
    a. *The Rite of Spring*
    b. *The Firebird*
    c. *Pulcinella*
    d. *Petrushka*

    Ans. c
    p. 268
    SG

85. Stravinsky's second phase is generally known as
    a. neoclassical
    b. primitive
    c. serial
    d. postromantic

    Ans. a
    p. 268
    SG

86. During the period 1920 to 1951 Stravinsky drew inspiration largely from
    a. eighteenth-century music
    b. Webern's serial techniques
    c. Russian folklore
    d. African sculpture

    Ans. a
    p. 268
    SG

87. In the 1950s Stravinsky dramatically changed his style, drawing inspiration from
    a. Claude Debussy
    b. Richard Wagner
    c. Anton Webern
    d. Russian folk music

    Ans. c
    p. 269
    SG

88. In the 1950s Stravinsky dramatically changed his style to favor
    a. the twelve-tone system
    b. neoclassicism
    c. primitivism
    d. jazz

    Ans. a
    p. 269

89. Which of the following statements is *not* true?    Ans. a
    a. Stravinsky's ballet *The Rite of Spring* may be considered an example    p. 269
       of his neoclassical style.
    b. Stravinsky's early ballets, *Firebird*, *Petrushka*, and *The Rite of Spring*, call for very
       large orchestras and draw on Russian folklore and folk tunes.
    c. Stravinsky drew on a vast range of styles, from Russian folk songs to baroque
       melodies, from Renaissance madrigals to tango rhythms, to create original music.
    d. Stravinsky's extensive output includes compositions of almost every kind,
       for voices, instruments, and the stage.

90. The deliberate evocation of primitive power through    Ans. d
    insistent rhythms and percussive sounds is known as    p. 269
    a. ostinato          b. Africanism          c. barbarism          d. primitivism

91. *Le Sacre du printemps (The Rite of Spring)* is an example of    Ans. b
    a. neoclassicism                    c. serialism    p. 269
    b. primitivism                      d. romanticism    SG

92. Stravinsky's *Rite of Spring* is scored for    Ans. c
    a. a small chamber group            c. an enormous orchestra    p. 270
    b. vocal soloists and orchestra     d. a wind ensemble    SG

93. The expressionist movement flourished in the years    Ans. b
    a. 1890-1914                        c. 1914-1941    p. 275
    b. 1905-1925                        d. 1920-1950    SG

94. The twentieth-century artistic movement that stressed    Ans. c
    intense, subjective emotion was called    p. 275
    a. impressionism     b. primitivism     c. expressionism     d. neoclassicism

95. Expressionism stressed    Ans. b
    a. subtle feeling                   c. reticence    p. 275
    b. intense subjective emotion       d. surface beauty    SG

96. The expressionist movement was largely centered in    Ans. c
    a. France                           c. Germany and Austria    p. 275
    b. Great Britain                    d. Russia    SG

97. Twentieth-century musical expressionism grew out of the emotional    Ans. d
    turbulence in the works of late romantics such as    p. 275
    a. Richard Wagner                   c. Gustav Mahler    SG
    b. Richard Strauss                  d. all of the above

98. Expressionist painters, writers, and composers used _____ to assault    Ans. b
    and shock their audience.    p. 275
    a. pastel colors                    c. clearly defined forms    SG
    b. deliberate distortions           d. vague nature scenes

99. Distortion is a technique used primarily in the _____ period.          Ans. c
   a. impressionist                      c. expressionist                      p. 275
   b. classical                          d. romantic

100. Which of the following statements is *not* true?                          Ans. b
   a. Twentieth-century musical expressionism grows out of the emotional turbulence    p. 275
      in the works of late romantics like Wagner, Richard Strauss, and Gustav Mahler.
   b. Expressionist artists favored pleasant subjects, delicate pastel colors,
      and shimmering surfaces.
   c. A stress on harsh dissonance, an exploitation of extreme registers, fragmentation, and
      unusual instrumental effects are all characteristics of expressionistic compositions.
   d. Expressionist painters reacted against French impressionism; they often used
      jarring colors and grotesquely distorted shapes to explore the subconscious.

101. Expressionism is an art concerned with                                    Ans. c
   a. depicting the beauties of nature    c. social protest                    p. 275
   b. emotional restraint, clarity, and balance    d. all of the above         SG

102. The expressionists rejected                                               Ans. a
   a. conventional prettiness            c. imagination                        p. 275
   b. reality                            d. morality                           SG

103. All of the following painters may be considered part of                   Ans. a
   the expressionist movement *except*                                         p. 275
   a. Claude Monet                       c. Oskar Kokoschka
   b. Ernst Ludwig Kirchner              d. Edvard Munch

104. Edvard Munch was an expressionist                                         Ans. b
   a. poet                               c. musician                           p. 275
   b. painter                            d. playwright                         SG

105. Expressionist music stresses                                              Ans. d
   a. harsh dissonance                   c. unusual instrumental effects       p. 275
   b. fragmentation                      d. all of the above                   SG

106. Expressionist composers                                                   Ans. b
   a. contributed many patriotic songs to the war effort                       p. 275
   b. avoided tonality and traditional chord progressions                      SG
   c. tried to capture atmosphere with rich, sensuous harmonies and pleasant subjects
   d. all of the above

107. In addition to being a composer, Schoenberg showed skill as a             Ans. b
   a. chemist                            c. music critic                       p. 275
   b. painter                            d. economist                          SG

108. Schoenberg's teacher was                                                  Ans. d
   a. Johannes Brahms                    c. Nikolai Rimsky-Korsakov            p. 275
   b. Richard Wagner                     d. himself                            SG

109. Schoenberg acquired his profound knowledge of music by                         Ans. d
   a. going to concerts                          c. studying scores                        p. 275
   b. playing in amateur chamber groups          d. all of the above

110. Alban Berg and Anton Webern were Schoenberg's                                  Ans. b
   a. teachers                                   c. predecessors                           p. 275
   b. students                                   d. jealous rivals                         SG

111. Schoenberg's personality inspired love and loyalty among                       Ans. b
   his students, including Alban Berg and                                           p. 275
   a. Igor Stravinsky                            c. Gustav Mahler
   b. Anton Webern                               d. Béla Bartók

112. Which of the following statements is *not* true?                               Ans. a
   a. Because of the hostility of the conservative Viennese public, Schoenberg      p. 275
      abandoned musical composition in 1908 and turned instead to painting.
   b. In Schoenberg's atonal music from 1908 to 1914, all twelve tones are used without
      regard for their traditonal relationship to major and minor scales.
   c. Schoenberg developed a more systematic method of organizing atonal music in the
      early 1920s, a system he called the "method of composing with twelve tones."
   d. Schoenberg's Five Pieces for Orchestra, Op. 16, illustrate his concept of tone-color
      melody, or succession of varying tone colors used as a musical idea in a composition.

113. Schoenberg's third period, in which he developed the twelve-tone system,       Ans. c
   began around                                                                     p. 277
   a. 1874            b. 1908            c. 1921            d. 1933                   SG

114. Because of the Nazis seizing power in Germany, Schoenberg                      Ans. d
   a. returned to Judaism                                                           p. 277
   b. emigrated to the United States
   c. was dismissed from the faculty of the Prussian Academy of Arts
   d. all of the above

115. When Schoenberg arrived in the United States after the Nazis seized power      Ans. c
   in Germany, he obtained a teaching position at                                   p. 277
   a. Harvard         b. Yale            c. UCLA            d. Columbia              SG

116. An eerily expressive kind of declamation midway between song and speech,       Ans. d
   introduced during the expressionist period, is                                   p. 278
   a. *Pierrot Lunaire*                          c. a cappella
   b. *stile rappresentativo*                    d. *Sprechstimme*

117. Which of the following statements is *not* true of Schoenberg's twelve-tone    Ans. b
   method of composition?                                                           p. 278
   a. The tones of a row may be presented at the same time to form chords.          SG
   b. Each tone of a row must be placed in the same register.
   c. The tones of a row may be placed one after another to form a melody.
   d. A tone row may be shifted to any pitch level.

118. Schoenberg developed an unusual style of vocal performance, halfway between speaking and singing, called
   a. *Klangfarbenmelodie*    b. *Sprechstimme*    c. atonality    d. serialism

Ans. b
p. 278
SG

119. The ordering of the twelve chromatic tones in a twelve-tone composition is called a
   a. series
   b. tone row
   c. set
   d. all of the above

Ans. d
p. 278

120. Which of the following terms is *not* used to describe the special ordering of the twelve chromatic tones in twelve-tone composition?
   a. polychord    b. set    c. tone row    d. series

Ans. a
p. 278
SG

121. A succession of varying tone colors used as a musical idea in a composition, used by Schoenberg in his atonal compositions, is known as
   a. *Klangfarbenmelodie*
   b. tone row
   c. *Sprechstimme*
   d. *schöne melodie*

Ans. a
p. 280

122. The text of *A Survivor from Warsaw*
   a. was written by Schoenberg
   b. is partly based on a direct report of a survivor of the Warsaw ghetto
   c. is set to a kind of speech-singing
   d. all of the above

Ans. d
p. 281
SG

123. *A Survivor from Warsaw* used three languages: English, German, and
   a. Italian
   b. French
   c. Hebrew
   d. Russian

Ans. c
p. 281
SG

124. Which of the following statements regarding Berg is untrue?
   a. He composed a great quantity of music in all forms.
   b. He synthesized traditional and twentieth-century elements.
   c. As in the music dramas of Wagner, there is a continuous musical flow within each act of his opera *Wozzeck*.
   d. He first attracted international attention with his opera *Wozzeck*.

Ans. a
p. 284
SG

125. When he was nineteen, Alban Berg began to study music privately with
   a. Anton Webern
   b. Igor Stravinsky
   c. Paul Hindemith
   d. Arnold Schoenberg

Ans. d
p. 284

126. Which of the following statements is *not* true?
   a. Typical of expressionist composers, Berg scored his opera *Wozzeck* for a small chamber orchestra.
   b. The vocal line in Berg's opera *Wozzeck* includes speaking, shrieking, *Sprechstimme*, distorted folk songs, and melodies with wide leaps that are difficult to sing.
   c. Though written in the early 1830s, Georg Büchner's play *Woyzeck* is amazingly modern in its starkly realistic dialogue and disconnected scenes.
   d. A novel feature of Berg's opera *Wozzeck* is that the music for each scene is a self-contained composition with a particular form or of a definite type.

Ans. a
p. 284

127. Which of the following is *not* a composition by Alban Berg?
   a. *Gurrelieder*                       c. *Lyric Suite*
   b. *Lulu*                              d. *Wozzeck*

Ans. a
p. 284

128. Georg Büchner's play *Woyzeck* was written in the
   a. 1830s                              c. 1920s
   b. 1890s                              d. 1940s

Ans. a
p. 284
SG

129. The vocal lines in *Wozzeck* include
   a. distorted folk songs               c. *Sprechstimme*
   b. speaking                           d. all of the above

Ans. d
p. 284
SG

130. Which musical form provides the basis for the last act of *Wozzeck*?
   a. variations                         c. passacaglia
   b. military march                     d. lullaby

Ans. a
p. 285
SG

131. Webern
   a. had little formal musical training
   b. taught himself piano and cello
   c. earned a doctorate in music history from the University of Vienna
   d. enjoyed frequent performances of his own music

Ans. c
p. 289
SG

132. The most important elements in Webern's music are
   texture, tone color, and
   a. tempo          b. rhythm          c. harmony          d. dynamics

Ans. d
p. 289

133. The least important element in Webern's music is
   a. texture                            c. dynamic level
   b. tone color                         d. tonality

Ans. d
p. 289
SG

134.. Webern's twelve-tone works contain many examples of
   a. long singing melodies              c. strict polyphonic  imitation
   b. melodic and harmonic repetition    d. homophonic texture

Ans. c
p. 289
SG

135.. Which of the following statements is *not* true?
   a. Composers in the 1950s and 1960s were fascinated by Webern's use of texture,
      tone color, dynamics, and register as unifying elements, and often imitated his
      deceptively "cool" sound.
   b. While very popular in his own lifetime, Webern's music has been neglected and
      forgotten since his death in 1945.
   c. The texture of Webern's music is delicate and transparent.
   d. Webern's twelve-tone works often contain strict polyphonic imitation.

Ans. b
p. 289

136. Webern's melodic lines are
   a. "atomized" into two- or three-note fragments
   b. reinforced by frequent tutti unison passages
   c. folklike, with narrow ranges and frequent repetitions
   d. basically in major and minor keys

Ans. a
p. 289
SG

137. Webern's Five Pieces for Orchestra are scored for    Ans. a
    a. a chamber orchestra of eighteen soloists    c. mandolin, harmonium, and strings    p. 290
    b. solo voice, chorus, and orchestra    d. the traditional large romantic orchestra    SG

138. Which of the following statements is *not* true?    Ans. d
    a. Like Stravinsky, Hindemith, and Schoenberg, Bartók emigrated to the United    p. 291
       States as a result of the rise of Nazism in Europe.
    b. During the early 1900s, Bartók spent most of his free time in tiny Hungarian
       villages recording folk music on a cylinder phonograph.
    c. The Concerto for Orchestra, Bartók's most popular work, is so named because it
       treats the individual orchestral instruments in a soloistic manner.
    d. Bartók arranged many Hungarian and Rumanian folk tunes, and quoted many
       folk melodies in his original works.

139. Bartók's principal performing medium was    Ans. b
    a. conducting    c. violin    p. 291
    b. piano    d. flute    SG

140. From 1907 to 1934 Bartók taught _____ at his alma mater,    Ans. a
    and gave recitals throughout Europe.    p. 291
    a. piano    b. cello    c. cimbalom    d. violin

141. Bartók was a leading authority on    Ans. a
    a. peasant music    c. American jazz    p. 291
    b. twelve-tone music    d. the music of ancient Greece

142. Bartók evolved a completely individual style that fused folk elements with    Ans. d
    a. changes of meter and a powerful beat    c. classical forms    p. 291
    b. twentieth-century sounds    d. all of the above    SG

143. While not rejecting any influence, Bartók emphasized that    Ans. c
    the strongest influence on his music was    p. 291
    a. American    b. Arab    c. Hungarian    d. Rumanian

144. Bartók's _____ are widely thought to be the finest    Ans. b
    since those of Ludwig van Beethoven.    p. 291
    a. symphonies    c. concertos
    b. string quartets    d. solo piano works

145. Bartók's six string quartets are widely thought to be the finest since those of    Ans. b
    a. Dmitri Shostakovich    c. Joseph Haydn    p. 291
    b. Ludwig van Beethoven    d. Igor Stravinsky    SG

146. The melodies Bartók used in most of his works are    Ans. b
    a. authentic folk melodies gathered in his research    p. 291
    b. original themes that have a folk flavor    SG
    c. reminiscent of nineteenth-century symmetrical themes
    d. exclusively Hungarian and Rumanian folk tunes

147. While remaining within the framework of a tonal center, Bartók often used
_____ in his music.
   a. harsh dissonances           c. tone clusters
   b. polychords                d. all of the above

Ans. d
p. 292
SG

148. Bartók's Concerto for Orchestra
   a. is his most popular work
   b. received its title because it was written for an orchestra of virtuosi
   c. is romantic in spirit because of its emotional intensity, memorable themes,
      and vivid contrasts of mood
   d all of the above

Ans. d
p. 293
SG

149. Charles Ives's father was a(n)
   a. insurance salesman         c. professional athlete
   b. physician               d. bandmaster

Ans. d
p. 294
SG

150. After graduating from Yale, Ives
   a. went into the insurance business    c. began teaching
   b. began playing the trumpet professionally    d. went into professional athletics

Ans. a
p. 294
SG

151. Which of the following statements is *not* true?
   a. Though experimental and far ahead of their time, Ives's compositions are
      rooted deeply in the folk and popular music he knew as a boy.
   b. Having learned many instruments as a youth, Charles Ives was a practical musician
      who created music that was well orchestrated and relatively easy to perform.
   c. The greatest influence on Charles Ives's musical training was his father,
      a bandmaster who loved to experiment with unusual sounds.
   d. Charles Ives's *Putnam's Camp, Redding, Connecticut* is the programmatic description
      of a child's reveries while on a church picnic one Independence day.

Ans. b
p. 295

152. During most of his lifetime, Ives's musical compositions
   a. were enthusiastically received in public performances
   b. were quickly published by a major firm
   c. accumulated in the barn of his Connecticut farm
   d. were sought after by musicians eager to perform them in public

Ans. c
p. 295
SG

153. Ives's music contains elements of
   a. revival hymns and ragtime       c. village bands and church choirs
   b. patriotic songs and barn dances    d. all of the above

Ans. d
p. 295
SG

154. Which of the following compositions is *not* by Charles Ives?
   a. *Three Places in New England*    c. *Concord* Sonata
   b. *An American in Paris*        d. *114 Songs*

Ans. b
p. 295

155. Ives's large and varied output includes works in many genres, but not
   a. symphonies              c. songs
   b. operas                 d. chamber music

Ans. b
p. 295
SG

156. *Putnam's Camp, Redding, Connecticut,* is a movement from Ives's
    a. *Three Places in New England*
    b. *Essays before a Sonata*
    c. *Concord Sonata*
    d. *The Unanswered Question*

Ans. a
p. 296
SG

157. A musical description of a child's 4th of July picnic and vivid imagination of Revolutionary events is
    a. *Appalachian Spring*
    c. *Putnam's Camp, Redding, Connecticut*
    c. *Porgy and Bess*
    d. *Survivor from Warsaw*

Ans. c
p. 296

158. *Putnam's Camp, Redding, Connecticut,* is a child's impression of
    a. a summer at camp
    b. a Fourth of July picnic
    c. a fishing trip
    d. army life in the war

Ans. b
p. 296
SG

159. *Putnam's Camp, Redding, Connecticut,* illustrates Ives's technique of quoting snatches of familiar tunes by presenting fragments of
    a. *Yankee Doodle*
    b. *The British Grenadiers*
    c. both a and b
    d. neither a nor b

Ans. c
p. 297
SG

160. George Gershwin grew up in
    a. New York, New York
    b. Charleston, South Carolina
    c. Anatevka, Russia
    d. Paris, France

Ans. a
p. 297

161. Gershwin left high school at the age of fifteen to
    a. become a pianist demonstrating new songs in a publisher's salesroom
    b. study theory and composition in Paris
    c. work in his father's store
    d. develop his athletic talents

Ans. a
p. 297
SG

162. Gershwin's first piano teacher was
    a. his brother Ira
    b. a public school teacher
    c. Maurice Ravel
    d. himself

Ans. d
p. 297

163. Which of the following musicals is *not* by George Gershwin?
    a. *Funny Face*
    b. *Funny Girl*
    c. *Of Thee I Sing*
    d. *Lady, Be Good*

Ans. b
p. 297

164. Which of the following works is *not* by George Gershwin?
    a. *Of Thee I Sing*
    b. *Porgy and Bess*
    c. *The Desert Song*
    d. *An American in Paris*

Ans. c
p. 297
SG

165. The Gershwin song that became a tremendous hit in 1920 was
    a. *La, La, Lucille*
    b. *I Got Rhythm*
    c. *Swanee*
    d. *Embraceable You*

Ans. c
p. 297
SG

166. George Gershwin usually collaborated with the lyricist
    a. Jerome Kern
    b. Irving Berlin
    c. Paul Whiteman
    d. Ira Gershwin

Ans. d
p. 297
SG

167. In addition to his musical skills, George Gershwin showed talent as a
     a. lyricist                              c. sculptor
     b. clarinetist                           d. painter

Ans. d
p. 298
SG

168. Which of the following statements is *not* true?
     a. Gershwin's career as a composer of music for the concert hall was launched by
        the triumphant premiere of his *Rhapsody in Blue* in 1924.
     b. Gershwin was an outgoing person, a sportsman, an art collector and amateur
        painter, and apparently irresistible to women.
     c. Gershwin's *Rhapsody in Blue* is not true jazz, but it employs jazzlike rhythms
        and melodies, and the orchestration suggests many distinctive sounds of jazz.
     d. Gershwin spent the last years of his life composing his most extended work,
        the opera *Porgy and Bess*, which he never lived to see performed.

Ans. d
p. 298

169. *Porgy and Bess* is a(n)
     a. Broadway musical                      c. rhapsody for piano
     b. opera                                 d. popular song

Ans. b
p. 298
SG

170. *Rhapsody in Blue* opens with
     a. a solo flute                          c. a muted trumpet
     b. the full orchestra                    d. a solo clarinet

Ans. d
p. 299
SG

171. Aaron Copland was born in
     a. Brooklyn, New York                    c. Anatevka, Russia
     b. the Appalachian mountains             d. Paris, France

Ans. a
p. 300

172. Which of the following statements is *not* true?
     a. In 1950 Copland turned to serialism, manipulating a tone row to create music
        that is completely personal in style, such as his *Music for the Theater*.
     b. To many composers in the late 1930s, including Copland, it seemed futile to write merely
        for a sophisticated elite, and they simplified their music to reach a wider audience.
     c. Copland's music reached a mass public through his scores for films and such
        patriotic works as *A Lincoln Portrait*.
     d. Aside from his numerous compositions, Copland has contributed to American music
        by lecturing, writing books and articles, teaching, and directing composer's groups.

Ans. a
p. 300

173. In 1921 Copland began a three-year period of study in
     a. Germany                               c. Italy
     b. Austria                               d. France

Ans. d
p. 300
SG

174. In 1921 Copland went to France, where he was the first
American to study composition with
     a. Virgil Thomson                        c. Maurice Ravel
     b. Nadia Boulanger                       d. Claude Debussy

Ans. b
p. 300

175. In 1925, after Copland returned from France, *American* music meant
     a. the eclecticism of Ives               c. primitivism
     b. the serialism of Schoenberg           d. jazz

Ans. d
p. 300

176. In 1925, and for a few years afterward, Copland's music showed the influence of    Ans. b
    a. impressionism                                 c. neobaroque styles          p. 300
    b. jazz                                        d. expressionism              SG

177. Copland's turn toward simplicity in the 1930s can be traced in part to    Ans. a
    a. the great depression                     c. the influence of Schoenberg    p. 301
    b. dissatisfaction with his own style       d. the influence of religion          SG

178. Copland's name has become synonymous with American music    Ans. d
    because of his use of    p. 301
    a. revival hymns, cowboy songs, and other folk tunes    SG
    b. jazz, blues, and ragtime elements
    c. subjects from American folklore
    d. all of the above

179.. Which of the following works was *not* composed by Aaron Copland?    Ans. c
    a. *Appalachian Spring*                    c. *An American in Paris*      p. 301
    b. *Connotations for Orchestra*          d. *A Lincoln Portrait*

180. Which of the following works was *not* composed by Aaron Copland?    Ans. a
    a. *Concord* Sonata                      c. *Billy the Kid*           p. 301
    b. *Rodeo*                                d. *Music for the Theater*    SG

181. An example of Copland's use of serialist technique is    Ans. b
    a. *Music for the Theater*              c. *Fanfare for the Common Man*    p. 301
    b. *Connotations for Orchestra*        d. *Appalachian Spring*          SG

182. In addition to his compositions, Copland made valuable contributions to music    Ans. d
    in America by    p. 301
    a. directing composer's groups        c. organizing concerts of American music  SG
    b. writing books and magazine articles    d. all of the above

183. *Appalachian Spring* originated as a    Ans. c
    a. program symphony                  c. ballet score            p. 302
    b. song cycle                         d. chamber opera           SG

184. *Appalachian Spring* originated as a ballet score for the    Ans. b
    great modern dancer and choreographer    p. 302
    a. George Balanchine                c. Vaclav Nijinsky
    b. Martha Graham                 d. Agnes De Mille

185. Copland depicted "Scenes of daily activity for the Bride and her Farmer-husband"    Ans. a
    in *Appalachian Spring* through    p. 303
    a. five variations on the Shaker melody *Simple Gifts*    SG
    b. intensely dissonant passages and humorous offbeat accents
    c. strings softly singing a hymnlike melody
    d. a joyful dance tune that is American in flavor

186. Since World War II, musical styles have
    a. taken many new directions and changes
    b. remained relatively stable
    c. returned to the styles of the nineteenth century
    d. concentrated on perfecting the twelve-tone system

Ans. a
p. 305

187. All of the following are major developments in music since 1950 *except* the
    a. spread of chance music
    b. increased use of the twelve-tone system
    c. continued composition of symphonies in the classical style
    d. composition of music in which tone color, texture, dynamics, and rhythm are
       as important as pitch

Ans. c
p. 305
SG

188. Composers began to shift from tonality to the twelve-tone system because
    a. they were bored with tonal music
    b. it was easier to write twelve-tone music
    c. they discovered it was a compositional technique rather than a special musical style
    d. they could make more money selling atonal compositions to a wider public

Ans. c
p. 306

189. The twelve-tone composer whose style was most imitated in
the 1950s and 1960s was
    a. Anton Webern       b. Arnold Schoenberg   c. Milton Babbitt        d. Alban Berg

Ans. a
p. 306

190. Serialism is a compositional technique in which
    a. the World Series was the unifying idea of a composition
    b. a series of five pitches could be constantly repeated
    c. a series of rhythms, dynamics, or tone colors could serve as a unifying idea
    d. a series of musical ideas would follow each other in quick succession

Ans. c
p. 306

191. A major composer associated with the serialist movement is
    a. Philip Glass                          c. George Crumb
    b. Milton Babbitt                        d. Ellen Taaffe Zwilich

Ans. b
p. 306
SG

192.. Twelve-tone compositional techniques used to organize rhythm, dynamics, tone
color, and other dimensions of music to produce totally controlled and organized
music are called
    a. chance music        b. minimalism        c. *Klangfarbenmelodie*   d. serialism

Ans. d
p. 306
SG

193. All of the following are proponents of serialism *except*
    a. Karlheinz Stockhausen                  c. Milton Babbitt
    b. Pierre Boulez                          d. John Cage

Ans. d
p. 306

194. In chance, or aleatory, music the composer
    a. takes a chance on which performers will perform the work
    b. chooses pitches, tone colors, and rhythms by random methods
    c. writes a rhythmic pattern but leaves it to the performer to determine the actual pitches
    d. writes the music in a traditional manner, but allows the recording engineer to make
       electronic changes

Ans. b
p. 306
SG

195. An example of aleatoric music is
   a. Arnold Schoenberg's *Gurrelieder* for orchestra
   b. Igor Stravinsky's *Soldier's Tale* for chamber ensemble
   c. John Cage's *Imaginary Landscape No. 4* for twelve radios
   d. Charles Ives's Fourth Symphony for orchestra

Ans. c
p. 307

196. Which of the following statements is *not* true?
   a. Chance music makes a complete break from traditional values in music, and asserts that one sound or ordering of sounds is as meaningful as another.
   b. Since the development of tape studios, synthesizers, and computers in the 1950s and 1960s, composers have had potentially unlimited resources for the production and control of sound.
   c. Minimalist music appeals to a very small select group, and especially to painters, sculptors, and other composers.
   d. After World War II tonality was gradually abandoned in favor of the 12-tone system.

Ans. c
p. 307

197. Which of the following is *not* primarily known as a minimalist composer?
   a. Terry Riley
   b. George Crumb
   c. Steve Reich
   d. Philip Glass

Ans. b
p. 307

198. Minimalism as an artistic movement was a
   a. way to create popular works quickly and with little effort
   b. reaction against the complexity of serialism and the randomness of chance music
   c. simplification of nonwestern thought and musical styles
   d. natural outgrowth of the late romantic style

Ans. b
p. 307

199. Minimalist music is characterized by
   a. the development of musical materials through random methods
   b. rapidly changing dynamics and textures
   c. a steady pulse, clear tonality, and insistent repetition of short melodic patterns
   d. use of twelve-tone techniques to organize the dimensions of music

Ans. c
p. 307
SG

200. Which of the following characteristics is *not* true of minimalist music?
   a. A fast rate of change.
   b. A clear tonality.
   c. A constant repetition of melodic and rhythmic patterns.
   d. A steady, driving pulse.

Ans. a
p. 307

201. Minimalist music grew out of the same intellectual climate as minimalist art, which features
   a. simple forms, clarity, and understatement
   b. deliberate distortion and violent colors to communicate the tension and anguish of the human psyche
   c. the effects of light, color, and atmosphere through collections of tiny colored patches
   d. three-dimensional objects and human figures distorted into planes

Ans. a
p. 307
SG

202. Many composers since the mid-1960s have made extensive use of quotations from       Ans. b
earlier music as an attempt to       p. 307
a. simplify writing original compositions       SG
b. improve communication between the composer and the listener
c. capitalize on the popularity of earlier works
d. continue and develop serialist techniques

203. Which of the following statements is *not* true?       Ans. a
a. Microtones are pitches produced electronically by means of a microphone.       p. 309
b. Scores for recent music often contain notes in new shapes, or new symbols, as
well as novel ways of arranging notation on the page.
c. Mixed-media presentations generally are intended to break down the ritual surrounding
traditional concerts and to increase communication between composer and audience.
d. During the 1920s and 1930s, Edgard Varèse pioneered in the exploration of
percussive and noiselike sounds, and wrote the first important work for
percussion ensemble, *Ionisation*.

204. Intervals smaller than the half step are called       Ans. d
a. quartertones       c. macrotones       p. 309
b. tone clusters       d. microtones       SG

205. *Ionisation*, the first important work for percussion ensemble, was composed by       Ans. b
a. John Cage       b. Edgard Varèse       c. Ellen Taaffe Zwilich  d. John Adams p. 311

206. Edgard Varèse's *Poème électronique*       Ans. d
a. was designed for the 1958 Brussels World Fair       p. 312
b. was one of the earliest masterpieces of electronic music created in a tape studio
c. was composed in collaboration with the famous architect Le Corbusier
d. all of the above

207. *Poème électronique* was designed for the 1958 Brussels World's Fair, and was       Ans. d
composed in collaboration with the famous architect       p. 312
a. I. M. Pei       c. Frank Lloyd Wright       SG
b. Walter Gropius       d. Le Corbusier

208. Ellen Taaffe Zwilich is a       Ans. a
a. Pulitzer Prize-winning American composer       p. 313
b. concertizing pianist
c. celebrated operatic soprano
d. promoter of young, upcoming American musicians

209. Ellen Taffee Zwilich won the 1983 Pulitzer Prize for Music for her composition       Ans. c
a. String Quartet       c. Symphony No. 1       p. 313
b. Double Quartet for Strings       d. Concerto for Piano and Orchestra       SG

210. *Concerto Grosso 1985* is an example of       Ans. b
a. total serialism       c. minimalism       p. 314
b. quotation music       d. chance music       SG

211. *Nixon in China* is set to a libretto by
   a. Alice Goodman            c. Richard Nixon
   b. John Adams             d. Chou En-Lai

Ans. a
p. 316
SG

212. Which of the following compositions is *not* by John Adams?
   a. *Harmonielehre*         c. *The Death of Klinghoffer*
   b. *Nixon in China*        d. *Concerto Grosso 1985*

Ans. d
p. 316

213. When a voice is answered by an instrument, or when one instrument (or group of instruments) is answered by a chorus, the pattern is referred to as
   a. jazz          c. polyphonic texture
   b. call and response     d. calling the beat

Ans. b
p. 320

214. Which of the following jazz elements is *not* derived from west African traditions?
   a. sophisticated harmonies     c. percussive sounds
   b. complex rhythms      d. strongly emphasized improvisation

Ans. a
p. 320

215. The immediate sources of jazz include
   a. the American band tradition    c. ragtime
   b. the blues        d. all of the above

Ans. d
p. 321

216. The "king of ragtime" is acknowledged to be
   a. John Philip Sousa     c. Scott Joplin
   b. Bessie Smith       d. Louis Armstrong

Ans. c
p. 321
SG

217. Which of the following statements is *not* true?
   a. King Oliver is generally acknowledged the "king of ragtime."
   b. Ragtime is a style of syncopated piano music that was popular from the 1890s to about 1915.
   c. When playing ragtime, the pianist's right hand plays a highly syncopated melody while the left hand maintains a steady beat.
   d. Ragtime music is generally in duple meter and is performed at a moderate march tempo.

Ans. a
p. 321

218. Ragtime is
   a. a style of composed piano music    c. generally in duple meter
   b. performed at a moderate march tempo    d. all of the above

Ans. d
p. 321
SG

219. Ragtime flourished in the United States
   a. just before the Civil War    c. from the 1890s to about 1915
   b. from the 1860s to about 1890    d. between the two world wars

Ans. c
p. 321
SG

220. The blues
   a. usually follow a pattern 12 bars in length    c. are traditionally a vocal genre
   b. are usually slow and sad    d. all of the above

Ans. a
p. 321

221. The chord progression usually used in the blues involves only three basic chords: tonic, dominant, and
   a. supertonic    b. mediant    c. subdominant    d. submediant

Ans. c
p. 321

222. Which of the following statements is *not* true?    Ans. a
   a. The subdominant chord is the triad based on the sixth step of the scale.    p. 321
   b. The lyrics of vocal blues consist of several 3-line stanzas, each set to a harmonic framework that is usually 12 bars long.
   c. The music of the blues is usually written in quadruple meter, with a 4/4 time signature.
   d. The most famous blues singer of the 1920s, known as the "empress of the blues," was Bessie Smith.

223. The chord progression usually used in the blues involves only three basic    Ans. c
   chords: tonic, dominant, and    p. 321
   a. supertonic                    c. subdominant    SG
   b. mediant                       d. submediant

224. Blues music is usually written in _____ time.    Ans. a
   a. 4/4                           c. 6/8    p. 321
   b. 3/4                           d. 2/4    SG

225. The most famous blues singer of the 1920s, known as the "empress of the blues,"    Ans. a
   was    p. 322
   a. Bessie Smith    b. Mahalia Jackson    c. Nina Simone    d. Diana Ross    SG

226. The "empress of the blues" was    Ans. c
   a. Lil Hardin                    c. Bessie Smith    p. 322
   b. Madonna                       d. Joan Baez

227. Two notable blues compositions are *Memphis Blues* and *St. Louis Blues*, by    Ans. b
   a. Bessie Smith                  c. Louis Armstrong    p. 322
   b. William C. Handy              d. King Oliver    SG

228. The poetic and musical form of the blues was popularized    Ans. c
   in the early years of this century through the publication    p. 322
   of *Memphis Blues* and *St. Louis Blues* composed by
   a. Bessie Smith    b. Louis Armstrong    c. William C. Handy    d. King Oliver

229. The backbone of a jazz ensemble is its    Ans. c
   a. director                      c. rhythm section    p. 322
   b. brass section                 d. clarinet section

230. The rhythm section of a jazz ensemble usually does *not* include the    Ans. c
   a. banjo/guitar                  c. vibraphone    p. 322
   b. piano                         d. percussion

231. A jazz sound results from    Ans. d
   a. its variety of pitch inflections    p. 323
   b. the type of vibrato employed
   c. the particular way tones are attacked and released
   d. all of the above

232. In jazz, each statement of the basic harmonic pattern or melody is called a
    a. riff                                   c. chorus
    b. phrase                            d. verse

*Ans. c*
*p. 323*

233. Which of the following statements is *not* true?
    a. Jazz is generally played by a small combo of three to eight players, or by a "big band" of ten to fifteen.
    b. Jazz can be described generally as music rooted in improvisation and characterized by syncopated rhythm, a steady beat, and distinctive tone colors and techniques of performance.
    c. Jazz can be notated as easily as any other musical form.
    d. Some jazz improvisations are based not on a melody but on a harmonic pattern, or series of chords.

*Ans. c*
*p. 324*

234. The major center of jazz from about 1900 to 1917 was
    a. Chicago                         c. New York
    b. New Orleans                 d. Kansas City

*Ans. b*
*p. 324*

235. New Orleans style Dixieland flourished in the United States
    a. from the 1860s to about 1890       c. from 1900 to 1917
    b. from the 1890s to about 1900       d. from 1917 to 1935

*Ans. c*
*p. 324*

236. The most distinctive feature of New Orleans style jazz was
    a. the use of a saxophone for playing the melody
    b. collective improvisation by the front line
    c. solo breaks by the rhythm instruments
    d. its lack of syncopated melodies

*Ans. b*
*p. 324*
*SG*

237. The "front line" of a Dixieland group included
    a. cornet, clarinet, and trombone      c. piano
    b. drums, bass, and banjo            d. all of the above

*Ans. a*
*p. 324*
*SG*

238. The melodic instruments, or cornet, clarinet, and trombone, of a Dixieland band were known as the
    a. stars         b. front line        c. rear line          d. combo

*Ans. b*
*p. 324*

239. The "king of swing" is generally acknowledged to have been
    a. Benny Goodman             c. Duke Ellington
    b. Glenn Miller                d. King Oliver

*Ans. a*
*p. 325*

240. Short repeated melodic phrases frequently used during the swing era are called
    a. riffs                                c. gigs
    b. breaks                         d. tags

*Ans. a*
*p. 325*
*SG*

241. To create tension and excitement, arrangers for swing bands often used a rapid alternation of brass and sax *riffs*, or
    a. free improvisational solos      c. short repeated melodic phrases
    b. short codas                 d. choruses

*Ans. c*
*p. 325*

242. One of the most important solo instruments of the swing era was the
    a. cornet
    b. guitar
    c. tuba
    d. saxophone

Ans. d
p. 325
SG

243. Duke Ellington was an important figure in
    a. swing
    b. ragtime
    c. bebop
    d. all of the above

Ans. a
p. 325
SG

244. The jazz style called *swing* flourished in America from
    a. 1900 to 1917
    b. 1917 to 1935
    c. 1935 to 1945
    d. 1945 to 1955

Ans. c
p. 325

245. The typical swing band had about fifteen musicians, grouped into three sections:
    a. saxophones, trumpets, and trombones
    b. saxophones, brasses, and rhythm
    c. trumpets, trombones, and rhythm
    d. saxophones, brasses, and piano

Ans. b
p. 325

246. The rhythm section of a swing band normally consisted of
    a. piano, percussion, guitar, and bass
    b. percussion, guitar, and bass
    c. piano, percussion, and bass
    d. piano, percussion, and guitar

Ans. a
p. 325

247. Which of the following statements is *not* true?
    a. Swing music was more composed than improvised and was arranged,
       or notated in written-out parts for the musicians.
    b. The guitar became one of the most important solo instruments during the swing era.
    c. Swing was performed mainly by big bands of about fifteen players.
    d. Edward Kennedy "Duke" Ellington, perhaps the most important swing composer,
       arranger, and conductor, ranks among the leading figures in the history of jazz.

Ans. b
p. 325

248. Bebop differed from earlier jazz forms in that it
    a. used simple harmonies
    b. was meant for attentive listening, not dancing
    c. used written arrangements with little improvisation
    d. all of the above

Ans. b
p. 326

249. A bebop performance generally began and ended with
    a. a statement of the main theme by one or two soloists in unison
    b. a statement of the main theme by the whole combo in unison
    c. improvisational sections by the soloists
    d. free sections by the rhythm instruments to set the beat and tempo

Ans. a
p. 326
SG

250. One of the greatest of all jazz improvisers and a
    towering figure among bebop musicians was the saxophonist
    a. Charlie Parker
    b. Thelonious Monk
    c. Cootie Williams
    d. Dizzy Gillespie

Ans. a
p. 326

251. In bebop, the beat of the music was mainly marked by the
    a. piano
    b. bass drum
    c. pizzicato bass
    d. trumpet

Ans. c
p. 326
SG

252. Which of the following statements about bop is *not* true?                     Ans. d
  a. Bebop performers often built melodies on chords containing six or seven          p. 326
     notes rather than on the four- or five-note chords used in earlier jazz.
  b. In bebop, the beat of the music was mainly marked by a pizzicato bass.
  c. Bebop melodies were often varied in length.
  d. Bebop performers were mainstream jazz musicians who enjoyed having other
     musicians sit in on their sets.

253. A typical bebop group might include                                             Ans. c
  a. two lead guitars, bass guitar, and drums                                        p. 326
  b. fourteen to fifteen musicians, grouped into three basic sections
  c. a saxophone, a trumpet, and a rhythm section of piano, bass, and percussion
  d. a cornet, a clarinet, a trombone, and a rhythm section of piano, bass, guitar,
     and percussion

254. Bebop was                                                                       Ans. d
  a. music with sophisticated harmonies and unpredictable rhythms                    p. 326
  b. usually played by small jazz groups                                             SG
  c. meant for attentive listening, not dancing
  d. all of the above

255. Bebop, as a musical style, developed in the                                     Ans. b
  a. 1930s          b. early 1940s          c. 1950s          d. early 1960s          p. 326

256. Which of the following is *not* associated with cool jazz?                      Ans. a
  a. Ornette Coleman              c. Stan Getz                                        p. 327
  b. Lennie Tristano              d. Miles Davis                                      SG

257. Cool jazz                                                                       Ans. a
  a. was related to bop but was calmer and more relaxed in character                 p. 327
  b. consisted of short pieces freely improvised                                     SG
  c. used traditional jazz instrumental combinations
  d. all of the above

258. Cool jazz emerged                                                               Ans. c
  a. between 1924 and 1935          c. during the late 1940s and early 50s           p. 327
  b. between 1935 and 1945          d. in the 1960s

259. Which of the following statements is *not* true?                                Ans. b
  a. The jazz style that was related to bop but was far more calm and relaxed in     p. 327
     character was called "cool jazz" in contrast to the "hot jazz" of an earlier era.
  b. Free jazz, like earlier styles, was based on traditional forms and established
     chord patterns.
  c. Jazz rock, or fusion, combines the jazz musician's improvisatory approach with
     rock rhythms and tone colors.
  d. The percussion section of a fusion combo often includes instruments from Africa,
     Latin America, or India.

260. The following can be said about free jazz:
    a. It disregarded regular forms and established chord patterns.
    b. It can be compared to chance music.
    c. It began in the early 1960s.
    d. All of the above are true.

Ans. d
p. 327
SG

261. The leading figures in the free jazz movement were
    a. Charlie Parker and Thelonious Monk     c. Joe Zawinul and Wayne Shorter
    b. Dave Brubeck and Lennie Tristano        d. John Coltrane and Ornette Coleman

Ans. d
p. 327

262. Which of the following is *not* a characteristic of fusion?
    a. The group typically includes acoustic instruments along with synthesizers,
       guitar, and bass.
    b. The percussion section is smaller than in earlier jazz.
    c. Rock rhythms and tone colors are combined with the jazz musician's improvisatory
       approach.
    d. Acoustic instruments are often used with electric attachments that expand the range
       of tonal effects.

Ans. b
p. 327
SG

263. The bebop musician who spearheaded developments in cool
jazz and then jazz rock is
    a. Miles Davis                              c. Thelonious Monk
    b. Meyer Davis                              d. Charlie Parker

Ans. a
p. 327

264. A major figure in the development of jazz rock or fusion was
    a. Miles Davis                              c. Louis Armstrong
    b. Ornette Coleman                          d. Stan Getz

Ans. a
p. 327
SG

265. A _____ is a type of theater that fuses a dramatic script, acting, and spoken
dialogue with music, singing, and dancing.
    a. vaudeville show      b. song cycle       c. musical comedy      d. revue

Ans. c
p. 328

266. Songs in musical comedies are usually in _____ form.
    a. 12-bar blues      b. 32-bar AABA      c. 24-bar ABA      d. 16-bar AB

Ans. b
p. 328

267. The introductory section of a musical comedy song is called the
    a. chorus            b. verse            c. introduction      d. vaudeville

Ans. b
p. 328

268. Generally, musical comedy is in _____ act(s).
    a. one               b. two              c. three             d. four

Ans. b
p. 328

269. The main section of a musical comedy song is called the
    a. chorus                               c. release
    b. verse                                d. all of the above

Ans. a
p. 328

270. In contrast to opera, the American musical tends to
    a. use simpler forms                    c. contain more spoken dialogue
    b. use simpler melodies and harmonies   d. all of the above

Ans. d
p. 328

271. Which of the following is *not* true of the American musical?   Ans. b
    a. It is usually in two acts.   p. 328
    b. It is generally set outside the United States.
    c. It embraces a variety of styles.
    d. It tends to use simpler harmonies, melodies, and forms.

272. Which of the following statements is *not* true of the musical comedy?   Ans. c
    a. It has music, singing, and dancing.   c. It is sung throughout.   p. 328
    b. It has scenery, costumes, and spectacle.   d. It has a dramatic script.

273. Which of the following is *not* true of the American musical?   Ans. c
    a. The songs in a musical generally have an introductory section (verse) and a main   p. 328
       section (chorus) in AABA form.
    b. Shows originally produced as musicals are sometimes later performed in opera
       houses and recorded by opera singers.
    c. The composer of a musical normally writes the lyrics as well as composes
       and orchestrates the music.
    d. Songs in musicals tend to be narrower in pitch range than operatic arias.

274. Which of the following statements *not* true?   Ans. b
    a. Operetta, or comic opera, combines song, spoken dialogue, and dance,   p. 328
       with sophisticated musical techniques.
    b. The main section of a musical comedy song is called the verse.
    c. The sources of the American musical include operetta, vaudeville, and the revue.
    d. A musical comedy aims to entertain through fusion of a dramatic script, acting, and
       spoken dialogue with music, singing, and dancing and with scenery, costumes, and
       spectacle.

275. Which of the following is *not* a source of the American musical?   Ans. b
    a. the revue   c. operetta   p. 328
    b. the minstrel show   d. vaudeville

276. A variety show with songs, comedy, juggling, acrobats, and animal acts,   Ans. a
    but no plot, is called   p. 329
    a. vaudeville   c. a revue
    b. an operetta   d. a concept musical

277. Vaudeville is   Ans. d
    a. an opera in English   p. 329
    b. a play with music, acting, and speaking, costumes and scenery
    c. a variety show with a plot
    d. a variety show with songs, comedy, juggling, acrobatics, and animal acts without a plot

278. Revues in the first decades of the twentieth century   Ans. d
    a. featured pretty, scantily clad young women who sang and danced   p. 329
    b. featured comedians who performed sketches
    c. were often satirical
    d. all of the above

279. A variety show without a plot but with a unifying idea is called
    a. vaudeville                      c. a revue
    b. an operetta                     d. a book musical

Ans. c
p. 329

280. William S. Gilbert and Arthur Sullivan were the writers of
    a. *Oklahoma!*                     c. *The Mikado*
    b. *Sunday in the Park with George*   d. *Sweeney Todd*

Ans. c
p. 329

281. *The Mikado*, widely performed in the United States around the turn of the century, was written by
    a. Cole Porter                     c. W. S. Gilbert and Arthur Sullivan
    b. Victor Herbert                  d. Richard Rodgers and Oscar Hammerstein

Ans. c
p. 329

282. A golden era of American musical theater was created from about
    a. 1776-1820                       c. 1920-1960
    b. 1850-1875                       d. 1980 to the present

Ans. c
p. 329

283. Some of the composers who contributed to the creation of the golden era of American musical theater were
    a. William S. Gilbert and Arthur Sullivan
    b. George Gershwin, Cole Porter, Richard Rodgers, and Frank Loesser
    c. Giacomo Puccini, Giuseppe Verdi, and Richard Wagner
    d. Stephen Sondheim and Andrew Lloyd Webber

Ans. b
p. 329

284. Which of the following statements is *not* true?
    a. Except for a few rock musicals, the musical was relatively unaffected by the "rock revolution" of the 1960s.
    b. The golden era in American musical theater was created by Gilbert and Sullivan in the late nineteenth century.
    c. *West Side Story* was an unprecedented fusion of song and dance with electrifyingly violent choreography by Jerome Robbins and Peter Gennaro.
    d. *Oklahoma!* by Rodgers and Hammerstein was a landmark in the integration of dance, songs, and plot.

Ans. b
p. 329

285. *Slaughter on Tenth Avenue*, the ballet used in the climax of *On Your Toes*, was choreographed by
    a. Stephen Sondheim                c. George Balanchine
    b. Mikhail Baryshnikov             d. Agnes de Mille

Ans. c
p. 329
SG

286. *Slaughter on Tenth Avenue*, choreographed by George Balanchine, was a ballet used in the climax of
    a. *The Mikado*                    c. *On Your Toes*
    b. *Cats*                          d. *Oklahoma!*

Ans. c
p. 329

287. Which of the following American musicals is *not* by Stephen Sondheim?
    a. *Sunday in the Park with George*   c. *Sweeney Todd*
    b. *Of Thee I Sing*                d. *Company*

Ans. b
p. 330

288. Which of the following statements is *not* true of Leonard Bernstein's music?   Ans. c
    a. It bridged the worlds of "serious" and popular music.   p. 331
    b. It is infused with jazz and dance rhythms.
    c. It is frequently atonal.
    d. It is enlivened by syncopations and irregular meters.

289. Leonard Bernstein was a well-known   Ans. d
    a. composer of orchestral and vocal works   c. conductor   p. 331
    b. author-lecturer   d. all of the above

290. The composer, conductor, and pianist who began his spectacular career as   Ans. d
    substitute conductor of the New York Philharmonic on only a few hours'   p. 331
    notice was
    a. Richard Rodgers   c. Steven Sondheim
    b. Cole Porter   d. Leonard Bernstein

291. Leonard Bernstein began his spectacular career as a   Ans. c
    a. writer of the successful Broadway musical *On the Town*   p. 331
    b. singer of operettas and musicals
    c. substitute conductor of the New York Philharmonic on only a few hours' notice
    d. television lecturer on educational programs

292. In addition to his famous musicals, Bernstein also wrote successful   Ans. d
    a. ballets   c. symphonies   p. 331
    b. choral works   d. all of the above

293. Leonard Bernstein was influenced, particularly in his ballets, by   Ans. b
    a. Delibes and Tchaikovsky   c. Bach and Handel   p. 331
    b. Stravinsky and Copland   d. Verdi and Wagner

294. Which of the following musicals is *not* by Leonard Bernstein?   Ans. b
    a. *West Side Story*   c. *On the Town*   p. 332
    b. *Cats*   d. *Wonderful Town*

295. The musical loosely based on Shakespeare's *Romeo and Juliet* is   Ans. a
    a. *West Side Story*   c. *Cats*   p. 333
    b. *Sweeney Todd*   d. *On Your Toes*

296. In *West Side Story*, the two star-crossed lovers are   Ans. c
    a. Anthony and Cleopatra   c. Tony and Maria   p. 333
    b. Tristan and Isolde   d. Bernardo and Maria

297. *West Side Story*   Ans. d
    a. is loosely based on Shakespeare's *Romeo and Juliet*   p. 333
    b. is set in the slums of New York   SG
    c. deals with the conflict between gang rivalry and youthful love
    d. all of the above

298. In *West Side Story* Maria and Tony are          Ans. c
    a. mother and son                    c. doomed lovers          p. 333
    b. arch enemies                      d. sister and brother

299. *West Side Story* contains          Ans. b
    a. a conventional range of popular styles          p. 333
    b. an unprecedented fusion of song and drama with electrifying violent choreography     SG
    c. less music than the average Broadway show
    d. all of the above

300. The lyrics for *West Side Story* were written by          Ans. b
    a. Oscar Hammerstein II              c. Jerome Robbins          p. 333
    b. Stephen Sondheim                  d. Leonard Bernstein          SG

301. Rock has been defined as          Ans. c
    a. a folk-like guitar-based style associated with rural white Americans          p. 335
    b. an African-American dance music that fused blues, jazz, and gospel styles
    c. vocal music with a hard driving beat often featuring electric guitar accompaniment
        and heavily amplified sound
    d. a blend of rhythm and blues and popular music

302. Early rock grew mainly out of _____, a dance music of American blacks          Ans. a
    that fused blues, jazz, and gospel styles.          p. 335
    a. rhythm and blues                  c. disco
    b. country and western               d. Motown

303. An African-American dance music that fused blues, jazz,          Ans. b
    and gospel styles is known as          p. 335
    a. country and western               c. rock
    b. rhythm and blues                  d. disco

304. A folk-like, guitar-based style associated with rural          Ans. a
    white Americans is known as          p. 335
    a. country and western               c. soul
    b. rhythm and blues                  d. Motown

305. Which of the following was *not* among the leading performers of rhythm and          Ans. a
    blues in the 1950s?          p. 335
    a. Aretha Franklin      b. Chuck Berry          c. Little Richard          d. the Platters

306. _____ has been described as a type of soul music that blended          Ans. d
    rhythm and blues with popular music.          p. 335
    a. country and western               c. gospel
    b. rhythm and blues                  d. Motown

307. Which of the following was *not* a member of the Beatles?          Ans. d
    a. John Lennon                       c. George Harrison          p. 335
    b. Paul McCartney                    d. Bob Dylan          SG

308. Which of the following statements is *not* true?
   a. During the 1960s, the popular music scene was basically confined to the English form of rock and roll.
   b. The Beatles were the most influential performing group in the history of rock.
   c. A new era in rock history began in 1964 with the American tour of the Beatles, an English group.
   d. The song cycle *Sgt. Pepper's Lonely Hearts Club Band* has a wide range of musical styles, including traditional rock and roll, a parody of a 1920s music-hall tune, a song featuring the exotic sounds of Indian music, and an old-fashioned melodramatic ballad.

Ans. a
p. 335

309. The Beatles's influence on American rock music may be seen through later performer's use of
   a. "classical" and nonwestern instruments
   b. new electronic and instrumental sounds
   c. unconventional chord progressions
   d. all of the above

Ans. d
p. 336
SG

310. The dominant dance music of the 1970s was
   a. the twist
   b. the mashed potato
   c. the bunny hop
   d. disco

Ans. d
p. 336
SG

311. Which of the following groups was *not* a part of the 1980s "second British invasion"
   a. Eurhythmics      b. Black Sabbath      c. Culture Club      d. Police

Ans. b
p. 336

312. A type of basic rock popular in the 1980s characterized by sexually explicit lyrics, bizarre costumes, and tremendous volume, is known as
   a. reggae      b. punk rock      c. heavy metal      d. funk rock

Ans. c
p. 336

313. A typical rock group consists of
   a. sections of brass, reeds, and percussion (rhythm)
   b. vocalist, two acoustic guitars, harmonica, and drums
   c. two electric guitars, electric bass, percussion, and electric keyboard
   d. vocalist, backup singers, and drums

Ans. c
p. 336
SG

314. A method of singing used by males to reach notes higher than their normal range is called
   a. freaky      b. Yeah! Yeah!      c. disco      d. falsetto

Ans. d
p. 337
SG

315. Rock is based on a powerful beat in quadruple meter with strong accents on _____ of each bar.
   a. the second and fourth beats
   b. the first and third beats
   c. the first beat
   d. all four beats

Ans. a
p. 337
SG

316. The harmonic progressions of rock are usually
   a. limited to only two chords
   b. the same as earlier popular music
   c. quite simple
   d. extremely complex

Ans. c
p. 339
SG

317. The Beatles's recording _____ can be considered a unified song cycle.     Ans. a
    a. *Sgt. Pepper's Lonely Hearts Club Band*     c. *The Beatles*                    p. 339
    b. *Abbey Road*                                d. *Lucy in the Sky with Diamonds*

318. Which of these recordings can be considered a unified song cycle?     Ans. b
    a. the "white album"                           c. *Magical Mystery Tour*           p. 339
    b. *Sgt. Pepper's Lonely Hearts Club Band*     d. *Abbey Road*                     SG

319. Which of the following statements is *not* true?     Ans. c
    a. Rock music is amplified powerfully, and the guitar is often manipulated     p. 339
       electronically to produce a wide range of tone colors.
    b. Though it includes diverse styles, rock tends to be vocal music with a hard, driving
       beat, often featuring electric guitar accompaniment and heavily amplified sound.
    c. The harmonic progressions of rock are usually quite complex, often using chromatic
       chord progressions and sophisticated harmonies.
    d. During the 1970s and 1980s, rock musicians exploited the ever-expanding capacities
       of synthesizers and computers, making it possible for a few performers to sound like
       a large ensemble.

# VII. NONWESTERN MUSIC

1. Which of the following statements is *not* true?                                Ans. c
   a. Music of the nonwestern world is too varied to allow easy generalizations.   p. 342
   b. Nonwestern traditions have been an important source of inspiration for       SG
      twentieth-century western music.
   c. Improvisation is nonexistent in nonwestern music.
   d. Some composers in the nonwestern world combine traditional elements with
      western forms and styles.

2. Which of the following statements is *not* true?                                Ans. b
   a. Nonwestern music is extremely varied.                                        p. 342
   b. The range of music is the same throughout nonwestern societies.
   c. Nonwestern music is usually transmitted orally.
   d. Nonwestern music is closely linked with religion, dance, and drama.

3. Nonwestern music is most often transmitted                                      Ans. a
   a. orally from parent to child or teacher to student                            p. 342
   b. through the imitation of radio broadcasts                                    SG
   c. through music notation
   d. all of the above

4. Singers in the middle east and north Africa cultivate a vocal timbre that       Ans. a
   a. has a nasal, intense, and strained tone    c. is relaxed and open-throated   p. 343
   b. can produce two sounds at the same time    d. is guttural and raspy

5. A nasal, intense, and strained tone is cultivated by singers from               Ans. c
   a. Peru                              c. the middle east and north Africa         p. 343
   b. Siberia                           d. sub-Saharan Africa                       SG

6. The main way of making music in most nonwestern cultures is by                  Ans. b
   a. playing native instruments        c. playing European instruments            p. 343
   b. singing                           d. playing the radio

7. Musical instruments whose sound generator is a stretched                        Ans. d
   skin or other membrane are classified as                                        p. 343
   a. aerophones                        c. idiophones
   b. chordophones                      d. membranophones

8. Musical instruments whose sound generator is a stretched string are classified as  Ans. b
   a. aerophones                        c. idiophones                              p. 343
   b. chordophones                      d. membranophones

9. Chordophones are instruments whose sound generator is a                         Ans. b
   a. stretched skin                    c. column of air                           p. 342
   b. stretched string                  d. drum                                    SG

10. Musical instruments whose sound generator is a column of air are classified as     Ans. a
    a. aerophones                                   c. idiophones                  p. 343
    b. chordophones                              d. membranophones

11. Musical instruments whose own material is the sound generator are classified as     Ans. c
    a. aerophones                                   c. idiophones                  p. 343
    b. chordophones                              d. membranophones

12. The choice of musical instruments in nonwestern cultures frequently depends on     Ans. d
    a. the musical style of a culture            c. religion                      p. 343
    b. the culture's geography                 d. all of the above

13. Nonwestern musical scales often contain _____ tones.     Ans. d
    a. five                                          c. seven                   p. 344
    b. six                                         d. all of the above            SG

14. Music that has a texture in which all parts perform the same basic melody,     Ans. a
    but in versions that differ in ornamentation or rhythm, is called     p. 344
    a. heterophonic                               c. monophonic
    b. homophonic                               d. polyphonic

15. Most of the music of sub-Saharan Africa features     Ans. d
    a. a wide variety of instrumental ensembles    c. percussive sounds        p. 345
    b. complex rhythms and polyrhythms        d. all of the above

16. Which of the following statements is *not* true with regard to sub-Saharan Africa?     Ans. a
    a. The most common type of instrument is the chordophone.     p. 345
    b. The human body is often used as a percussion instrument.     SG
    c. The people speak over 700 different languages.
    d. Music is usually performed outdoors.

17. Which of the following statements is *not* true with regard to sub-Saharan Africa?     Ans. b
    a. Many African languages are "tone languages," in which the meaning of a     p. 346
        word is determined by the relative pitch at which it is spoken.
    b. Nonwestern music primarily employs the same major and minor scales as western
        music.
    c. Sub-Saharan Africa includes several thousand peoples with different religions, social
        customs, and ways of life, speaking over 700 different languages.
    d. There is no written notation.

18. Which of the following statements is *not* true with regard     Ans. b
    to the music of sub-Saharan Africa?     p. 347
    a. Idiophones are the most common musical instruments.
    b. The music is mostly monophonic in texture.
    c. Music permeates virtually every aspect of African life.
    d. The human body is often used as a percussion instrument.

19. A performance style in which the phrases of a soloist are
    repeatedly answered by those of a chorus is known as
    a. yodeling                              c. polyphony
    b. call and response                     d. campfire singing

Ans. b
p. 347
SG

20. The *mbira* may be described as a(n)
    a. hourglass-shaped drum
    b. African form of string instrument
    c. form of xylophone used in orchestras
    d. melodic idiophone with tongues of metal or bamboo attached to a sounding board

Ans. d
p. 348
SG

21. A melodic idiophone with tongues of metal or bamboo attached to a
    sounding board, used in sub-Saharan Africa, is known as the
    a. vina                                  c. mbira
    b. talking drum                          d. akadinda

Ans. c
p. 348

22. Vocalists in Africa often use the _____ to accompany themselves.
    a. mbira                                 c. xylophone
    b. nose flute                            d. pressure drum

Ans. a
p. 348
SG

23. Drums in sub-Saharan Africa
    a. come in a wide variety of sizes, shapes, and forms
    b. are essential to many religious and political ceremonies
    c. are usually played in groups of two to four
    d. all of the above

Ans. d
p. 348
SG

24. Drums in sub-Saharan Africa are often considered
    a. symbolical of power and royalty
    b. sacred or magical
    c. the property of the group, rather than of an individual
    d. all of the above

Ans. d
p. 348

25. Traditional Japanese classical music includes
    a. works for orchestra, chamber ensemble, and soloists
    b. vocal and instrumental works
    c. theater music
    d. all of the above

Ans. d
p. 350

26. The _____ is a Japanese instrument with thirteen strings
    stretched over a hollow sounding board.
    a. samisen                               c. shakuhachi
    b. koto                                  d. kengyō

Ans. b
p. 350

27. Most masterpieces of traditional koto music were composed
    a. during the Edo period (1615-1868)     c. in the tenth century
    b. in the Meiji period (1868-1912)       d. between 650 and 750

Ans. a
p. 351
SG

28. *Kengyō* refers to
    a. a family of famous koto performers and composers
    b. the highest rank, "master of koto," bestowed on performers
    c. a style of playing the koto
    d. all of the above

Ans. b
p. 351
SG

29. The shamisen is a(n)
    a. instrument with three strings that are plucked
    b. end-blown bamboo flute with five holes
    c. two-headed barrel drum
    d. instrument with thirteen strings stretched over a hollow sound board

Ans. a
p. 351
SG

30. The _____ is a Japanese instrument with three strings that are plucked.
    a. shamisen                          c. shakuhachi
    b. koto                              d. kengyō

Ans. a
p. 351

31. The shakuhachi is a(n)
    a. instrument with three strings that are plucked
    b. end-blown bamboo flute with five holes
    c. two-headed barrel drum
    d. instrument with thirteen strings stretched over a hollow sound board

Ans. b
p. 351
SG

32. When instrumental or vocal parts perform the same basic melody but in
    versions that differ in ornamentation or rhythm, the texture is
    a. polyphonic                        c. heterophonic
    b. monophonic                        d. call and response

Ans. c
p. 352
SG

33. Heterophonic texture occurs when instrumentalists or vocalists perform
    a. two different melodies at the same time
    b. the same basic melody but in versions that differ in ornamentation or rhythm
    c. the same basic melody without variation
    d. a basic melody and a subordinate accompaniment

Ans. b
p. 352

# ANSWER KEY
## FOR THE UNIT QUIZZES

Contained in the *Study Guide and Student Workbook* that accompanies
Kamien: *MUSIC: An Appreciation* (second brief edition)

### UNIT QUIZ I, ELEMENTS

1-k, 2-s, 3-c, 4-f, 5-i, 6-h, 7-t, 8-a, 9-o, 10-m, 11-l, 12-n, 13-g, 14-b, 15-p, 16-j, 17-q, 18-e, 19-r, 20-d, 21-c, 22-b, 23-a, 24-b, 25-d, 26-c, 27-a, 28-b, 29-d, 30-b, 31-j, 32-a, 33-h, 34-d, 35-c, 36-f, 37-i, 38-e, 39-g, 40-b.

### UNIT QUIZ II, THE MIDDLE AGES AND RENAISSANCE

1-i, 2-d, 3-k, 4-m, 5-e, 6-l, 7-a, 8-c, 9-b, 10-f, 11-g, 12-h, 13-j, 14-c, 15-d, 16-e, 17-a, 18-b, 19-b, 20-a, 21-b, 22-b, 23-c, 24-c, 25-a.

### UNIT QUIZ III, THE BAROQUE PERIOD

1-j, 2-q, 3-k, 4-h, 5-l, 6-a, 7-c, 8-d, 9-f, 10-p, 11-e, 12-m, 13-b, 14-g, 15-i, 16-n, 17-o, 18-r, 19-a, 20-d, 21-a, 22-a, 23-c, 24-a, 25-f.

### UNIT QUIZ IV, THE CLASSICAL PERIOD

1-c, 2-d, 3-a, 4-c, 5-b, 6-b, 7-a, 8-a, 9-a, 10-d, 11-c, 12-c, 13-c, 14-b, 15-a, 16-exposition, 17-development, 18-recapitulation, 19-introduction, 20-coda (codetta), 21-c, 22-b, 23-c, 24-a, 25-c, 26-c, 27-b, 28-a, 29-a, 30-c.

### UNIT QUIZ V, THE ROMANTIC PERIOD

1-a, 2-m, 3-g, 4-l, 5-g, 6-n, 7-h, 8-l, 9-a, 10-j, 11-k, 12-b, 13-l, 14-i, 15-f, 16-d, 17-n, 18-c, 19-e, 20-l, 21-c, 22-b, 23-d, 24-b, 25-a, 26-a, 27-d, 28-b, 29-b, 30-c, 31-j, 32-a, 33-h, 34-b, 35-c, 36-d, 37-f, 38-e, 39-i, 40-g.

### UNIT QUIZ VI, part 1, THE TWENTIETH CENTURY

1-j, 2-e, 3-i, 4-f, 5-d, 6-h, 7-m, 8-l, 9-k, 10-a, 11-c, 12-b, 13-g, 14-c, 15-a, 16-b, 17-d, 18-c, 19-b, 20-b, 21-c, 22-c, 23-a, 24-d, 25-c, 26-e, 27-a, 28-d, 29-f, 30-b.

### UNIT QUIZ VI, part 2, JAZZ AND ROCK

1-i, 2-d, 3-c, 4-m, 5-j, 6-f, 7-g, 8-e, 9-a, 10-b, 11-h, 12-k, 13-l, 14-c, 15-a, 16-a, 17-a, 18-h, 19-k, 20-f, 21-d, 22-m, 23-k, 24-c, 25-l, 26-m, 27-g, 28-i, 29-c, 30-g, 31-a, 32-m, 33-j, 34-b, 35-l, 36-e, 37-c, 38-b, 39-h, 40-a.

### UNIT QUIZ VII, NON-WESTERN MUSIC

1-e, 2-i, 3-b, 4-h, 5-g, 6-j, 7-d, 8-f, 9-a, 10-c.

# - NOTES -

- NOTES -

- NOTES -

- NOTES -

- NOTES -